A Lover's Quarrel

A Lover's Quarrel

A Theologian and His Beloved Church

JOE R. JONES

CASCADE Books • Eugene, Oregon

A LOVER'S QUARREL
A Theologian and His Beloved Church

Copyright © 2014 Joe R. Jones. All rights reserved. Except for brief quotations in critical publications or reviews, no part of this book may be reproduced in any manner without prior written permission from the publisher. Write: Permissions, Wipf and Stock Publishers, 199 W. 8th Ave., Suite 3, Eugene, OR 97401.

Cascade Books
An Imprint of Wipf and Stock Publishers
199 W. 8th Ave., Suite 3
Eugene, OR 97401

www.wipfandstock.com

ISBN 13: 978-1-62564-226-4

Cataloguing-in-Publication data:

Jones, Joe R.

    A lover's quarrel : a theologian and his beloved church / Joe R. Jones.

    xxvi + 202 pp.; 23 cm. Includes bibliographical references.

    ISBN 13: 978-1-62564-226-4

    1. Theology, Doctrinal. 2. Church. 3. Christianity and culture. I. Title.

BT79 .J79 2014

Manufactured in the U.S.A.

*In gratitude for the emphatic and faithful voices
and vigorous lives
of daughters
Lynda Serene Jones
Kindanne Carole Jones
Verity Augusta Jones
and niece
Krista Marie Jones*

Contents

Foreword by Stanley Hauerwas   ix
Preface   xiii
Acknowledgements   xix
Introduction   xxi

Part One: Ecumenical Theologizing with Ecclesial Friends

1. The Shape and Contours of the Christian Life   3
2. On Being the Church of Jesus Christ   14
3. Spiritual Formation and Christian Discourse: The Shaping Power of Christian Discourse   23
4. Salvation: Mapping the Salvific Themes of Christian Faith   37
5. Yoder and Stone-Campbellites: Sorting the Grammar of Radical Orthodoxy and Radical Discipleship   54
6. World Communion Sunday: Why?   77

Part Two: On Being Mugged by Politics but Lifted by Gospel Hope

7. Venturing into Blogging   87
8. Following Jesus and Worshipping Jesus in Rivalrous Times   89
9. Capitalism, Democracy, and Health Care: A Response to Family and Friends   91

Contents

10 Narratives: Sociopolitical, Personal, Perhaps Theological? 99

11 How Might *We* Get On with Politics—but Who Are *We*? 104

12 A Letter to the Churches After 9/11/2011 107

13 Troublings: Campaign Rhetoric, Voting, Democracy, and Truth-Telling 111

14 Our American Agony 114

Part Three: Fragments from Times Past and Emerging Hopes

15 Spiritual Notes on Growing Up in Oklahoma 119

16 A YDS Reflection: Remembrance of Things Past and Present Discontent 143

17 Spinoza, H. Richard Niebuhr, and Ben and Me 152

18 Owen Died, K. Died, Bodies Age, Madge Writes a Christmas Letter 155

19 In Transition but Hopeful 158

20 On Hearing a Sermon 161

Part Four: Sermons Ventured on Behalf of the Witness of the Beloved Church

21 On Being Identified as Ambassadors for Christ 167

22 Jesus, the Family, and the Summons of the Kingdom 174

23 Behold, the Lamb of God 182

24 Remembering a Friend: Charles E. Jones 189

25 Purity of Heart and the Vicissitudes of Aging 193

26 In Gratitude for Gary Byrkit: Pastor Theologian Par Excellence 197

Foreword

This is not going to be easy. In his lovely chapter, "Spiritual Notes on Growing Up in Oklahoma," Joe Jones makes clear that he not only was born and raised in Oklahoma, he is an Oklahoman "all the way down." Yet I am a Texan. As I hope I make clear in my memoir, *Hannah's Child: A Theologian's Memoir*, I am a Texan all the way down. I am not only a Texan, but I am from North Texas. Folks from Texas, particularly folks from North Texas, just do not "get on" with folks from Oklahoma. I can assure you the feeling is mutual. Folks from Oklahoma only grudgingly acknowledge that there is a land just south of them called Texas that is peopled by folk they doubt are sane. They are called Texans.

So how does it come about that this Texan is writing a "Foreword" for this book of essays by Joe Jones? The only way to explain this strange occurrence is that Jones and I, by God's good grace, have been made more than our origins through the work of the Holy Spirit. Put as simply and directly as I can: the reason I am able to write the "Foreword" for this engaging book by Jones is that he and I have somehow along the way been made Christians. In one of the pieces Jones has included in this book he reflects on the personal and social significance of narratives. That chapter makes explicit the governing grammar of this book, by which Jones helps us see through quite diverse genres how the story of Christ can join us in a common story called discipleship.

Before I had read *A Lover's Quarrel: A Theologian and His Beloved Church* I had felt Jones and I shared much in common, but reading this book made me realize just how deep that commonality goes. Jones, of course, is from Oklahoma and from higher cotton folk than was my family. His folk had gone to college and his father was a judge. My mother was from dirt-poor Mississippi and my father was a bricklayer. Jones was a good baseball and basketball player. I loved baseball, but could not play during the summer because I had to work. But nonetheless our lives followed a similar path.

Foreword

We were raised by good Christians. We, for some reason, took seriously the fact we were Christians. We both discovered a love of philosophy in college. We both, early on in our development, fell in love with Tillich. We both went to Yale Divinity School and were stunned by the work of Barth in Mr. Hartt's Systematic Theology course. We both were shaped by reading Wittgenstein with Mr. Holmer. What we learned at Yale led us both to take seriously the work of John Howard Yoder. In short, we have been pursuing quite similar agendas that hopefully are different enough to make for an interesting comparison.

If I were to name, however, what I think is the deepest commonality between us it would be the fact that we both understand ourselves to be theologians for the church. Jones, for example, describes himself as an ecclesial Neanderthal because he still goes to church. I also still go to church. Indeed I find that going to church is the most important thing I do if I am to be not only a theologian, but a human being. For as Jones makes clear throughout this book, the training necessary to be a Christian is to undergo the disciplines necessary to acknowledge our humanity without regret.

Jones and I, however, go to different churches. I am an Episcopalian and he is a Disciples of Christ, but we share some fundamental convictions about the challenges before our respective churches. Jones thinks his church, if it is to sustain the commitment to the formation of disciples, has to recover the significance of creedal orthodoxy. I think if my church is to sustain its commitment to creedal orthodoxy we must recover the significance of discipleship. Both agendas reflect our common Christological commitments.

I hope those reading this "Foreword" will not think me self-indulgent for calling attention to our similar backgrounds, as well as how Jones and I have come to similar judgments. Rather I hope by calling attention to what we share I have highlighted some of the virtues of how Jones thinks, as well as the conditions of possibility for how he thinks. For I think for anyone who reads through this book will find what makes Jones's way of construing the Gospel so compelling is his commitment to being a friend. It is not accidental that he addresses those to whom he writes in his pieces as "Friends." That Joe claims me as a friend is not only a great honor, but an indication that we have common work to do.

That friendship is crucial for how Joe goes about his work in this book also accounts for another aspect of the essays, to which I want to call attention. These essays manifest Jones's passion for the concrete. Jones never retreats into abstractions. He writes with disarming directness. This is true not only in the work he does in his blogs, but also in the more "academic" essays in Part One. His account of the shape and contour of the Christian life is at once compelling and frightening because Jones makes unmistakable what we must be and do if we are to be followers of a crucified savior.

I call his account frightening because we are not sure any of us are capable of living lives of faithfulness. Jones is, of course, well aware that none of us are so capable, but that is why we need friends. The heart of Jones's account of the Christian life is the presumption that of course we cannot be what we have been called to be in Christ alone. We need all the "ecclesial friends" we can get. Accordingly, though Jones writes determinatively within the tradition of the Disciples, he does so with a sense of how that tradition at once has Catholic and Anabaptist gestures. Jones's chapter on Yoder, and in particular Yoder's need for a more fulsome account of the Trinity, is a model of how theology can be done in an ecumenical mode.

Jones is a master of the craft of theology. His wonderful creed-like statements of what the Gospel and church are invite the kind of ongoing reflection that you cannot help but find fruitful. His accounts of growing up in Oklahoma and his reflections on his time at Yale Divinity School not only help us better understand him but the world in which we find ourselves. All of which adds up to my gratitude that this man from Oklahoma saw fit to claim me, Texan though I be, for a friend.

Stanley Hauerwas
Gilbert T. Rowe Professor of Theological Ethics
Duke Divinity School

Preface

Upon retiring from Christian Theological Seminary in Indianapolis, Indiana in June 2000, my wife, Sarah, and I took up habitation in a family cottage on Ft. Gibson Lake in eastern Oklahoma. There in the grand solitude of rural lakeside life, I was able to bring my years of lecture notes in systematic theology into a publishable form. That was achieved with the publication in 2002 of my *A Grammar of Christian Faith: Systematic Explorations in Christian Life and Doctrine*, 2 vols. (Rowman & Littlefield). In conjunction with this publication, I also established a website—www.grammaroffaith.com—to post some previous essays, sermons, prayers, and to continue doing more into the future. In 2005 a collection of such writings was published as *On Being the Church of Jesus Christ in Tumultuous Times* (Cascade). And in 2010 I reframed the website and began for the first time to post blogs and have continued posting various other writings.

With only two exceptions, all the writings included in this new book have been written since my last book was published in 2005. And the writings have various contexts and purposes that I think are consistent with the overall perspective conveyed in the *Grammar* volumes but were occasioned by time-specific personal and public events, politics, and church life.

Essays in Part One: *Ecumenical Theologizing with Ecclesial Friends* are products of a series of unplanned invitations to contribute to ventures undertaken by friends from the various strands of the Stone-Campbell movement. Two of the essays were in direct conversations with friends from the Churches of Christ. An essay on the grammar of salvation talk was written for a Christian Church project on Disciples Theology. It was especially pleasing to write an essay for a gathering of such friends to evaluate the theological work of the great Mennonite theologian of the last decades of the twentieth century, John Howard Yoder. Readers should be assured that this essay is a major theological exploration for me in these later years. The

Preface

last entry is a sermon given on World Communion Sunday in October of 2012.

Part Two is essentially a selection of some blog postings begun in 2010, when I reorganized my website. They are mostly as I wrote them, but some significant editing and combining of postings have been performed. The central question cascading through all of these writings is how might a Christian—being formed by a faith that undergirds and guides *how* one lives—grapple with the sociopolitical world in the United States and beyond. Anyone who has studied the *Grammar* should understand that being-a-Christian and being-church always happens *somewhere* and *sometime*, and those spaces and times are quite simply the *world*. There is an irremovable dialectical tension between the church and the world in which it exists. The temptation for the church, almost from its beginnings, is to become a mirror image of whatever world in which it exists. Almost all of my writings and my teaching have aimed at giving the church a sharper theological self-understanding in order to cope with the overwhelming powers of the world. The New Testament refers to these as "principalities and powers" and "the elemental spirits."

Though I too sometimes use the expressions "right" and "left," that use concedes too much to a demonic misunderstanding of how the church is called to exist, wherever and whenever it exists, as shaped by the Gospel of Jesus Christ. To be sure, Christians wherever they exist are confronted with the ecclesial and personal questions of *how* they exist: *how* do they put together *being disciples of Jesus Christ* in their actual lives amidst the sociopolitical powers of their time? For the church that is first a *theological* discussion that bears on *politics*, rather than a politics seeking a theological justification. That's really hard to grasp! Perhaps Christians often get *mugged by politics* and lose sight of *Gospel hope*. On the other hand, how can such Gospel hope ever be grasped except in the midst of living in a messy sociopolitical world?

In Part Three: *Fragments from Times Past and Emerging Hopes*, I take some risks in making excursions into the past and venturing into some graces, laments, and hopes even now as my eighth decade of life rushes by. The first essay, "Spiritual Notes on Early Years in Oklahoma," has never appeared before in public print. Coming to grips with being raised by my family in Oklahoma has been disarming, wrenching, and upbuilding, but still inadequate to the subtle and elusive intimations of the Spirit. It is not quite a so-called autobiography. I hope including these notes in this book will be helpful to others.

Preface

In preparation for the fiftieth reunion in 2011 of my 1961 BD class at Yale Divinity School, we were invited to reflect on how our lives and hopes have unfolded in these past fifty years. That was a big but alluring task in a limited space! My struggles with writing the reflections became as well the troubling revisiting of an extremely turbulent time in my life, during which the church and the nation were both in a sociopolitical crisis that still reverberates today in both church and nation. Believing, being faithful, and sustaining a life are not precise and punctual matters, as became apparent as I wrote my reflections. It turns out that the reunion was modestly attended—many had already died—but my reflection piece created some good conversation. But, sadly, so many of my dearest student colleagues were absent because of their growing disenchantment over the years with the church and the diminution of their own theological appetite and belief.

The remaining writings in this section are, I hope, expressive of Sarah's and my struggle to be church and Christian as our health was declining, and we were being compelled by such to move back to our hometown, Oklahoma City. As expressed in the last writing in this section, we heard a sermon and found a congregation intent on being the church of Jesus Christ. We are hopeful day by day and grateful for the many gifts of work and friendships over the years. And I hope that readers of this book will hear some words and sounds of a Gospel that is sheer gift, never quite earned or deserved, but the deep ground upon which we humans are invited to stand—wherever and whenever!

Part Four: *Sermons Ventured on Behalf of the Witness of the Beloved Church*, are sermons/homilies given since 2005, with one exception. I recently was able to recover from virtually defunct computer files a sermon I preached at the ordination of our youngest daughter, Verity Augusta Jones, in October of 1995. The others stand on their own for a variety of occasions. But the last one, "In Gratitude for Gary Byrkit: Pastor Theologian Par Excellence," was given on the recent occasion of the funeral of our beloved new pastor, Gary Byrkit. Our grief is still real and we are grateful for the ministry he provided his congregation for over twenty-eight years and for us some fourteen months.

Since my "retirement" in 2000, I have been blessed with many conversation-partners—pastors, laity, professors—who stay in regular communication and often in "study groups" variously organized and located here and there. The following were noteworthy conversation-partners in study groups: Jim Caton, Charles and Laurel Ragland, Larry and Linda

Preface

Hahn, Les Brown, Robert Weitzeil, Dick and Lura Cayton, Tom Russell, Owen Cayton, Kevin Tully, Fred Turner, Charles Green, Jeannie McMahan, Craig Stinson, Jim Williams, Kent Dorsey, Don Bohlcke, Ron Wright, J. C. Mitchell, and Jim and Judy Payne. Some former students have continued to bless me with regular email exchanges and face to face conversations: Kent Ellett, Mark Nation, Bob Noble, Ben Dillon, Mary Moorman, Janet Hoover, Rakesh Peter Dass, Ned Mulligan, and Bill Pegg. A new friend, Chip Kooi, Professor of Theology at Oklahoma Christian University in Oklahoma City, has been exceptionally stimulating in inviting me to co-teach a seminar on my *Grammar* and in our regular lunches over this past year. As will also be apparent in these texts, my cousin Jon Rex Jones and my childhood friend, Tom Spear, have been engaging conversation-partners on important matters of public concern.

Hardly a week goes by that my retired Christian Theological Seminary colleague, Gerry Janzen—one of the great biblical theologians of our time—doesn't enlarge my understanding of biblical passages, render soaring accounts of Samuel Taylor Coleridge's theologizing, and provide his own inimitable reflections on the grand themes of Christian theologizing and living.

And then there is that strange collection of folk who sometimes read my web postings and respond with arresting insights and challenges. I am blessed by all of these friends and the others who remain unmentioned but not forgotten.

I especially appreciate Stanley Hauerwas, not only for his providing the foreword to this book, but for his invariably stimulating publications over these many years. From time to time his theological steadfastness and boldness have been encouraging to me.

There is great joy in dedicating this book to four women of considerable distinction in how they are pursuing their lives with exemplary courage and dedication. Eldest daughter Serene Jones, a world-renowned systematic, political, and feminist theologian, is Johnston Family Professor of Religion and Democracy and President of Union Theological Seminary in New York City. Middle daughter Kindy Jones is a distinguished lawyer now serving as Chief of Litigation in the Office of the Attorney General of Oklahoma. Youngest daughter Verity Jones is an ordained minister in both the Christian Church (Disciples of Christ) and the United Church of Christ, now serving as Executive Director of the Center for Pastoral Excellence at Christian Theological Seminary in Indianapolis. Dr. Krista

Preface

Jones, daughter of my deceased brother, the Honorable Charles Jones, is a renowned dentist in Edmond, Oklahoma, vigilant advocate on behalf of the poor and distressed, and elected to the Edmond Hall of Fame in recognition of her community leadership.

This family of women, including now my dear wife Sarah, each with her own unique voice and presence, has been an abundant blessing to me—both as sure anchors in deep and controversial waters and as vigorous conversation partners—over these many years.

As mentioned earlier, we moved to Oklahoma City in quest for medical care for Sarah. Late in 2012 she was diagnosed with a rare neurological disorder: Progressive Supranuclear Palsy. She has been suffering from the disease for at least three years, perhaps even longer. No cure is available, but her spirit and the care-giving of the many means we cope daily in hope.

The folks at Cascade Books have been immensely kind and helpful in getting this book into print. Rodney Clapp was the editor assigned to my text, and his suggestions, critiques, and other judgments were wise and upbuilding. What more could one expect from a fellow Oklahoman!

Joe R. Jones
August 2013

Acknowledgments

Chapter One: "The Shape and Contours of the Christian Life." A series of articles in *The Indiana Christian*, 2008–2009. Used with permission.

Chapter Two: "On Being the Church of Jesus Christ." *Leaven: A Journal of Christian Ministry*, 15/1 (First Quarter 2007) 6–11. Used with permission.

Chapter Three: "Spiritual Formation and Christian Discourse: the Shaping Power of Christian Discourse." In *Spiritual Formation and the Future of Stone-Campbell Churches*, 1–20. Bloomington, IN: Ketch Publishing, 2008, Used with permission.

Chapter Four: "Salvation: Mapping the Salvific Themes of Christian Faith." In *Chalice Introduction to Disciples Theology*, edited by Peter Goodwin Heltzel, 190–202. St. Louis: Chalice, 2008. Used with permission.

Chapter Five: "Yoder and Stone-Campbellites: Sorting the Grammar of Radical Orthodoxy and Radical Discipleship." In *Radical Ecumenicity: Pursuing Unity and Continuity after John Howard Yoder*, edited by John C. Nugent, 107–28. Abilene, TX: Abilene Christian University Press, 2010. Used with permission.

Chapter Twenty-One: "Jesus, the Family, and the Summons of the Kingdom." *Encounter*, 67/2 (Spring 2006) 199–206. Used with permission.

Introduction

Why The Church and Why the Quarrel?

Well-meaning friends over many years have expressed curiosity about my continuing concern about church and theologizing in the context of the church. They often ask: why be concerned about the church when there is so much in the nation and world and their politics and theories that need careful attention and construal? After all, the church is idiosyncratic and provincial, while philosophy, political theory, religious studies, etc. are broad and universal in intent, dealing with real issues of life and death, justice and hope. Yes, I do admit that these disciplines and topics of daily life and politics percolate repeatedly and sometimes heatedly in my mind.

But I have over the years been "given" and have embraced the task of educating ministers for the church. Living in the midst of the church, however frustrating from time to time, I have found that it is also the only site or community in which the Gospel of Jesus Christ is assumed to be at the center of its *discourses and practices*. Drop out that Gospel and whatever one might mean by "church" will be under the control of what I call the "principalities and powers" of the world. It is the Gospel that intrudes on those powers and bears on what we humans might call our *destiny*. And it bears on whatever we might mean by the word *God*, and everyone knows or should know that that English word is bereft of any primordial context and agreement in human history otherwise. But there is, however contested it may be, a deep Christian use of that word that is at the irremovable heart of the church and is tethered to the Gospel of Jesus Christ.

Friends also ask why I speak such strange language as "the grammar of" and refer repeatedly to "discourses and practices." My primary conviction here is that human beings, wherever and whenever, are distinctly formed by the language—the *discourses*—in which they construe, have, and live in a world. Yet, it is not merely the discourses-as-language, but in those *practices*—those multitudinous ways of acting and repeatedly acting in social agreement and disagreement with others. Two primal convictions are pivotal here. First, it is by virtue of their discourses and practices, with others, that human beings have-a-world. Second, whatever might be meant by "church," it must pivot around some understanding—some discourses and practices—identifying the Gospel of Jesus Christ.

We cannot even get started in probing this further discussion without candidly admitting that we, today, are dependent upon traditions of usage that we did not create. We can and do interrogate those traditions and we may even reject or prescind from this or that in the traditions' discourses and practices, but we cannot presume to step aside or jump outside of the traditions and construct on our own a Gospel of Jesus Christ. There is a particularity here that cannot, or should not, be erased or cancelled. Those traditions upon which we are dependent are primarily *church traditions*.

Simply in the context of these considerations, it should be clearer why there are communities of folk who are *disciplined* in the discourses and practices of being the sort of people who confess that the Gospel of Jesus Christ is at the center of their life. And that their "life" is inconceivable to themselves without being intrinsically a life of *witness*—of witness to that Gospel and the God made known in it and the grace so generously given thereby. So, the church, as some tradition of witness in history, always precedes someone becoming a confessing adherent to the Gospel of Jesus Christ. And it is intrinsic to the church that it deals with the *norms* for its discourses and practices concerning that Gospel and who God is and what it means to be a human confessing the Lordship of Jesus.

I do admit that any contemporary savant is free on her own to look around and observe that there are many persons and many groups of folk who claim to be followers/disciples of Jesus Christ, and who claim to be church. Such an observer is free to make whatever remarks she pleases about the claims expressed in their discourses and practices. Simply as a casual observation she might say that the discourses and practices of many of these folks and their communities are not only odd and subversive but unworthy of any intellectual or practical assent from an "educated" person. In our time, that judgment by others is such a given that I have further proposed that Christians boldly *admit* that the church's discourses and practices are at their very heart *confessional* in character. When intellectual push comes to shove the church has no knock-down argument that intellectually compels anyone to believe or to become a follower of Jesus.

I think it quite intelligible to thoughtful and disciplined Christians that they live in a world in which many others believe that "Christians" are simply gullible and intellectually dense and perhaps even ignorant, hateful, misanthropic, and arrogant. I tend to agree that many self-described Christians are embarrassingly ignorant, hateful, misanthropic, and arrogant, and such is evident in how they express and give an account of the apparent faith that is within them. In fact, the painful anomaly often appears that self-identified Christian witnesses seem *incompetent* and *illiterate* in those discourses and practices that are essential to the life of the church, but that is a judgment internal to the life of the church as it develops norms and procedures for understanding and living the Christian life.

So, for the sake of that contemporary observer/critic who takes time to inspect the discourses and practices of various groups of folk who claim to be the church of Jesus Christ, I propose that those of us immersed—or somewhat immersed—in the discourses and practices of the church need to aim at some agreement among ourselves about a theological characterization or definition of the church in which the Gospel of Jesus Christ is at the grammatical center of its discourses and practices.

Since our return to Oklahoma in 2000 it has been my good pleasure to teach an Introduction to Theology course in the Commissioned Ministry Training Program for the Oklahoma Region of the Christian Church (Disciples of Christ). The persons in the program do not intend to go to seminary but hope to provide various forms of ministerial leadership. But please note: it is a challenging task to dissuade these laypersons from thinking that *theology* is a subject matter that is the exclusive preserve of persons called *theologians*. I suggest to them that all of the language of the church is primordially intended as *witnessing to God* and therefore should be construed as *theological language*. Hence, *theologizing* is already going on in the church's discourses and practices and is not, therefore, something invented by esoteric folk called *theologians*, over which they have exclusive domain. All Christians, in their speaking and acting—in their discourses and practices—are doing theology as they witness to the reality of God. All Christians are in some basic sense *theologians* as they witness to God. Of course, the ongoing self-critique of the church bears on whether that language is true and faithful.

Introduction: Why The Church and Why the Quarrel?

Yet, just as each Christian is called to grow in his/her understanding and practice of faithful witness, so too theological reflection becomes a disciplined practice. Over the centuries this inherent movement internal to being-Christian has been called the movement of *faith seeking understanding*.

Yet over many years of engaging the church and church people in the discourses and practices of Christian witness, I have found myself stumbling into the disarming discovery that so many of the folk who publicly claim, in some definite sense, to be Christian are in fact quite *unskilled* or *illiterate* in speaking, teaching, and living Christian faithfulness. Such illiteracy is present in both the ordained and the laity.

Yes, perhaps that sounds arrogant and condescending. But even granting that it is a profound and almost universal human trait to regularly fake and burke at some of the simple processes of living with honesty and discipline, it is staggering that the precious words of the faith get so mangled and cheaply used by folk who proudly claim to be Christian and would find it an insult to be criticized by a snobbish and radically orthodox former seminary professor.

Well, there you have it. I would be reduced to silence—which is a temptation—if I thought I could just opt out of church life and do my own thing in philosophy, politics, economics, and life. But I am stalked by an undeserved but overwhelming sense that there is good news—a Gospel—arising out of the biblical witness that the God of Israel, incarnate in Jesus of Nazareth, and alive in the Holy Spirit is graciously weaving down through human history and is determined to have the ultimate word on human destiny and meaning. Hallelujah! Who can believe it? Perhaps an ecclesial folk, gathered here and there, might keep such good news alive by witnessing to it in discourses and practices. And even in their own missteps and misunderstandings they might be empowered to convey a sense that God will not leave us alone to go to war and to kill under the pretense that we are kingdom-folk simply preserving that absurdity called "Christian America" as the foundation of American free-enterprise worship.

Might this proposed statement of the Gospel help us understand the deep roots of the church's life?

> The Gospel of Jesus Christ is the Good News
> that the God of Israel, the Creator of all creatures,
> has in freedom and love become incarnate
> in the life, death, and resurrection of Jesus of Nazareth

Introduction: Why The Church and Why the Quarrel?

> to enact and reveal God's gracious reconciliation
> of humanity to Godself, and
> through the Holy Spirit calls and empowers human beings
> to participate in God's liberative and redemptive work by
> acknowledging God's gracious forgiveness in Jesus,
> repenting of human sin,
> receiving the gift of freedom, and
> embracing authentic community by
> loving the neighbor and the enemy,
> caring for the whole creation, and
> hoping for the final triumph of God's grace
> as the Triune Ultimate Companion of all creatures.

Folk who believe this are folk who also understand that the U.S.A. is not a Christian nation nor a Christian church. Yet many are the folk who live in the midst of the U.S.A. who have the audacity to confess being captured by the Gospel of Jesus Christ that conveys a harsh judgment on human selfishness and death-dealing and yet an almost unfathomable grace and forgiveness that always places the church on the side of the least of these in human societies, whenever and wherever. Might the least of these occasionally be malingerers and indolent and perhaps violent? Yes, but if the world treats them as the great failures in the enterprises of life, are they not in fact the lost sheep who just might be able to hear a grace they know they do not deserve? And might that Gospel grace be a gift that the rich and famous might presume they neither need nor want? Well, the Gospel and the church, at their very best and clearest, are odd but unnervingly consumed by grace.

Hence, to keep the church repentant and faithful, consider this proposed definition of the church:

> The church is that liberative and redemptive
> community of persons
> called into being
> by the Gospel of Jesus Christ
> through the Holy Spirit
> to witness in word and deed
> to the living Triune God
> for the benefit of the world
> to the glory of God.

Looking back, perhaps it is true what my friend Gerry Janzen said: I have been blessed over many years to have a *lover's quarrel with the church*. What else might one have expected, given the church is called into being by the Gospel of Jesus Christ to witness in word and deed to the living Triune God and yet the actual lives of empirical churches seem so ill-formed and chaotic. But it is a *lover's* quarrel, and this lover still struggles to understand how to live before the sheer beauty, miracle, and bounty of the unearned grace of God and in and with other sojourners struggling to be faithful.

Might it also be apparent that I have a *lover's quarrel* with the world and its principalities and powers! Yet it too is a *lover's* quarrel. After all, my proposed definition of the church does affirm that the purpose of the church is "to witness in word and deed to the living Triune God *for the benefit of the world* to the glory of God." Quite simply, God loves the world! For the church a defining issue for its life of witness is *how to love the world faithfully*.

Part One

Ecumenical Theologizing
with Ecclesial Friends

1

The Shape and Contours of the Christian Life

A version of this essay first appeared as six articles written for the The Indiana Christian *in 1997–98. This sort of careful thinking through how we talk about the Christian life I also refer to as examining the grammar of Christian discourses. The proposal herein is to explore the shape of the Christian life as Life in the Church, Life in the Spirit, Life in Faith, Life in the Works and Passions of Love, and Life in Hope.*

Life In The Church

It is not uncommon that we so accentuate our American individualism that we fall into the trap of thinking the Christian life is simply an individual endeavor and can be quite easily pursued in utter independence of the life of the church. But this is not the way the New Testament talks about the faithful life: faith requires the support of the community of the faithful, rather than the lonely and isolated journey of the singular individual. We need other persons to teach us, to mentor us, to worship with us, to pray with us, to converse with us, to practice with us, to love with us, if we are to grow in faithfulness.

While the church is always at least a group of folk who have some institutional relations, the church is primarily a *community of persons called into life by the Gospel of Jesus Christ*. The New Testament refers to this community as a *koinonia* of persons in liberative and redemptive fellowship with each other and with God. We need to keep our focus on the church as a distinctive sort of community with a distinctive way of life and mission in the world.

In contemporary Christian theological reflection we are developing a new way of describing the nature and mission of the church. The emphasis is on the church as a community constituted by its distinctive *discourses and practices.* Under the word "discourses" we include the wide array of linguistic expressions of the faith in the life of the church: we pray, we sing, we read scripture, we preach and hear sermons and lessons, we confess our sins, and much more. It is in these discourses, when they are functioning well and truthfully, that we identify who God is, characterize the human situation before God, and characterize the way Christians are called to live in the world. Persons come to faith by encountering these discourses, and it is in the use of these Christian concepts, images, and stories that faith comes to have content and character. And when these discourses, in given communities of the church, are in disarray or confusion or said emptily, then it becomes difficult for the Christian life to take decisive shape in the hearts of the people.

Under the word "practices" we are simply pointing out that the discourses, as actions of speaking, are themselves practices of faith, and that such speaking shapes the practices of worshiping and living that are essential to Christian life. We learn in the church how to speak the language of faith, how to practice faithful speech, and how to put faithful speech into action in our relations with others, with God, and with the world. The Christian life is something definite and authentic only in its concrete practices.

Hence, Christian living requires that the individual be in the community of faithful discourses and practices that aim at forming her life in relation to herself, in relation to others in the church and in the world, and in relation to God. None of us can teach that to ourselves by ourselves: we require the church as the community of distinctive discourses and practices in which we can *learn how to be faithful.*

It is in the church that we learn how to be grateful for God's grace in Jesus Christ, learn the depth and content of that grace, learn how to become lovers of Christ who are empowered to love the world in a new way, and learn how to become witnesses to the triune God for the benefit of the world. Persons do not become Christians by accident of birth or ethnicity or nationality.

They become Christians through their own authentic appropriation of the discourses and practices of the church of Jesus Christ.

Life In The Spirit

Consider the Christian life as *life in the Spirit*. It is everywhere evident in the New Testament that the disciples of Jesus Christ—those who say "yes" to his life, death, and resurrection as God's gracious good news of new life—are empowered to say "yes" by the Holy Spirit. Indeed we can say that it is *the Holy Spirit that is the foundational dynamism of the Christian life.*

The Holy Spirit is variously named "the Spirit of your Father" (Matt 10:20), "the Spirit of his Son" (Gal 4:6), "the Spirit of Jesus" (Acts 16:7), "the Spirit of Christ" (Rom 8:9; Phil 1:19; 1 Pet 1:11), "the Spirit of life" (Rom 8:2), "the Spirit of grace" (Heb 10:29), and "Spirit of truth" (John 14:17) and many times simply the "Holy Spirit." To live in Christ is to live in and by the Spirit of Christ, which is none other than the Spirit of the Father who is the God of Israel and the Creator of all things.

It is the Spirit that comes upon, descends upon, is poured out on persons and the church; that speaks to and through persons, teaches and reveals to persons in witness to Christ and the Father; that dwells within persons; that sanctifies persons; that intercedes in prayer; that gives wondrous gifts. Among these gifts of the Spirit are *new life* (John 6:63; Rom 7:6; 8:11; 1 Cor 3:6), *freedom from sin* (Rom 8:2; 2 Cor 3:17), *living, speaking, and doing the truth* (John 4:24; 14:17), *the creating, building up and giving unity to the church* (Acts 2; 1 Cor 12:1–13; 14:12; 2 Cor 13:13; Eph 4:3–4; 1 Pet 3:8), and the *bestowing of the wonderful fruit of Christian living* (Gal 5:22: "love, joy, peace, patience, kindness, generosity, faithfulness").

There is no aspect of the life of the individual Christian and the church that does not seem to be empowered and shaped by the Holy Spirit. Hence, we can say that the Spirit is that power graciously given to persons that works within their lives to shape and form them in conformity to God's triune life as the One who creates and governs all things, as the One who became incarnate in Jesus of Nazareth, and as the One who moves within creatures to bring new life.

It is because we say these words so meaningfully and responsibly that the church has from its foundations been set on a trinitarian trajectory. We acknowledge the Spirit as the Spirit of the Creator and the Reconciler when we confess God's trinitarian life with us and for us. This confession also reminds us that the Holy Spirit is never the possession of individual persons or the church but is the One who freely and lovingly possesses persons and the church.

Hence, there is never any opposition between life in the Spirit and life in Christ. Life in the Spirit is tested by its having the "mind of Christ" (1 Cor 2:14–16). To live in Christ and become his disciple in witness to God's love for the world is precisely to live in and by the Spirit.

Persons who live in the Spirit pray for God's continuing guidance and are bold to believe that the Spirit will be their counselor through the trials and joys of life. But living in the Spirit is living in the community of church where the discourses about and in the Spirit are uttered and learned and where the practices of worship, of education, of love, and of outreach to the world are cultivated regularly. The Spirit promises to empower and to dwell *within* those discourses and practices when they are faithfully performed and lived. Come Holy Spirit, come!

Life In Faith

The Christian life can also be understood as life-in-faith. We should not expect to arrive a simple definition of the term *faith*. In the New Testament the term *pistis* and its derivatives are variously translated "faith," "belief," "believing," and "having faith." To capture these biblical senses, some theologians have invented the word "faithing," comparable to "believing." But we can save ourselves some confusions about meanings if we admit up front that "faith" [and *pistis*] is a term that has a *family of uses* that are interconnected but not reducible to a simple definition. In general we can say that "faith" can refer both to the whole of the Christian life and to some particular aspects of that life.

First, let us consider "faith" as used to refer to the whole of the Christian life as an orientation to God: the life of saying "yes" to what God has done in Jesus Christ for the salvation of the world. In this sense, faith is a whole *way of life* or *form of life* that is given its shape by God's self-revealing life. It is the orientation of the whole person's heart, mind, and will on God's saving life.

As such, faith involves distinctive beliefs, actions, and passions. Faith is the comprehensive *how* of the person's life: how one lives before God's abundant grace and under the summons of God's command to witness and to love. In this connection, faith is a matter of *being faithful* to God and to the life God has summoned us to live.

Second, faith, both as the basic orientation of the Christian and as particular aspects of that orientation, is always to be thought of as a *gift* of the Holy Spirit (1 Cor 12:9; Eph 2:8). God's gift evokes gratitude to God and worshipful praise for God's loving grace in Jesus Christ. Therefore, faith is never to be thought of as a human achievement about which boasting might be appropriate. With this combination of thankfulness and worship, we can say that faith is *doxological gratitude* to God.

Third, faith obviously involves some aspects of what we ordinarily call *belief*. Faith involves believing something about God, believing that God is characterized in some definite ways. In particular it focuses on God's being characterized by the life of Jesus Christ. So, faith is always at least belief that God is characterized as the Almighty Creator of all things, as the Reconciling Lover in Jesus Christ, and as the Redeeming Spirit. Indeed there are many distinctive Christian beliefs about God, about humanity, and about the world.

But, fourth, faith is not belief in any easy or superficial sense. This is clear when we consider that it is impossible to have Christian faith, in the sense of believing a statement about God to be true, in any neutral or merely detached fashion. When we believe that God is the One we know in Jesus Christ, we are also *having faith in God*. We are trusting in God; we are staking our life on God. This personal trust in God keeps faith from ever being understood as mere belief that some statement is true of God.

Thus, we can see how *faith as belief that* and *faith as trust in* are mutually interrelated and never to be separated or opposed. We cannot trust in God if there is not some belief as to who God is, and we cannot truly believe something about God without trusting in God. Christians do not trust in an unknown cipher presumably at the depths of things.

Fifth, putting belief and trust together helps us understand how faith can be seen as a *personal knowing of God*. In faith we encounter God with belief and trust, with a consuming passion for the life of God and for the life God has called us to live. In faith we meet God as gracious and holy friend.

So, the Christian life is life-in-faith to the extent we believe God's self-revealing declarations to us in Israel and in Jesus Christ through the Spirit and to the extent that we trust the whole of our life to God.

To recapitulate, it is in the church that we hear the Gospel of Jesus Christ and are called to live in the Spirit of Christ. This living-in-the-Spirit is living-in-faith: believing that God is as the Gospel of Jesus Christ says God is, and trusting in God with the whole of our life.

Life in the Works and Passions of Love: Part 1

The word *love*, of course, has many uses in English, and we will have to think diligently in order to sort out the distinctive Christian understanding of love. We know we are into perplexing issues when we recognize that in ordinary language *love* can refer to a *feeling* or to an *action* or to a *relationship*. How does Christian theology tie these concerns together? And what are we to make of people who say that Christian love for another is not something that can be commanded or made obligatory but is something that arises spontaneously from the affections?

Well, the New Testament should help us here. If anything is clear, it is that Jesus and the New Testament authors regularly adopt the Hebraic form of *divine command* when speaking of love:

> "Your *shall* love the Lord your God with all your heart, and with all your soul, and with all your mind, and . . . you *shall* love your neighbor as yourself." (Matt 22:37–39; Mark 12:31–33; Luke 10:27)

> "You *shall* love your neighbor as yourself." (Matt 19:19; Rom 13:9; Gal 5:14; Jas 2:8)

> "But I say to you . . . love your enemies, do good to those who hate you." (Luke 6:27, 35; Matt 5:43–44)

These compelling passages don't say: "wait to love until you feel like it" or "love when it arises spontaneously in your heart" or "love is such a precious internal feeling that it could never be commanded." Rather, love of God and love of neighbor are commanded by God, and therefore the Christian has an *obligation to love God and neighbor.*

Yet it is true that the love commandments do not just emerge from nowhere. They emerge from an encounter with the Gospel of Jesus Christ: that God loves human beings and summons them to a life of love. Hence, Christians are motivated and empowered to love by God's prior love for humanity. In Jesus Christ God teaches us *how to love*. (See John 3:16; 13:34; 15:9; Rom 5:8; Gal 2:20; Eph 5:1–2; 1 John 3:16; 4:9–11,19; Rev 1:5.) And this love becomes love in our hearts and minds and wills under the empowerment of the Holy Spirit (Rom 5:5).

As God in Jesus Christ has been self-giving and compassionate with the world of humans, so too we are called to give of ourselves in relation to the neighbor. But an extraordinary stretching of meaning is taking place in the life of Jesus: the *neighbor* is not just *persons from the neighborhood* but now includes the enemy. Since God's love is indiscriminate and given to all, so too the Christian's love is summoned to be indiscriminate, excluding no one. No person falls outside that group of those whom Christians are commanded to love.

What then does it mean to love *indiscriminately* all persons? It means at least that we are not called to love only those for whom we are already have some familial and friendly feelings and relationships. We are commanded to love the enemy, and this at least means that we are to regard the enemy's life as of the same value as our own. The enemy's life is not expendable in the hands of Christian love.

In relation to the neighbor, then, we are to perform the works of love on his or her behalf. That is, we are to love the neighbor *for her own sake*, and not for the sake of some larger cause or for our own sake. We are to engage in those actions that build up the neighbor in his life situation and promote his good before God. Because love involves works on behalf of others, we can never reduce Christian love merely to having private affectionate feelings towards others.

Life in the Works and Passions of Love: Part 2

We have discussed the sense in which love, Christianly understood, is commanded by God in Jesus Christ. This love that is commanded is also empowered by God's prior love for us in Jesus Christ through the Spirit. And this love involves doing works for the good of the universal neighbor, including our enemies. The Greek term in the New Testament for this love is *agape*.

If we keep our eyes clearly focused, we can learn more about this *agape* love by contrasting it to another Greek term for love, *eros*. In general, *eros*, or what I call *erosic love*, involves our being *attracted to* some person or object. This enormous power of attraction is crucial to human life and lies at the root of most of our desires. Insofar as we are attracted to the object of love, then, we desire some form of union with or possession of the object.

Think of how erosic love "befalls" us when we are romantically smitten by and attracted to another person. The pull toward the person is

PART ONE—Ecumenical Theologizing with Ecclesial Friends

powerful, and it disposes us to have all sorts of feelings and to engage in sometimes strange actions. Often the feelings and emotions of erosic love simply overwhelm us.

But there are myriad of ways in which erosic love affects us and a myriad of objects that can be attractive to us. We can be attracted to persons whom we call "friends," attracted to family members, attracted to heroes and heroines, attracted to some future goal, such as becoming a first rate musician, etc. Common to all these "loves" is the given fact that they are *preferential* to the individual lover. That is, our erosic loves express our preferences. And obviously, contrarily, there are many persons and objects for which we have no preferential love. Indeed, there are many persons that are repulsive to us.

Erosic love in its many forms is important for human life, and in itself is not bad. But it is not *agape* love. Rather, *agape* love is commanded by God and therefore has a normative structure built in to it: we are to seek the good of the neighbor, regardless of whether we find the neighbor attractive and a preferential object of our desires and passions. *Eros*, being geared to the preferential and attractive, does not have such a normative structure inherent in it. We can erosicly love another without having regard for the other's good as an end in herself. In contrast, *agape love does not command us to find the other preferentially attractive, but it does command us to see to the well-being of the other.*

Yet, *agape* love is not without feelings and passions. We are commanded to love one another with all our *heart*, which means we are to have a *passion* for the good of another, even if that other is not particularly attractive to us—even if the other is repulsive and threatening to us! This passion, which is a feeling of concern, means that we have compassionate openness to the other, that we feel the other's situation and are affected by the other's pain, plight, struggle, joy, and happiness.

Yet what about the command to love the neighbor as yourself? Does this imply that we all love ourselves in a good fashion and can therefore imitate this in loving the other? I suspect not. We are confronted with the unavoidable biblical recognition and contemporary insight that persons typically don't know how to love themselves in the *agape* sense. In an age of rampant narcissism, we confront the paradox of the narcissist: utter self-absorption coupled with self-loathing.

Hence, there is, Christianly understood, an *illicit self-love* and an *illicit self-contempt,* both of which are to be overcome. Illicit self-love happens when we make ourselves and our desires the center of the universe and all things are judged in relation to "myself." Illicit self-contempt happens when we have utter disgust and disregard of ourselves and consider ourselves of no value to anyone or to God.

Agape love intends the overcoming of both of these demonic possessions so common in our world. In Jesus Christ we learn that we are loved and valued by God and that God has an eternal destiny in store for us. In learning of God's love for us, we are empowered to love ourselves for the first time in a legitimate and non-selfish way. And we are thereby empowered to love the neighbor and the enemy.

Christians who know God's love for themselves do not have to find their value at someone else's expense, and they don't have to loath themselves. Oddly enough, at the heart of Christian faith is knowing oneself to be a sinner who regularly engages in illicit self-love and illicit self-contempt, and yet it is also a knowing oneself as forgiven and loved by God. To know this, is to be empowered to love oneself as one is loved by God. To know this, is to have a redemptive joy and hope.

Life in Hope

We have basically determined that the Christian life is life-in-the-church and life-in-the-Spirit. As such life, we have also determined that it is life-in-faith and life-in-love. It should now be no surprise that we will conclude our discussion by describing the Christian life as *life-in-hope*.

Hope, of course, has to do with our orientation to the *future*. We hope for possibilities in the future, and such hoping is in general essential to human life. Persons who have no hope are persons in despair about the future: they perceive the future as uninviting or threatening or utterly indifferent to them. Such *hopelessness* is devastating to human well-being.

But the Christian faces the future as that which is in all respects under the sovereign rule of the God they know in Jesus Christ. While there may be many other questions about how the future will affect us, Christians are sure of one fundamental belief: *there is no future that can separate them from the love of God they know in Christ Jesus.*

Paul says this powerfully in Rom 8:32–35, 37–39:

> If God is for us, who is against us? . . . It is Christ Jesus . . . who intercedes for us. Who will separate us from the love of Christ? Will hardship, or distress, or persecution, or famine, or nakedness, or peril, or sword? . . . No, in all these things . . . I am convinced

> that neither death, nor life, . . . nor rulers, nor things present, nor things to come, nor powers, . . . nor anything else in all creation will be able to separate us from the love of God in Christ Jesus our Lord.

Could any of us have made a more comprehensive list of the sort of things that might threaten our future? No, Paul's list covers it all, and apparently Paul thinks any of these threatening events might happen to the Christian, without thereby catapulting the Christian into thinking he or she is being forsaken by God. Rather Paul believes that even if these realities do happen to us, not one of them will be able to separate us from the love of God. Here is the point: these terrible realities may indeed happen to us in our present and future, but it is the love of God that is the most important thing in the life and future of the Christian.

Hence, Christians face the future as the time in which they will meet the love of God, come what may. So, Christians do not have the Pollyannish hope that everything in their life will be a blessing and beyond harm's way; rather, they have a sober realism that all sorts of difficult threats might happen. But they trust in God's sovereign love and therefore they have hope in God about the future.

To live with this kind of hope is, therefore, to have a compelling *freedom* about how one lives. We can give up all those fears that seem to define us daily and to threaten our perceived well-being. We can be *free from* those fears that enslave us.

Consider death: most of us live in utter fear of death as the worse threat we can imagine. Hence, we hope continually to avoid or postpone death, and we are enslaved by that fear. Scripture is clear that we will all die, but it is possible to face the future with the following belief and hopefulness expressed by Paul: "whether we live or whether we die, we are the Lord's" (Rom 14:8).

We are free from the power of death over our lives because we hope in the Lord as the One who resurrects the dead and confers new life. The Christian hope in the *resurrection of the dead* affirms that in whatever future in life and death we will finally meet and be embraced by the eternal love of God. Death is not a power that can finally hold and determine us.

Because our hope is finally in God, the Christian life can live sprightly into the future as the time over which the triune God reigns. The principalities and powers of the world may appear to have the power to determine our future and the meaning of our life, but we Christians believe that in the cross and resurrection of Jesus Christ God has given us a future not under the control of other powers.

This future for the Christian is also a future for all our brothers and sisters in the world. They too, whether they know or not, are caught up in the cross and resurrection of Jesus Christ, and we Christians abide in the hope that ultimately they will know the grace and love of God.

Hence, *Christians are those folk who hope in the ultimate triumph of God's grace as the triune Ultimate Companion of all humans and of the whole creation.* That sums up the Christian life as that grateful and faithful life made possible by Jesus Christ through the Holy Spirit in the community of the saints in the church; this life is altogether *life in hope that is free to love the neighbor and the enemy.*

2

On Being the Church of Jesus Christ

This essay was written for a special issue on ecclesiology among the traditions of the Stone-Campbell Movement for the journal Leaven, *vol. 15, no. 1 (First Quarter 2007), 6–11.*

It is indeed a happy occasion for me to be invited to contribute an article on ecclesiology in collaboration with other brothers and sisters from the Stone-Campbell Movement, otherwise called the Restoration Movement. That folk involved in the Movement could identify themselves as part of a movement presupposes that the Movement had some discourses and practices that gave definition to the Movement itself. I think the following self-designations were central to nineteenth-century folk's capacity to speak of a new and particular movement of restoration.

First, the intent to *restore*[1] New Testament Christianity expressed itself in such discourse as "Where the Bible speaks, we speak, and where

---

1. Here and in the following chapters, the reader should be aware that I use italicized words to emphasize points and to draw attention to that particular use of the word or words. Also, I will use single and double quotes in special ways. Single quote marks [' . . . '] are used to indicate one of three signals. (1) It can signal that we are talking *about* a word or sign, as in the sentence "The word 'language' is used to refer to the natural languages of persons." (2) It can signal that we are highlighting a special use of a word or locution, as in "The actions of 'perichoresis' are crucial to church life." (3) It can signal that we are talking about the meaning of the sentence itself that is included within the single quotes, as in the two sentences used above. Functions one and two of the single quotes can also be accomplished by use of *italic* type. Double quote marks [" . . . "] are used when I am actually quoting from another text or some person's actual speech. These writing practices may seem peculiar, but they are ways in which I am intending to

the Bible is silent, we are silent." Of course, that was mainly understood as "Where the New Testament speaks..."

Second, implicit—and often quite explicit—in this intention to restore New Testament Christianity is the belief that the history of the church since New Testament times had been a steady and disastrous decline from and corruption of the distinctive and normative New Testament discourses and practices.

Third, not the least of the reasons for restoring New Testament Christianity was the desire to recover the real Jesus, uncluttered and obscured by centuries of creedal statements and controversies. Hence, the slogan, "No creed but Christ" served the purpose of putting Jesus at the center of the faith, and yet now a Jesus apparently detached from any ecclesial creed.

Fourth, the intent was also to restore the organization of the New Testament church, believing earnestly that there was *one* administrative pattern evident in the texts. Already imbued with the "Free Church" trajectory of American individualism and anti-clericalism, the Movement identified the church as comprised of baptized adult believers who have confessed, "Jesus is the Christ, the Son of the Living God, and my personal Savior and Lord." Hence, the church is not dependent for its reality on any 'apostolic clerical successors,' who are given the authority to guide and teach the church and to baptize.

Given that these four passionate trajectories were there in the originating decades of the Movement, it should be intelligible to us now that some inevitable perils were lurking therein and would lead to the later fragmentation of the Movement. The assumptions that the New Testament discourses and practices contained one and only one pattern of belief and one and only one pattern of authoritative church organization were simply unsustainable by increasing historical scholarship.[2]

However, the emphasis on the church as a voluntary community comprised of baptized believers was commensurate to the taken-for-granted way in which the church existed in the first three centuries of its life. It was only when the church came under the protection and promotion of the Roman Empire in the fourth century—becoming thereby 'established' by the

---

remind the reader that words having varying uses that are often unnoticed in ordinary styles of writing.

2. For an insightful discussion of the variety among the churches in New Testament times, see Raymond E. Brown, *The Churches the Apostles Left Behind* (New York: Paulist, 1984).

PART ONE—Ecumenical Theologizing with Ecclesial Friends

governing authorities—did the possibility even exist that a person might become or be called a 'Christian' as a matter of governmental geography.

Yet, by discounting later church traditions, including creedal developments, the Restoration Movement deprived itself of the capacity to deal with differences within the New Testament discourses and practices. This became particularly painful with regard to how to interpret Jesus Christ. Wanting a Jesus without any creedal identification led to the Movement's most divisive issue: in what sense is Jesus divine and in what sense human and in what sense our Savior? Incapacitated to develop and affirm any common confessional or creedal statement about Jesus, the Movement was left either to the dogmatic declarations of individual pastors and professors or to the dogma that only the individual believer can decide for herself who Jesus is—Jesus dissolved into the private preferences of the individual believer! Is it any wonder that a restoration movement of this character would find itself breaking apart into differing traditions?

It is my hope that this issue of *Leaven* will lead these differing wings into a robust and self-critical ecclesiology that might reaffirm some of the admirable concerns of the Movement's earlier forebears and yet lead to rethinking theologically some of the disagreements that have plagued our past conversations.

Let me confess at the outset of this essay that I was raised in what is known as the 'Disciples' branch of the originating Movement. And I spent twenty-five years teaching in and administering two Disciples institutions of higher education. It seems commonplace these days to refer to the Disciples as the 'liberal' wing of the Movement, and however problematic that moniker might be, it is the Disciples wing that has deliberately pursued ecumenical discussions and relationships to other church traditions. Yet, the state of ecclesiology among Disciples, either as an explicit theological statement or as actually discussed and practiced in congregations, regions, and the general manifestation, seems to me cluttered with confusion and bewilderment.[3] Yet it may be that the roots of these problems are present

---

3. The Commission on Theology of the Council on Christian Unity of the Christian Church (Disciples of Christ), on which I served for more than two decades, completed a long-term study on ecclesiology in a report to the General Assembly in 1997. This final report and previous reports are contained in eds. Paul A. Crow Jr. and James O. Duke, *The Church for the Disciples of Christ: Seeking to be Truly Church Today* (St. Louis: Christian Board of Publication, 1998). That the report fell promptly into oblivion and neglect is but an understatement of the problems in current Disciples theological self-understanding. My recent book, *On Being the Church of Jesus Christ in Tumultuous Times* (Eugene, OR: Cascade, 2005) contains a wide range of reflections on the present state of Disciples; see especially the Introduction and chapters 1, 2, 3, 4, 12, and 14.

On Being the Church of Jesus Christ

even in the Movement's originating decades and therefore may be common to all three wings.

How, then, do we get back on track in developing an ecclesiology? Here I want to make some proposals that might help.

First, I propose that we recognize that any community, but especially the church, lives and has its practical identity in and through its characteristic and distinctive *discourses and practices*. It is within these discourses that the community identifies itself, acknowledges a common purpose, and devises procedures and practices—a politics—that facilitate and even constitute the community as just this community among many other communities. When those discourses and practices are lacking in basic agreement and flounder in disarray, we can understand why the community itself might be suffering profound confusion about itself and its identity.[4]

Second, I propose we embrace our early Movement's desire to give primacy to the New Testament witness, but I propose that we study the New Testament as the emerging *discourses and practices* of the Jesus movement. And we must understand these discourses and practices as throughout *theological*: they intend to witness to Jesus as the Savior of the world and they intend thereby to identify him as bound-up-with and/or tethered-to and/or one-with the reality of the God of Israel. When the post-apostolic church sorted out the New Testament texts as authoritative canon, it primarily meant that the discourses and practices in these texts are authoritative and informative for succeeding followers of Jesus. Put another way, the witness and conversations manifest in these texts are the conversation-partners for all future conversation that should be forming and informing that emerging social reality called *ekklesia*—the summoned and assembled and gathered people of God.[5]

One consequence of this proposal is that we can affirm that the New Testament discourses are already theological and therefore we can give up the notion that *doing theology* is somehow a misleading practice for the church. If the New Testament discourses are to live in the church today, then the church is itself constituted by its peculiar theological discourses

---

4. In my systematic theology, *A Grammar of Christian Faith: Systematic Explorations in Christian Life and Doctrine*, 2 vols. (Lanham, MD: Rowman & Littlefield, 2002), I discuss the importance of language to the life of the church (1–19); see especially the ten theses on language on pages 17–18.

5. In my *Grammar* book, chapter 11 is on the Doctrine of the Church. Pages 596–602 contain an account of the rich variety of images of the church in the New Testament, which I based on the work of Paul Minear.

PART ONE—Ecumenical Theologizing with Ecclesial Friends

and the peculiar practices that are both represented in and formed by the New Testament discourses.

Third, we can now admit that our own contemporary Restoration tradition could not exist without the discourses and practices of the church in the succeeding centuries after the New Testament. We can, therefore, engage these previous traditions and their contemporary descendants in serious theological discussion without fear that we are somehow forsaking the New Testament witness.[6]

Fourth, apparently without sustained consistency and clarity of intention, the Movement did seem to identify being-the-church with being-disciples-of-Jesus. In this way it might be possible that discipleship to Jesus would entail *doing church* differently as an *alternative community* to the ways of other churches and to the ways of the world.

To further this discussion of an ecclesiology in which the church is an alternative community, I will now propose a theological definition of the church, which I have been using for over two decades.

> The church is that liberative and redemptive
> community of persons
> called into being
> by the Gospel of Jesus Christ
> through the Holy Spirit
> to witness in word and deed
> to the living triune God
> for the benefit of the world
> to the glory of God.

What then is the church as a social reality in the world? It is a *liberative and redemptive community of persons*. It is a community—a *koinonia*—in which persons are being liberated and redeemed from those conditions in their lives that prohibit and inhibit the love of God and the love of neighbor. Here we can affirm that the church is throughout its life and work a *soteriological* community: responding to God's salvific work in and for the world. The church's distinctive discourses and practices are themselves the *means of grace* through which the church and the world receive and learn how to live under the grace of God. They are not, however, the means by which we are to earn God's grace. The prior grace of God in Jesus Christ empowers

---

6. See *Grammar*, 111–48, for a discussion of the authority of the Bible in relation to church traditions.

the church to be liberated by grace and to be liberating in communicating that grace and forgiveness.

But it is a community that is *called into being by the Gospel of Jesus Christ*. Clarity about who or what calls a community together is essential, and the way we have put the call of the church is such as to deny that the church is called into existence by any other agent or cause than the Gospel of Jesus Christ. It is the Gospel that summons the church into existence, and when some church community can no longer agree as to who calls it or even what the Gospel is, there we have a church community that has lost both its calling and its purpose.[7]

In the Restoration tradition, there has been continuing agreement, even in the midst of our disagreements, that there is a Gospel that is rooted in the life, death, and resurrection of Jesus of Nazareth. It is, however, my hope that all wings of the Movement might agree that Jesus is the very reality of God-become-flesh and moving among humans in reconciling patterns of speaking and living. While the Disciples wing has not been able to sustain a common trinitarian understanding of God, and the other wings are hesitant at the prospect, a nontrinitarian understanding will miss the mark and Jesus will be reduced to a prophet of some importance but not the incarnate life of God reconciling the world to Godself.

The Gospel of Jesus Christ summons the church into being and through the continuing activity of the Holy Spirit gives the church its *defining purpose and mission: to witness in word and deed to the living triune God for the benefit of the world*. In all that it is and does, in its words and deeds, in its discourses and practices, the church is bearing witness to the reality of God as the One who created the world and covenanted with Israel, as the One who became incarnate in Jesus of Nazareth for the salvation of the world, and as the One who moves within creaturely life to redeem the world. There is no other God than this triune God, and the church exists to witness to what this God has done as Creator, Reconciler, and Redeemer of the world.[8] Hence, the church itself exists for the *benefit of the world*—as that creaturely world God is intent on redeeming.

Once again we must grasp the importance of the discourses and practices of the church: it is in the words of the discourses that the church

---

7. It seems to me that every church must continually be asking itself just what the Gospel is. For my statement of the Gospel, see *Grammar*, 7, 112–14.

8. See my *Grammar*, 166–98, for an extended argument for the inescapability of trinitarian belief for any church that believes Jesus is divine and human.

construes for itself and for the world who God is, what the Gospel of Jesus Christ is, what it means to be God's beloved creature graced and loved by God, and what the church can hope for in the future before God. Yet, we must not forget that the discourses live in and through the distinctive practices of the church.

The ecclesiology that I am unfolding now aims to identify the sort of communal body the church is as the *body of Christ* in the world—a new *social reality* in the world intending the transformation of human life and the worlds in which they live as the worlds that God loves and is intent on redeeming. Herein being the body of Christ centers on discipleship to Jesus as the one who proclaimed the kingdom of God, who advocated love of neighbor and enemy, and who commanded a nonviolent way of life. *This is the body of Christ as an alternative community living an alternative way of life to the ways of the world.*

Consider how the witness of the church in discourses and practices can be understood in three interrelated spheres of the church's life. These spheres are what I call the *Sphere of Church Nurture*, the *Sphere of Church Outreach*, and the *Sphere of Church Administration*. Let us be clear: the church is witnessing to the triune God in all three of these spheres and not just in the Outreach sphere. In each of these spheres there is a host of distinctive practices that are essential to the church being the sort of community the Gospel of Jesus Christ summons it to be.

Briefly, in the Sphere of Nurture the church engages in the distinctive ways of *worshiping* God, of *educating* itself and passing on the faith, and of *communal care* in the practices of love that see to the needs of the gathered folk. The church is that community that practices baptizing persons in the name of the Father, the Son, and the Holy Spirit as the gracious good news that their sins have been forgiven and they are called to live a new life of neighbor love. The church practices the celebration of the Lord's Supper as the encounter with the living Jesus Christ as the Lord of History and hope for the world. The church practices reading the Bible *as* Holy Scripture and preaches and teaches the Word known in the Bible. Without these concrete practices in which the nurture of the church itself takes place in and through its distinctive language, the church flounders in its life. Throughout these practices, of course, the church is embodying a witness to the world, declaring that God is graciously summoning the people of the world to receive God's grace and live in peace with one another.

In the practices of the Sphere of Outreach the church aims directly to act upon and within the world for the world's transformation. Such practices include *evangelism*, being at the side of the neighbor as one who needs to hear of God's reconciling life in Jesus. The church also engages in the practices of *prophecy*, intending to identify those principalities and powers in the world that subjugate human beings and exclude them from the goods of life that encourage hope and generosity. In the practices of *emancipation* the church, often in cooperation with other similar spirits and groups, seeks to perform works that seek to emancipate the least powerful of our human brothers and sisters from those social conditions that enslave them. In the practices of *vocation*, in and through individual Christian lives in the world, they seek to inhabit places of home and neighborhood, of economic work, of citizenship, and of recreation as places in which God is at work and summoning them to truth-telling, promise-keeping, and nonviolence.

What then are we to make of the Sphere of Administration? While I think our forebears searched for a simpler organization in the New Testament than is actually there, there are some definite beliefs and practices we in the Free Church tradition can clearly embrace. First, we must acknowledge that how the church organizes itself, how it has a polity and a politics, is itself a form of witness to the world. Second, the church can never forget that any organizing it does within itself is subject to the criterion of whether it facilitates the mission of witness. In that respect, the processes and practices of administering the life of the church are not ends in themselves; they are means to the end of the faithful and truthful witness of the church in the totality of its life. Thirdly, the Restoration tradition should refuse to relinquish its belief that the New Testament church is not a hierarchically ordered community dependent on its 'overseers' for its ongoing identity and legitimacy. Whatever we might make of the distinction between ordained ministers and laity, we should never construe it as a hierarchical distinction essential to the life and witness of the church.

There is not space here to discuss *in extenso* that the administration of the church includes trying to understand how the church of Jesus Christ is *one* church, one body, wherever it might exist. By what criteria are we to recognize that the church existed in traditions prior to and outside of the Restoration Movement? Can any tradition properly administer its witness to the world if it abstains from the theological, and therefore the practical, quest for Christian unity? Let us not suppose that the unity of the church universal will await or even linger along the byways while the wings of the

Restoration Movement worry how to recognize—how to construe—the living vitality of Christ's presence among themselves![9]

In concluding this essay I want to highlight a possibility—I would even call it a *mandate*—that the church so understands itself under the Lordship of Jesus Christ that it feels obliged periodically and publicly to *confess its faith in clear statements*. Such confessional statements must not be understood as infallible and irreformable, but they can be definite theological statements to the world of what the church itself regards as the essence of the Gospel of Jesus Christ. Unwillingness to produce such confessional statements, requiring, as they must, vigorous discussion within the church, is a sure sign that the church is willing either to suffer chaos in its public witness or to resort to less visible means of coercing and controlling that public witness.

Having an ecclesiology is simply to have a set of discourses and practices that identify what sort of community the church intends to be. The Restoration Movement's uneasiness about *doctrine* and *creeds* has unhappily obscured from itself that it does have—and must of practical necessity have—definite *teachings*. In linguistic fact, it would be an oxymoron to suppose that any community could claim to be the church of Jesus Christ in the absence of any particular teachings about who Jesus Christ is and what he does that is salvific for humankind, teachings about what it means to be a disciple of Jesus, and therefore some teachings about how such disciples live together and the purpose of their living and working together, and teachings about the purpose of their community they call 'church.' Let it thereby be clearly declared: *no community can be the church of Jesus Christ in the absence of definite teachings embodied in distinct discourses and practices that are constitutive of its communal life and purpose.*

So, abandoning the excuse that we have no doctrines, let us get on with the arduous but joyful task of identifying, critiquing, and testing the actual ecclesiology that already exists in the lives of the churches of the Restoration Movement and thereby assume responsibility for what we believe, teach, and do in our intention to be the church of Jesus Christ.

---

9. I sustain a consistently free-church theological perspective on administering the church in *Grammar*, 634–48.

3

Spiritual Formation and Christian Discourse

The Shaping Power of Christian Discourse

An address given at a Stone-Campbell Conference at Speedway Church of Christ in Indianapolis, Indiana in August of 2007. Published in Spiritual Formation and the Future of Stone-Campbell Churches *(Bloomington, IN: Ketch Publishing, 2008), 1–20. Edited herein.*

It is an extraordinary pleasure and blessing to be participating in this conference with brothers and sisters bound together as participants in and heirs of the Stone-Campbell Movement. It is a further joy to be invited here by my good friend and former student, Kent Ellett. The sheer delight of having him as that special sort of student who thinks clearly, believes deeply, and isn't afraid to speak up remains vivid in my memory. But to continue to have him as a conversation-partner in these years of my so-called retirement summons me to gird up my loins and engage his most probing questions and earnest proposals.[1] For you who are members of Kent's congregation here in Speedway, however much he may prod, probe, and challenge you to reach beyond your previous habits of thought, be reassured by me that he speaks with the authority and wisdom of angels and with the power of a divinely gracious passion.

---

1. Some folk may be interested in seeing an exchange between Kent and myself that is posted on my website, www.grammaroffaith.com, under "Responses" in the menu.

Part One—Ecumenical Theologizing with Ecclesial Friends

As a seventy-year-old third generation member of the Disciples branch of the Stone-Campbell movement, I have over the years encountered many from the Churches of Christ and Independent branches—encountered them as my students and as folks in the larger American ecclesial culture who are earnest about the authority of the Bible, the independence of the congregation, the unflinching inclusion of laity in church governance, and the unswerving conviction that there is a Gospel rooted in the life, death, and resurrection of Jesus of Nazareth.[2]

But how might I engage my Movement friends to preserve this passion for the Gospel and the Bible, while easing them out of that oft-unspoken but troublesome conviction that the Bible and the 'facts' of the Bible have authority only if the whole of the Bible is *inerrant*. Of course, many are they in the Movement who have seen their brothers and sisters relinquish that conviction only to tumble right off the spectrum of traditional Christian beliefs. Take a roll in a Unitarian congregation and you will find many of the broken-hearted who once tabernacled among the Stone-Campbell Movement but lost an authoritative and salvific Christ to a "Jesus of history" who died inadvertently but nevertheless left behind sayings of considerable moral and symbolic value.

It is also continually troubling to me that the Stone-Campbell Movement has been so focused on the Bible, in particular the New Testament, that it easily falls into the habit of thinking that *tradition* and *theology* are temptations to be avoided. Just stick with the Bible only and all will be well. The tradition that folk have in mind when they think this way is the tradition of the early ecumenical creeds and what came to be called the Roman Catholic Church. However, it is virtually unnoticed that all the branches of the Movement are themselves continuing *traditions*—as in the traditions of local congregations with their distinctive ways of ordering their life and thought; as in the traditions by virtue of which they could identify other congregations as included in their particular 'brotherhood.' The Movement might have rejected some past traditions, but it was practically impossible to reject all traditioning because they could not continue on into the future without a sense of who they were, who else was like them, and who else was faithful in ways that could be trusted.

---

2. In another format I recently addressed issues of ecclesiology with others in the Stone-Campbell Movement in an essay entitled "On Being the Church of Jesus Christ" in *Leaven*, vol. 15, no. 1 (First Quarter 2007), 6–11.

In this same connection, *doing theology* was typically considered *speculating* beyond what the Bible itself might say. 'Speculating' is the right word here, for it was a name for that apparent human reasoning and invention that went beyond the Bible and sought an authority and truth independent of the Bible. This negative sense about doing theology was also tied to a troubled mind about 'doctrines' and 'creeds.' If theology is be pursued it must be simply 'biblical theology'; the Bible and the plain and intelligible 'facts' of the Bible are the 'givens' for all church theologizing and teaching. Yet this suspicion about *reasoning and theologizing* often obscured from Movement folk the obvious fact that they are *reasoning* all the time as they interpret and infer points from Scripture, make arguments, draw distinctions, and so on.[3]

Closely linked to these dimensions of our heritage was our wariness of talking about the Spirit and certainly our reluctance to talk about 'spirituality.' To be sure, along with many in American Christianity, we talked excessively and effusively about faith being a 'private matter between the individual and God,' though sometimes we would fall into that American idiom of saying 'the individual and *his* God.' Even today, when many other church traditions regard 'spirituality' as an urgent topic for the Christian life, Movement folk still put the emphasis on the individual and tend to ignore that the individual Christian always lives in some tradition in the midst of some formative community.

Some Proposals about Spiritual Formation and Christian Discourses

These previous comments are simply intended as appetizers for the topic I have been assigned for this conference: Spiritual Formation and Christian Discourse. This actually is a wonderful topic, rich in possibilities of making

---

3. That some folk in the Movement nevertheless thought they were just interpreting the facts of scripture in a manner of "inductive reasoning," see Richard T. Hughes and C. Leonard Allen, *Illusions of Innocence: Protestant Primitivism in America, 1630-1875* (Chicago: University of Chicago Press, 1988) and Mark A. Noll, *The Scandal of the Evangelical Mind* (Grand Rapids: Eerdmans, 1994), especially 96-98.

For the reader/listener who is interested in further exploration on various theological topics, I will refer them to my systematic theology, *A Grammar of Christian Faith: Systematic Explorations in Christian Life and Doctrine*, 2 vols. (Lanham, MD: Rowman & Littlefield, 2002), hereinafter referred to as GCF. See GCF, 117-19 for a discussion of "reason." See GCF, 121-30 for a discussion of the authority of scripture, and 131-35 for a discussion of "tradition."

Part One—Ecumenical Theologizing with Ecclesial Friends

some pertinent and hopefully useful remarks about the Christian life and the church. I propose the following for our consideration:

1. There is no Christian life or spirituality that is not formed by some tradition or traditions of discourse. Hence, the word "discourse" here simply refers to the many ways in which a tradition lives in and through its distinctive ways of speaking and acting, of construing and judging, of thinking and believing, feeling and imagining. Take away these distinctive linguistic practices and you nullify the tradition as well. In making these points I am reminding us that the spirituality the church is concerned about is itself a *construction* of the language of the church.[4]

2. All of the primary discourses—the language—of the Christian church are *theological* in intent and scope: it is language *about* God and human life *before* God or language directed *to* God. Thus the constitutive language of the church is theological from beginning to end. The hymns we have sung this evening are theological. Our prayers are theological. Hence, let us give up the pretense that we are not doing theology or speaking theologically. The real question, however, is whether what we are doing and saying is good, true, and faithful theology, and that is a vexing but inescapable question that requires prolonged and demanding conversation and inquiry.

3. While the discourses of the Bible—what we call the Old and New Testaments—are the given discourses from which later traditions learn who God is and what God has done and is doing, it has never been the case that the discourses of the Bible were available to anyone apart from some contemporary ecclesial community of interpretation. As almost all of us Protestants have come to agree, the ecclesial tradition arising from first-century Israel in the proclamation, crucifixion, and resurrection of Jesus of Nazareth is the tradition that brought forth and determined what would constitute the authoritative canon of the New Testament. The church's discourses over the centuries have always been discourses intending to teach us what the Bible *really says*, but now really says according to the community's own study and interpretation. Hence, there is no easy answer to the question of which came first, the church or the New Testament. It was the early apostolic and post-apostolic church that wrote, preserved, and decided what would count as canonical texts for the church's life.

---

4. I grant that it may seem peculiar to put this emphasis on language and discourse, but see my prolonged discussion of these concepts in GCF, 1–19.

4. When we talk now as Christians about spiritual formation, we are relying on the distinctive ways in which the church talks about the shape of the Christian life. In ways conceptually interchangeable, talk of *spiritual life* is simply talk about how human life comes be shaped, formed, transformed, and enlivened by the Holy Spirit. Along with most church traditions, we have agreed that spiritual formation entails two overarching prongs of emphasis, both rooted in the prior forgiving grace of God in Jesus Christ: being formed by a relationship of love to God and being formed by a relationship of love for the neighbor.

Such formation could also be called *discipleship* to Jesus Christ as Lord and Savior. To be spiritual in the Christian sense is to be a disciple of Jesus—a follower of Jesus and a believer in Jesus' Gospel. When we tie spirituality to discipleship to Jesus, we should be able to grasp why spiritual formation is inextricably tied to some distinctive *beliefs* and distinctive *actions and feelings*. These beliefs and actions/feelings are what can also be called the *what* and the *how* of the Christian life. Saying it another way, in becoming members of the church as the body of Christ, persons are being formed by the incarnational narrative of Jesus Christ as the Son of God and Savior of the world. The Holy Spirit that moves within persons in the church is simply the Spirit of Jesus Christ and the Spirit of the Father.[5]

In ways that I hope will become clearer in our conversation together, I will be contending that the *what* and the *how* of Christian life are intricately and complexly intertwined and interdependent. Hence, to suppose one can have the *whats*—the beliefs, the Gospel, the incarnational narrative—without the *how*—the way of life, or the *how* without the *whats* is to erroneously suppose that either can be had without the other.

5. The theological task of sorting out the *whats* of Christian faith is crucial to Christian spirituality. It is important in this regard to notice that every tradition of the church believes there is at the center of its faith a *Gospel*—a good news about what God has done for human salvation—and that Gospel centers on Jesus Christ. What is that Gospel? Over many years of teaching theology courses in seminaries I have insisted that each student must be

---

5. I think one of the reasons the Stone-Campbell Movement in all of its strands has been short on developing a doctrine of the work of the Holy Spirit is that we have hesitated at the development of a robust trinitarian doctrine of God. See GCF, 483–509, for an attempt at retrieving such a robust doctrine of the Spirit. Note as well how trinitarian conceptuality connects spirituality, Christian life, and the church in GCF, 511–91, 593–653.

involved in the process of identifying as clearly and succinctly as he or she can just what that Gospel is. If we cannot come to some agreement about the Gospel, then it is irrelevant whether we believe the Bible is inerrant or not. Further, I propose that how we identify the Gospel will also give us a clue to how we ought to be reading the Bible. Talk of spiritual formation will itself fall into disarray if there is substantial disagreement about what is the Gospel. I want to recommend that all of us here for this conference, pastors and laity alike, try our hand [or should I say try our tongue] at saying what the Gospel is. To put it strongly for emphasis sake: it is the Gospel that ought to be guiding our reading of the Bible rather than our assumption that the Bible is what we must first "believe in" and then we can find the Gospel in the Bible.

6. Here is my try at formulating the Gospel—as the *Gospel of Jesus Christ*—as a way of clarifying for us what is involved in that spiritual formation that is summoned and formed by the Gospel:

> The Gospel of Jesus Christ is the Good News
> that the God of Israel, the Creator of all creatures,
> has in freedom and love become incarnate
> in the life, death, and resurrection of Jesus of Nazareth
> to enact and reveal God's gracious reconciliation
> of humanity to Godself, and
> through the Holy Spirit calls and empowers human beings
> to participate in God's liberative and redemptive work by
> acknowledging God's gracious forgiveness in Jesus,
> repenting of human sin,
> receiving the gift of freedom, and
> embracing authentic community by
> loving the neighbor and the enemy,
> caring for the whole creation, and
> hoping for the final triumph of God's grace
> as the triune Ultimate Companion of all Creatures.

I hope it is discernible that this Gospel statement is meaningless apart from the rich biblically-formed and tradition-sustained discourses and practices of the church. But I believe this statement might also give us some understanding of what sort of spiritual formation is important for the life of the church.

7. These points can position us to grasp an essential truth about faith and spiritual development: it is impossible—even unintelligible—that anyone

can become a Christian without *learning how to be a Christian* and such learning is dependent on being formed by the distinctive *discourses* and *practices* of the church. It is this *learning how* that we can also call *being spiritually formed by and conformed to Christ*. The Christian life itself is simply the life of this *being formed and conformed*. To grow in spiritual life it is necessary to acquire the skills involved in thinking and practicing faithfulness. In learning these skills the Christian becomes *wise* in the ways of God.

If this sounds odd to us, let me put it another way: however intense an experience of some sort a person might have had, without awareness of some available Christian language, it would be strictly impossible that the person could understand her experience as an experience of the Holy Spirit of the risen Jesus Christ. Certainly one might later *learn* to construe a previously compelling experience as an experience of the Spirit of God, but this construal is itself dependent on the language the person has come to possess. Could Paul have recognized Jesus on the road to Damascus if he had never heard of Jesus nor heard any language about Jesus of Nazareth?

8. Central to this spiritual formation is that persons come to have an *identity* before God. It is an identity that is superior to any other identity the person might also have. This is the identity of knowing oneself loved and forgiven by God and called by God to life in and through the church as witness to God's grace. The practice of baptism both bestows this identity and signals the acceptance of that identity by the baptizee and her promise to grow more deeply into that identity in the unfolding future.[6]

9. In light of these points, I trust it is now obvious why I firmly believe that the church as the body of Christ is intrinsically an *alternative community* from the communities of the world and yet that sort of alternative that lives on behalf of the world. It lives on behalf of the world, yet not on the world's terms. Rather, the church lives on its own evangelical terms as a redemptive community summoned by God to witness to God's gracious Life for the redemption of the world.

10. Two further points follow from these. First point: the church is itself the *site* where the conversation occurs as to what are the distinctive and important beliefs of the faith. Accordingly, that conversation is joyfully *theological*

---

6. See GCF, 662–70 for what my Disciples friends think is a surprising defense of the Movement's emphasis on "believer's baptism."

and involves that struggle whereby the church and all its members are engaged in that inescapable movement of *faith seeking understanding*. Second point: when that conversation internal to the church falls into disarray and confusion or becomes captive to concepts and beliefs alien to the Gospel of Jesus Christ, then the spiritual formation of its members becomes confused and disordered.

11. If what I have just outlined is helpful in thinking about spiritual formation and Christian discourses, then I hope we can now discern that the *theological content* of the discourses and practices of the church are truly important. It really does matter, then, how those discourses construe who God is and what it means to be human. Hence, we are confronted with the obvious implication that not everything anyone in the church, whether minister or layperson, says is good and truthful theology—that is, good and truthful construal of who the God is who comes to us in Israel, becomes incarnate in the life, death, and resurrection of Jesus of Nazareth, and in the Holy Spirit summons us to life in the church. Professed earnest intentions to speak of God do not of themselves guarantee truthful theological construals. Further, simple citations of the Bible do not guarantee faithful and truthful construals.

Before going further with this inquiry and before you get too nervous as to where I am going with these points, trust that I believe the God we know in Jesus Christ through the Spirit is the One who can work with and through broken and misleading and unfruitful discourses and practices. Many are we who were moved by the Spirit through language that we no longer believe is either true or upbuilding but was nevertheless the grist by way of which the Spirit moved us to greater maturity and spirituality. But that is no reason to be complacent about those discourses and practices in the church that are broken and unhelpful or even false and unfaithful. As Paul says, "When I was a child, I spoke like a child, I thought like a child, I reasoned like a child; when I became an adult I put an end to childish ways" (1 Cor 13:11).

Christian Identity, Spiritual Malformation, and the Discourses of the Church

If spiritual formation, as I have been arguing, is itself dependent on some discourses and practices that claim to be Christian, isn't it also the case

Spiritual Formation and Christian Discourse

that sometimes persons even in the church are *malformed* by discourses and practices that might seem to be heretical? The concept of spiritual formation thus contains within itself its contrary: *spiritual malformation*. I worry—and I confess this must sound arrogant—that many are the folk in our time who are being seriously malformed spiritually by discourses and practices within the church that are simply false or in contradiction to the Gospel of Jesus Christ.

We all know that it is exceedingly demanding to be an *alternative community called and formed by the Gospel of Jesus Christ*. Why is it so demanding and troubling? How does it come about that the church itself repeatedly succumbs to being just another mirror image of the world in which it exists? It is a continuing circumstance of the church that it is always and everywhere a community that exists in the midst of some other world/culture/society in whatever place or whenever time. All these other cultures/societies have their own principalities and powers that organize their life together, or strenuously try to organize their life. Repeatedly, however, it is these principalities and powers that exert continual pressure to *form* persons and to tell them who they are and what they are worth and what their place is in the larger order. In short, the worldly powers intend to give persons an *identity* that will inculcate loyalty to the powers and to living on behalf of the powers. These powers want their subjects to answer, "I am an Oklahoman" or "I am an American" or "I am a German" or "I am a Democrat" or "I am a Republican," for example, as the decisive markers of *person's self-understanding and worldly identity*. In ways exceedingly complex, these powers are unceasingly intent on subverting the church as an alternative community and are unceasingly intent on assuring that the church will be a community that serves the interests of the ruling powers of the world. It takes no imagination for each of us to fill in the blanks here.[7]

The church, then, in its discourses and practices of spiritual formation is continually tempted by these seductions and the history of such seducery is long and distressing. Ask this question of our tradition today here in the U.S.A.: am I an American who happens to be a Christian, or am I a Christian who happens to be an American? *Which identity orders which?* That is the disarming and crucial question. It should be apparent to us that the church must maintain a vigorous self-critical dialogue within itself if it

---

7. See GCF, 47–52, 648–53 for a discussion of what I call 'the dialectic between church and world,' in terms of which I explain three interrelated uses of the term 'world.'

is to sustain its identity as the body of Christ and an alternative community to the world.

I would here call your attention to a wonderfully insightful book by one of our distinguished lecturers here, namely, Professor Philip Kenneson's *Life on the Vine: Cultivating the Fruit of the Spirit in Christian Community*.[8] His book is a precise and subtle diagnosis and exploration of the many obstacles to Christian spiritual formation in our present American culture. The mirror he holds up to us in the Movement is a mirror that brings to light our hidden beliefs and inclinations and enjoins us to cultivate a distinctive way of life in the church of Jesus Christ.

Many are the ways in which the church's discourses and practices have been malformed by the powerful influences of the world, and we might also infer that such malformation has infiltrated and often confused the spiritual life of the members of the church body.

If we are in any doubt about the perils to which I am referring and about the ways in which appeals to an inerrant Bible have succumbed to these perils, then consider how many brutal wars and battles have been fought defending the belief in the divine authority of kings—an authority repeatedly defended as grounded in the biblical language of kingship or the unrivaled and God-ordained authority of rulers. Yet today, the question of the authority of kings as representatives of divine rule and judgment simply does not arise. It is not a live question. Why was it a live and therefore deadly question for millions of folk over many centuries? How did it happen that seemingly sincere Christians construed their primary discourses as counseling them to be obedient to and defend the rightful authority of kings and other rulers? And to kill on behalf of the king and the maintenance of the king's realm?[9]

Consider the status of chattel slavery. It was for centuries defended by many Christians as directly authorized by the Bible or at least permitted by biblical teaching and practice. And many were they who suffered as slaves and many were they who died to defeat slavery and died to defend slavery. There was the Bible—God's Word—being read in such different ways. Is there any one here today who would like to defend the right to buy, possess,

---

8. Downers Grove, IL: InterVarsity, 1999.

9. Of course, Paul in Romans 13:1–7 is typically invoked in these matters, almost in utter disregard for everything else he says in this epistle. I will say here, though I recognize its insufficiency, that sorting through these issues of "government" and "politics" is a major project for my future work.

Spiritual Formation and Christian Discourse

and sell human beings as slaves? Let us hope it is a non-issue for Stone-Campbell Christians today.[10]

Rising beyond issues of kingships and slavery, consider the overwhelming fact of history that Christians have for centuries gone to war when rulers determined it was necessary to go to war. Surely the Christians knew that there was not a scintilla of evidence anywhere in the New Testament that Jesus called followers to kill in his name or for the sake of his Kingdom. Nor does the New Testament anywhere teach that it is morally necessary and obligatory to kill others in order to defend the boundaries of a nation or a people. In fact the preaching of Jesus was replete with commands about loving and praying for the enemy and turning the cheek. How then does it happen that persons in the church become spiritually formed to think that killing others is somehow warranted by the one they call their Savior?

Let all of us affirm that it does really matter who we think God is, how we identify the reality and activities of God. The word "God" gets used in many different ways in the English language and in other languages as well. For Christians the crucial question is what do we mean when we use the word "God." Are we referring to that terrible god vowing to destroy and burn this fallen world and to rejoice in the suffering of the condemned? Are we referring to the god who demands loyalty to the state from all the citizens of each of the nation-states in our time? Which of these gods is the One who comes to us in Christ Jesus?

Friends in Christ, I am affirming that, if the discourses of the church are crucial to the spiritual formation of its members, then it matters what the contents of those discourses are—it matters what we believe and say about God and human life and the Gospel of Jesus Christ—and it matters to how we live and are formed as the body of Christ. It matters too whether we serve and are inspired by the Holy Spirit or by some other animating spirit.

---

10. Anyone who is tempted to think of herself as affirming biblical inerrancy must read the sobering account by the church historian Mark Noll of the terrible infelicities embedded in the church's discussion of slavery because of some biblical passages that seemed to permit slavery. See Noll's *The Civil War as a Theological Crisis* (Chapel Hill: University of North Carolina Press, 2006). Does anyone here today doubt that the ghosts of those debates and that war are hovering around us still?

PART ONE—Ecumenical Theologizing with Ecclesial Friends

Some Discourses and Practices that Involve Spiritual Perils

While many in our tradition have believed that theologizing is itself inimical to the faith, that belief itself has the consequence of hiding from ourselves that we hold deep beliefs about God that are formed by no other source than prejudiced kinfolk or a twisted and untutored pastor or a civic organization we might have joined or by a television evangelist we find congenial to our tastes or what we might have thought up in our own kitchen.

Consider now these beliefs quite common among the folk I encounter in church on Sunday mornings and in their crises around death and suffering. Many believe that everything that happens in the world is directly willed by God and that every event bears a particular divine purpose. So, if one loses one's child in an automobile accident, then God must have had a purpose in willing that accident to happen—though it remains hidden from us that if that is so, then we cannot really call it an 'accident'; it was a necessity willed by God. So we are utterly bewildered by the loss of the child and are perhaps rightly angry with God as to why God willed this to happen. Had we more time we could explore the nuances in this line of reasoning, but you would be foolish to suppose that this belief that everything happens for a divine purpose is not formative for many a Christian. I want to suggest to you that this belief really matters in *how* persons construe their lives, but I propose to you that it is profoundly misleading about the God we know in the cross of Jesus Christ. Perhaps we should phrase the matter this way: God does create and sustain a world of creatures in continual interaction with each other and therewith *permits* many destructive events to occur, while continually working in the world to be bring good out of evil.[11]

Think further about how persons often construe praying—sometimes under the impetus of questionable construals of New Testament accounts of Jesus' preaching and teaching.[12] It goes something like this: God is eager to reward those who trust in God and will give to the faithful whatever the faithful ask in prayer, *if* they just have enough faith. Hence, hunker down and have enough faith and God will give you what you want. Prayer gets you what you want. God the Cosmic Fetcher doing what the faithful want!

---

11. See further the lengthy discussion in chapter 5: "God the Creator: Creation, Providence, and Evil" in GCF, 233–92.

12. I have in mind such passages as Mark 11:22–24; Matt 7:7–11; 21:21–22. But see how Luke changes the meaning in Luke 11:13. See my extended discussion of prayer in GCF, 676–88.

Spiritual Formation and Christian Discourse

And, when the person who so prays does not get that for which she prayed, then the obvious conclusion is that she did not have enough faith. Consider what this means for persons who pray for the recovery of their dying loved ones who yet go on and die in spite of the prayers. What confusion and bewilderment: did the loved one die because we did not pray with enough faith? Perhaps it would have gone better and the loved one escaped death if we had gotten a hundred earnest persons praying? So, God awaits to be persuaded [bribed?] by the prayers of the faithful but the persuasion does not work if there is not the requisite amount of faith? Who is this "God" anyhow? How much more devastating can life be than to lead the sick and dying to believe that if they just have enough faith then God will cure them? So now these presumably Christian beliefs and practices spiritually form the dying to bear the additional guilt that they are dying because they did not have enough faith?

How do beliefs like these get such a hold on us? Why did we miss that Jesus' interest was teaching us that God is indeed gracious toward us and eager to bestow blessings on us. But we will only understand what the requisite blessings are when we understand that Jesus is teaching us what we ought to desire if we intend our desires to be commensurate with the Kingdom he is preaching and bringing. Pray for these blessings and God will surely be gracious. Pray for the blessing of being one who hungers and thirsts for righteousness's sake. Pray for the blessing of being a peacemaker. How generous God is to peacemakers. Pray for the blessing of a pure heart and be blessed in seeing God deeply. Pray for those who revile and persecute you, those enemies that intend you harm, and you will be blessed. The world may not bless you with honor and esteem, but God will.

Friends, I am not calling into question our praying those intercessory prayers that are vital to our faith. But I do worry about the deep corruption involved in the beliefs and practices of supposing we can pray to God to give us what we want and never question whether our wants and desires are appropriate to the presence of the Kingdom. What passes today under the slogan of the 'Gospel of Wealth' is a heretical encouragement to use the practice and discourses of prayer as a means to the really important 'blessing' of being wealthy. Why is it that we forget to pray for those goods that Jesus taught us to desire or to pray as Paul did that "whether we live or whether we die, we are the Lord's" (Rom 14:8)?

Yes, people in the church use the Bible in debilitating ways. I once heard a sermon based on Psalm 91 urging us to believe that this Psalm was the soldiers' prayer that God will protect them from the enemy, instilling the belief that if a soldier truly trusts in God he will be brought safely home, for God always protects the truly faithful. In that perfunctory greeting line after the sermon, I asked the preacher whether he was aware that precisely this Psalm had been cited by many of the Jewish faithful as the compelling reason why Jesus could not have been the Messiah. How could anyone be construed as the Messiah of God, the one most blessed, if he had been crucified and killed by the enemy? Surely a true Messiah would have been saved by the God of Israel from death and harm at the hands of the enemy. The pastor looked at me as though I was a quarrelsome professor picking on a sincere preacher just doing his duty of proclaiming God's word. Friends, this is the stuff of spiritual formation and malformation. Persons in the church are often being formed by just these beliefs and just these practices. It is sobering and counter-cultural to think people in the church should be formed in faith by believing in a God who dies on a cross for the salvation of the world. That is odd, very odd, and we dare not forget just how odd that story is and how the Gospel is tethered to it—and how the church's soul depends on its being tethered to that crucifixion and that salvation.

Friends, it matters what you believe about God. It matters to your own spiritual formation whether you believe God's aim for the world is ultimate destruction of the many and salvation for the few. It matters whether you believe God called America to be a light to the nations and therefore America is always justified in the purity of its motives and its own going to war against enemies as the enemies of God. It matters whether you believe Muslims are included in that category of the neighbors and strangers we are to love.

Think about it. It may be that our spirituality is at stake in what we believe or do not believe. It matters whether we are formed in Christ or malformed by the spirits of the world.

4

Salvation

Mapping the Salvific Themes in Christian Faith

An essay written in 2006, published in ed. Peter Goodwin Heltzel, Chalice Introduction to Disciples Theology *(St. Louis: Chalice, 2008), 190–202.*

From biblical times to the present, the discourses and practices of the Christian church have pivoted around the central conviction that the God of Israel, the Creator of the world, became incarnate in the life, death, and resurrection of the Jew Jesus of Nazareth for the salvation of the world. It is this central conviction that gave content to the joyful belief that there was a *Gospel*—good news about the salvation of the world. Drop out this conviction and this Gospel and the discourses and practices of the church lose their coherence and continuity. But having firmly said this, I must acknowledge that the meaning of the word 'salvation' has been more variegated and multidimensional than the church has often been willing to admit.

The purpose of this chapter is to explore the various uses of salvation language in the life of the church, identifying some differentiated uses and their interconnection with other doctrines or teachings, and to propose some ways of understanding how the church might understand salvation in relation to who God is, what it means to be human and sinful, and how the church is to witness to the salvific work of God.[1] I am hopeful that

---

1. It will not have escaped the reader's notice that I do not think the topic of 'salvation' can be explored without discussing, at least and minimally, the doctrines of God,

PART ONE—Ecumenical Theologizing with Ecclesial Friends

this chapter will provide a diagnostic and constructive map of how salvation language properly should work in the discourses and practices of the church's life and witness.²

Some Orienting Remarks and Distinctions

While the church, even in biblical times, talks much about *salvation*, that word is related to other words and uses, such as *deliverance, liberation/freedom, redemption, reconciliation, atonement, sacrifice, rescue, justification, righteousness, forgiveness, sanctification, regeneration, justice, restoration,* and *healing*.³ All of these words play differentiated and interconnected roles in the church's discourses about salvation, or what we might now call *soteriology*: how is it that persons and communities come to be saved. And none of this could be discussed without reference to God's love, grace, judgment, and forgiveness.

To gain some traction on these matters, let us recall how biblical words in Hebrew and Greek are initially rooted in ordinary language. In such ordinary language we can discern that salvation-type words have their meaning in relation to a presupposed contrasting condition. To be saved is to be *saved from* some perilous and threatening condition and thereby *saved to* or *saved for* some safer or more hopeful condition. This basic contrastive character of salvation talk stays with us even today: 'I was saved from death by the rapid response of the emergency room staff.' It should be lucid to us as well how such words as *liberation* and *freedom* have similar contrasting

---

humanity, sin, Christology, ecclesiology, and eschatology, topics also discussed in other chapters of this book. Perhaps it might be interesting to discern ways in which there is agreement and disagreement among the various authors of the essays in this book.

2. Most of the issues discussed in this essay have been more extensively discussed in my two-volume systematic theology, *A Grammar of Christian Faith: Systematic Explorations in Christian Life and Doctrine* (Lanham, MD: Rowman & Littlefield, 2002), hereinafter referred to as GCF, and in a collection of my writings published as *On Being the Church of Jesus Christ in Tumultuous Times* (Eugene, OR: Cascade, 2005), hereinafter referred to as BCJC. An earlier essay, "Schematic Reflections on Salvation in Jesus Christ," explored many of the themes and issues in this chapter and is reprinted in 3CJC, 104–22.

3. Useful studies of many of these biblical words can be found in: George Arthur Buttrick, ed., *Interpreter's Dictionary of the Bible*, 4 vols. (Nashville: Abingdon, 1962); ed. Gerhard Kittel and Gerhard Friedrichs, *Theological Dictionary of the New Testament*, abridged edition, edited and translated by Geoffrey W. Bromiley (Grand Rapids: Eerdmans, 1985); and ed. David Noel Freeman, *The Anchor Bible Dictionary*, 6 vols. (New York: Doubleday, 1992).

conditions: to be liberated or freed is to be liberated or freed *from* some oppressive or restraining condition. Notice also how *deliverance* language fits neatly into salvation language: a person or a community of persons is delivered *from* a perilous situation *to* a safer situation. We can carry these diagnostic comments further by imagining the contrastive conditions that make reconciliation and redemption intelligible to us.

It will be helpful in our further discussion to keep this contrastive character of the many types of salvation language in mind. Of course, in ordinary language the characteristics of the contrasts are so numerous as to defy exhaustive definition. However, in the church's discourse we can gain some leverage on the nature of the basic contrasts by recognizing that they pivot around the many ways in which humans are being *saved from sin and the consequences of sin*. We need, therefore, to have some grasp of sin and its consequences in order to understand the sort of salvation themes that are central to Christian faith. We must understand that the relevant concept of sin is a *theological concept*, which means that it cannot be articulated without identifying who God is and what it means to be a human being living before God.

Identifying God, Human Being, and Sin

It is a basic Christian confession that God the Creator of all things has been normatively self-revealing and self-manifesting in the election and liberation of Israel, in the life, death, and resurrection of Jesus of Nazareth, and in the empowering work of the Holy Spirit in the summoning of the church into life. It is this understanding of God as having an interactive Life with the world that has entailed for the church identifying God in triune ways: God the Creator of the world; God the incarnate Reconciler in Jesus Christ; God the Redeeming Spirit. It is this triune God that the church has always confessed is the *Savior of human beings otherwise lost in sin*.[4]

What sort of being, then, is human being? I propose that Christian discourse's understanding of human being can be usefully understood in these interrelated ways. First, human being is *creaturely being*, created by God as a creature among countless other creatures. To be a creature is to be interdependent with other finite, embodied creatures under the temporal and spatial conditions of life: no human exists without this interdependence

---

4. See GCF, chapter 4, 149–232, for a fuller discussion of the doctrine of the Trinity.

upon other creatures. Further, to be a creature means that human being is not God.[5]

Second, human being is a peculiarly *personal being*, but intimately formed by social interdependence with other persons. As a person, human being is an *I*—a subject, a self—that can construe a world through language and is thereby capacitated to speak to and listen to other persons. Personal being is endowed with the gift of finite freedom to make decisions and can encounter other persons as subjects who also can make decisions. While no person is simply reducible to relations to other persons and creatures, no person exists without some interdependence with other persons and creatures.[6]

Third, human being is *spiritual being*, that sort of creaturely embodied person who is made in the *image of God* and thereby summoned by God to live in obedient relationship with God and in loving mutuality with other humans, now construed as *thous*. It is the human spirit, as originally endowed by grace, that can discern and hear God's summons into authentic community, in which mutual flourishing is possible and the plentiful creation is the scene of joyful and peaceful begetting, laboring, sharing, and friendship. As spiritual being, a human can grasp her life as a gift from God and therefore as one loved by God. In short, human spirits are created and summoned to enjoy life together in the Kingdom of God as friends of God.[7]

While these points are only briefly noted here, they are deeply encoded in the distinctive discourses and practices of Christian communities. We should not suppose, however, that these concepts are the common property of the secular discourses today that propose to tell us what it means to be human. Christians construe human being in ways often different from—sometimes in conflict with—the regnant theories and opinions of the secular world.

We are now ready to identify the characteristic respects in which humans are sinners in need of God's salvific interaction. Sin is that absurd corruption of God's purposes in creating a world of creatures, of persons, and of spirits. Sin is that disruption and disorder that penetrates into the human individual and social life and thwarts those conditions of fulfillment and gladness ordained by God. Sin disrupts the human relationships

---

5. See GCF, chapter 6, 293–364, for a fuller discussion of "Human Being as Created and Sinful." See esp. 296–99 on creaturely being.

6. See GCF, 300–322 on personal being.

7. See GCF, 322–36 on spiritual being.

to God, to other creatures and persons, and to oneself that were intended by God in creating human being.

At the heart of human sin is *unbelief*—that devastating practical refusal to believe in God in which humans rebelliously want life on their own terms, utterly unbeholden to God. From this basic rebellion and unbelief, Christian discourse has identified the following faces of sin: 1) *pride or hubris*—that incessant self-centeredness and selfishness in which the individual and/or the individual's social group are the center of all valuing of life and death; 2) *concupiscence*—that disordering of desire in which the goods that can confer blessing and peace are rejected under the urgency and compulsion of the quest for immediate sensual satisfaction; 3) *sloth*—that unwillingness, that despair about being a self accountable to God and summoned into a future of responsibility; 4) *lying*—that refusal to care about the truth and that willful telling of lies about others and oneself.

The consequences of sin—the sin that individuals enact and the sins of others that are enacted against them—are in their multiple forms and faces *socially systemic* and corruptive of human life. Humans are incessantly stalked by their own alienation from God, their alienation from their own created nature, and their alienation from other creatures and especially other person-spirits. Rivalry for goods thought too scarce to be shared provokes enmity, violence, and deadly conflicts, resulting in much subjugation and oppression of others. Fear of death and the consequential fear of others who might harm or kill become the dominating dispositions and passions of human life in its individual and social forms.[8]

It is this shabby and frightful life that Christian discourse identifies as life under sin and its consequences, which stands under the *judgment* of God as that condition that is powerless to confer the goodness and blessing the Creator intended from the beginning. This is *not* how life was created to be, and it is a life, which left to its own devices, is a living hell. God says 'no' to sin as that human quest to determine on its own what creaturely powers are the real keys to life and death and therefore are worthy of their loyalty and obedience. Idolatry is the irrepressible urge of human life in and under the powers of sin.

---

8. See GCF, 343–64 on sin. Søren Kierkegaard and Reinhold Niebuhr are the great diagnosticians of sin in the modern world. See Søren Kierkegaard, *The Sickness Unto Death*, ed. and trans. Howard V. Hong and Edna H. Hong, *Kierkegaard's Writings*, vol. 19 (Princeton, NJ: Princeton University Press, 1980); and Reinhold Niebuhr, *The Nature and Destiny of Man: A Christian Interpretation* (New York: Scribner, 1949).

PART ONE—Ecumenical Theologizing with Ecclesial Friends

What is God to do about the fact that humans live in such a way that they *deserve* the alienating consequences of their lives together? Enmity and violence, despair and fear, pain and suffering, the unrelenting dominance of death over life, emerge as the sad tale of human life under sin. Does the just God simply accept that the order of *justice* requires these devastating consequences of human sin: a destiny of the futile human efforts to attain peace and fulfillment? Is it simply the case that humans either get their act together by their own free striving and live in peace or they face endless conflict and alienation? Having created and summoned human spirits into relationship with Godself and fruitful fellowship with others, does God simply leave it all up to humans to achieve whatever relief or salvation might be achieved? How, then, shall we construe the salvific acts of God in Israel, in the life, death, and resurrection of Jesus Christ, and in the movements of the Holy Spirit?

The Enactment of Salvation in Jesus Christ as the Incarnate Life of God

The Bible is the primitive narrative of how the God who creates all things acts upon and in the created world to save the world, especially humans but not only humans, from sin and the consequences of sin.

In brief, we can identify the basic salvific acts of God—all of which are the acts of God's grace—as the election of and covenanting with Israel, the incarnation of God in Jesus the Jew, and the empowering work of the Holy Spirit in calling the church as an alternative community witnessing to and living under the summons of God's grace.

The primacy of the life, death, and resurrection of Jesus of Nazareth must be understood as the fundamental self-revelation of God's work of salvation. It is in Jesus that the God of Israel decisively takes up the human peril under sin and enacts that gracious work that limits the effects of sin and opens up a new future. Essential to Jesus' salvific work is that the reality of his life, crucified death, and glorious resurrection from the dead are understood as also the work of God. Affirming that Jesus is both human and divine means that God has become active in and vulnerable under the conditions of the humanity of Jesus' life. God, living as a Jewish human being, is taking up the cause of humans living under those conditions that are the consequences of human individual and social sin. In affirming these

Salvation

claims about Jesus, we are affirming that the *Person* of Jesus is both human and divine.[9]

But merely to say 'Jesus is God incarnate' is not yet to characterize what he does that is salvific for humans, which the traditions have called the *Work* of Jesus. Yet the Person and Work cannot be separated: *Jesus is who he is as the one who does what he does.* What then does Jesus do that is salvific? I will use a reworked understanding of the three-fold offices of Jesus as *Prophet, Priest, and Victor*. In performing all of these offices Jesus is that human being loving God and loving other humans in the ways summoned by God in creating human life, and he is God loving humans in those reconciling ways of forgiveness and grace.[10]

As *Prophet* Jesus proclaims the coming Kingdom of God as that community of peacefulness and mutuality, not torn by enmity, jealousy, violence, and oppressive domination of one human by another. Since it is God who is bringing the Kingdom, Jesus does not summon folk to bring in the Kingdom by their own earnest efforts, though he does counsel folk about the sort of responses appropriate to the Kingdom's imminence: loving the enemy and the neighbor, renouncing violence, turning the other cheek, forgiving one another, refusing that exercise of power that intends to dominate and coerce others. Those who so respond to Jesus' prophetic invitation become his disciples and the vanguard of the Kingdom.

As *Priest* Jesus is the one who submits to the exercise of coercive and subjugating power by those principalities that rule in human empires, perpetuating human oppression and domination. These powers claim to be the rulers that determine life and death and under what conditions humans are allowed to live. In the name of orderly peace and security against enemies, these powers enslave their subjects and murder unruly enemies. These powers murder Jesus on a brutal cross as a sign of his criminal status—he is an enemy of and a threat to the empire's 'peace and security.'

To his disciples Jesus' crucifixion initially appears as a sure sign that the Kingdom he proclaimed and lived is an illusory hoax brutally cancelled by the powers of human empire. Only in their encounter with the resurrected Jesus do the disciples come to understand that Jesus is the Priest who lays down his life, like the sacrificial lambs of the temple, for the sake of reconciliation. Jesus is the Christ, the divine/human reality that takes the full brunt of the powers of sin—as they presume to administer life and

9. See GCF, chapter 7 on "The Person of Jesus Christ."
10. See GCF, chapter 8 on "The Work of Jesus Christ."

death—upon and into the divine Life itself, thereby depriving those powers of their claim to be the determiners of human life and destiny. The human pretense to live life in repudiation of the summons of their Creator—to live life on their own terms—is exposed as a lie. It is in Jesus' resurrection from the dead that his followers understand that he is indeed the *Victor* who finally and truthfully lives without sin and has overcome the consequences of sin, thereby ruling over life and death, over sin and the forgiveness of sin. Jesus is the one who enacts and reveals God's salvific grace in overcoming God's own alienation from the alienating lives of sinners.

Jesus' faithfulness, his love, his unwillingness to seize the sword against enemies, and his forgiving of enemies as they crucified him become that pattern of life that can repudiate sin as that way of life that is unavoidable and necessary to human beings in their sociality. Jesus' followers are summoned by the Spirit into a community of faith, love, and hope, living an alternative way of life to the ways of life of the world still bedeviled by sin—that is the summons of the Holy Spirit, as the Spirit of Christ, to be the church as the body of Christ in and for the world.

For Christians, then, talk of salvation will pivot around what God has done in Jesus Christ for the salvation of a world caught up in and being torn apart by the doing of sin and the being undone by sin. What we might call the *Way of Salvation* is intimately related to the life, death, and resurrection of Jesus and the calling of the church.

The Shadow of Dual Destiny

Before proceeding further to examine the way of salvation, we must acknowledge what I will call a shadow that looms heavily over much of the past discourses of the church. As we have seen earlier in our discussion, salvation-type words always have a contrasting condition. This clearly implies that there is a crucial conceptual distinction between being-saved and not-being-saved. If we further assume that there must be persons who are in each category of saved and not-saved, we seem confronted with the conclusion that there is a *dual destiny* among humans: some persons are saved and some are not-saved or are damned. Dual destiny language then forces us to inquire about how it comes about that some persons are saved and some are damned.

Along this line of inquiry, the church invoked the language of God's justice wherein such justice is understood to be *retributive* in character:

Salvation

God administers to humans what they justly deserve, whether that be reward and blessings or punishment and rejection. This is justice as *just deserts*. When these concepts structure salvation language, it inevitably appears that those who are saved in some sense *deserved* their salvation, just as those who are damned deserved their damnation. This sort of salvation language is deeply hedged in by such concepts as *earning* or *winning* or *achieving* one's salvation. Yet what is it that the saved *do* that deserves or earns their being saved? It would appear, then, that this logic of salvation is veering in the direction of that sort of *works righteousness* that Paul and others thought denied that persons are saved by the *grace of God*.[11]

Not wanting to openly embrace a works righteousness understanding of salvation, we might retrieve some sense of grace by saying that Jesus met the just demands of God and satisfied God's judgment against sinners.[12] Hence, sinners no longer have to meet God's just demands in order to be saved. But, how then do we avoid slipping into saying that all persons are saved by the grace of God in Jesus Christ because Jesus took the place of sinners before God and met God's just demands? Dual destiny thinkers, finding that belief abhorrent and presumptuous, rush in to re-establish dual destiny by saying that persons must do or feel or have an attitude that accepts Jesus as one's savior in order thereby to be saved. It is almost impossible for this line of thinking to avoid the subtle belief that salvation is finally up to the individual: either one accepts Jesus as savior and thereby *earns* being-saved or one refuses to accept Jesus—or just remains in ignorance of Jesus—and therefore *deserves* damnation. However this view twists and turns, the retributive justice image of God remains dominant and somehow something persons do determines their salvation. It remains obscure, then, just what it might mean to say one is saved by the grace of God. If grace is a free gift, then how could one also be said to have earned the gift? One earns rewards, not free gifts.

It is no accident that popular Christianity embraces a dual destiny view something like this: human life in time is a trial—pivoting around accepting Jesus as savior—that will determine whether one is saved to a life beyond death or is damned to a life in hell.

---

11. See Gal 2:15–21 for Paul's incisive discussion of the issue of works righteousness under the law. See also GCF, 513–19.

12. St. Anselm undertook to explain the salvific work of Jesus along these lines in "Why God Became Man," in *A Scholastic Miscellany: Anselm to Ockham*, ed. and trans. Eugene R. Fairweather, *Library of Christian Classics*, vol. 10 (Philadelphia: Westminster, 1956), 100–183. See GCF, 443–45, 453–54, for a critique of Anselm.

Assuming, however, that we are committed to the dual destiny language but want to avoid a just deserts understanding of salvation, we could, with Augustine and Calvin, affirm that anyone who is saved is saved only by the grace of God. Since everyone already deserves the damnation inherent in sin, anyone actually saved from this damnation is saved only by the gracious and inexplicable decree of God. To try to explain why this person is saved and that person is not is impossible by appeal to any criterion of just deserts. But this view that salvation and damnation are already dually determined in God's eternal predestination seems strangely detached from any understanding of salvation being brought by Jesus Christ. The singular virtue of this view of salvation is its firm grasp that salvation is first and last the work of God's grace. Perhaps the conundrum we are facing here is rooted in the attachment to retributive justice, just deserts, and dual destiny as the baseline concepts for understanding salvation.[13]

On Resisting Some Recent Temptations

In the last two hundred years—a period of wrenching critiques and disagreements within the theological discourses of churches—there has been a tendency to focus on one aspect of salvation language at the expense of other aspects. Hence, the rich diversity and interconnected language of salvation gets reduced to one defining image of what salvation really is. It will be instructive, I hope, to review briefly some of these temptations to reduce salvation to a single defining image.

Salvation as Existential Authenticity: Claiming that the eschatological vision of salvation as eternal life beyond death has been devastated by modern thought, Christian faith can still identify that feature of human existence that is determinative of the meaning of salvation, namely, the deep existential *how* of a person's life in time. Interpreting sin as inauthentic life manifesting itself in the all-consuming fear of death, the sinful *how* of a person's life results in much lying, self-deception, and deep despair. But in Jesus' call to faith and in the gracious bestowing of faith, persons come to live authentically, accepting God's forgiving grace as proclaimed in the Gospel and candidly facing their own deaths without resort to the myths of immortality. Eternal life is, therefore, not some future life after death;

---

13. See GCF, 709–24 for an extended discussion of issues involved in affirming dual destiny.

rather it is that state or event in some individual's life in which authentic response to God's grace is realized. Salvation is to be identified precisely in this qualitative way in which a person puts her life together. Obviously, there is still a dual destiny, though not perhaps of just deserts: some receive the grace and are transformed and some do not receive and therefore are not transformed. This view of salvation is similar to all those views that collapse the whole meaning of salvation into a primary concern with the transformation in time of the individual's relationship to God. Yet this view lacks a vivid sense for the restoration of human community and the way in which the Gospel summons persons to live in liberating ways on behalf of their neighbors. Further, it too cavalierly repudiates life beyond death.[14]

Salvation as Social Liberation: Largely as a critique of existential individualism, the liberation theme emphasizes that Christian life is the liberation of persons from social oppression to a situation of justice and freedom. Where the powers of the world enslave persons and deprive them of their just share of society's goods, there is no justice and therefore no liberation and no meaningful sense of salvation. Liberation thinkers have helpfully discerned the many ways in which sin is a socially systemic problem and that political/economic realities must be engaged if there is to be actual social salvation for the oppressed. While this is a word that is needed by the church, it does seem to imply, when it is understood as the only or primary meaning of salvation, that the socially oppressed are simply in all respects determined by their oppression and therefore lacking any meaningful sense of salvation. This also implies that the oppressed of the past—who never knew liberation from social oppression—have somehow missed the saving work of God in the world. As a necessary theme in Christian faith, liberation from social oppression is uneliminable; yet, as the primary or defining theme of salvation, it is devastating to our understanding of the limits of God's salvation. It needs an appreciation of how Paul in jail and a host of oppressed Christians of the past felt also liberated by God's grace with a hope in God that transcends any particular conditions of human life in time.[15]

---

14. Rudolf Bultmann dominated discussions about salvation during the 1950s and 1960s. See his *New Testament and Mythology and Other Basic Writings*, edited and translated by Schubert Ogden (Philadelphia: Fortress, 1984).

15. Liberation theology is more variegated than this brief excursus suggests, ranging from Latin American liberation theologians, to African-American theologies, to feminist theologies. The common theme of all these theologies is that liberation from oppression

Millennial Salvation: This theme emerges out of the Book of Revelation (20:4–6) in which a thousand-year reign of Christ seems to be prophesied. While that notion itself seemed misleading to many in the first centuries of the church's life and even threatened the final inclusion of Revelation in the New Testament canon, it does reappear time and again in the life of the church. The central point of the millennial theme is that there will be a thousand-year reign of Jesus in *human history*. It is a vision of peace and well-being actually being lived out by humanity under the gracious reign of Jesus. Premillennialists believe that Christ will return and usher in the reign of peace, at the end of which the final judgment of all things will be rendered. Postmillennialists believe Christ will come at the end of the thousand years and judge all things. We should appreciate the emphasis of the millennialists on the concreteness of the kingdom in history, which is similar to the liberationists concern for tangible social justice. However, two perils lurk in millennialism: 1) it can devolve into emphasizing that the Christians must themselves bring in the kingdom by their righteous efforts or at least their righteous efforts will be the precondition for Jesus bringing in the kingdom; or 2) the beginning or the ending of the millennium becomes bathed in violence, either the violence of slaughtering the evildoers in order to bring in the kingdom or the violence of slaughtering at the end. This violence language seems inevitable when this vision of salvation rests primarily on the Book of Revelation, which is replete with violent language about the conflict between good and evil.[16]

---

is some state of affairs in human history in which justice is achieved and oppression is dismantled in all its forms. The concept of justice that functions as the goal of liberating and emancipating work often seems unstable and imprecise. See the sympathetic but sobering critique of Latin American liberation theology by Daniel M. Bell, Jr., *Liberation Theology After the End of History: The Refusal to Cease Suffering* (New York: Routledge, 2001). See also GCF, 505, 528–36, 630–33, 699–709.

16. It is one of the strange silences among descendants of the nineteenth-century Stone-Campbell Movement, that it has forgotten that Alexander Campbell, one of the pioneering movers, understood himself as a millennialist and for years he published the journal entitled *Millennial Harbinger*. Campbell did seem to believe that the restoration of New Testament Christianity that he was advocating was beginning to show signs of progress that suggested that the reign of Christ might be near historically. However, Campbell's millennialism completely lacked the emphasis on a violent return by Christ to destroy the evildoers, which seems so prominent in today's world. But the terrible conflict of the Civil War devastated Campbell's confidence that the movement of 'restoration Christianity' and the providential ordering of American democracy were harbingers of an almost 'imminent' kingdom of God. See the fine discussion of Campbell's millennial concerns in Robert Frederick West's *Alexander Campbell and Natural Religion* (New Haven, CT: Yale University Press, 1948), esp. 163–222.

All of these views, in their tendency to insist that the center of the church's understanding of salvation is defined by their particular emphasis, can mislead the church about the differentiated and interconnected range of meanings available in a full-orbed understanding of the salvific work of the triune God. The following section will propose a map of salvation issues and concerns that comprehensively fit together without obvious self-contradiction.

The Spheres of the Way of Salvation: A Proposal

In the Gospels' narratives, Jesus is confronted by a rich young man who asks: "Good Teacher, what good deed must I do to inherit eternal life?" After the young man avers that he has kept "the commandments," Jesus summons him to sell his "possessions, and give the money to the poor… and come, follow me," to which the man goes away "grieving, for he had many possessions." The puzzled disciples ask: "Then who can be saved?" to which Jesus replies: "For mortals it is impossible, but for God all things are possible." (See Matt 19:16–20; Mark 10:13–16; Luke 18:18–30.)

In great proximity to this text, it is often asked, 'what must I do to be saved?' The accent is on *what must be done* in order to gain salvation, here understood as 'eternal life.' This picture of salvation and the earning-of-salvation has exercised a tight grip on much Christian imagination for centuries. That same picture, of course, ignores the further words of Jesus: "For mortals it [viz., inheriting eternal life] is impossible, but for God all things are possible." Salvation, inheriting eternal life, is impossible for mortals by the powers of their own actions? Many are the issues lurking in this passage, which we will now try to unfold.

To make sense out of this passage and to overcome some of the unsatisfying lacunae in the just deserts/dual destiny language, I propose to differentiate the language of salvation among the following spheres of salvation issues, while still grasping the deep interconnections of the theme of the triune God's gracious salvation in Jesus Christ and the summoning of the church through the Spirit. It is through the language and realities of the spheres that we will be able to appreciate the complex and differentiated ways in which the church can talk about salvation.

The **first sphere**, in the language of *incarnation, atonement, reconciliation, and justification*, emphasizes what was done—what was achieved—in the life, death, and resurrection of Jesus Christ. Something happened in

PART ONE—Ecumenical Theologizing with Ecclesial Friends

this particular human's historical career—what he did and what was done to him—that has a sovereign reality not simply dependent on the response of believers or followers. Indeed, who Jesus was and what he did—as has been identified in our previous discussion—are the fundaments of whatever else the church might say about God, human life, and salvation.[17]

However, this sphere can fall into disarray if we do not hold together and appreciate the interpenetration of Jesus' work as Prophet, Priest, and Victor. He is the Prophet of the Kingdom that is crucified on the cross and raised as the Victor over life and death. He is the vulnerable Priest who proclaims a Kingdom of peace and nonviolence and was murdered by the principalities and powers—imperial political and religious leaders—that murder in order to dominate and subjugate. He is the Victor raised from the dead who is the presence of and the forerunner of a Kingdom of peace. In all these offices, Jesus is the incarnate life of God graciously taking the sins of the world upon and into the divine Life and thus disarming them of their power to determine human meaning and destiny *before God*.

So, who is saved in this sphere? All humans are saved from the condition of being condemned by their sins before God to the condition of being graciously forgiven and justified in ways beyond their deserts. This gracious forgiveness stands there just on its own, independent of its acceptance and appropriation by any person, though its acceptance and appropriation bring the forgiveness and justification home to the believers.

The **second sphere** of salvation language pertains to the actual ways in which persons subject to sin find their lives forgiven, graced, healed, and transformed by the Spirit of Christ. The centering focus of this transformation is how persons *appropriate* in their lives and communities *what* Jesus revealed and accomplished for them. This is the sphere in which life in the church and the discipleship to Jesus become decisive themes. This sphere we will call *historic redemption* as what is taking place in what I will also call *historic destiny*: how life unfolds in the spatiality and temporality of human history. The special role of the church in historic redemption is that it is the body of Christ in the world and the bearer of the *means of grace*—embodied in its distinctive discourses and practices—by way of which persons come to know and appropriate the grace of God revealed and enacted in Jesus Christ. Distinctive Christian life becomes an *ethics of grace*: given what God has done in Jesus Christ, Christians live under the summons to

---

17. See GCF, 433–35, 473–80, for discussions of the benefits of Christ and human salvation.

Salvation

be peacemakers and forgivers, lovers of neighbors, strangers, and enemies. This is not an ethics of how to earn God's grace but an ethics of how to live in conformity to grace freely given and freedom conferring. Indeed, being liberated from the destiny determining power of sin, Christians can live for others without fear of death or the threat of death.

Hence, in its distinctive discourses and practices the church bears a witness to the gracious salvific acts of the triune God, intending in every way to be a alternative community of faith, love, and hope living for the benefit of the world otherwise entangled in sin. The church's life unfolds amidst the dynamic interaction of its *nurturing practices*—worship, communal care, and educational formation in faith—and in its *outreach practices*—evangelism, prophetic critique of the worldly powers of domination and oppression, and the actual engagement in works of love on behalf of the world. It is in these outreach practices that the church enacts a liberating dismantling of the many individual and social forms of sin in the world. It should be apparent that *all of these works of the church in historic redemption are from beginning to end salvific in character and purpose.*[18]

Having now affirmed this work of God in historic destiny, we must also admit that many are the individuals and the socio/political arrangements and communities that never respond to the work of forgiveness in Jesus and the work of transformation in the Spirit. In some sense, then, we must admit that in historic destiny, some folk know no healing and loving God of grace. If historic destiny is the complete *scope* of human life before God, we would have to admit that many are they who die in time having lived lives ravaged by sin—their own sin and the sins of others against them—without any apparent experience of God's salvific grace. Because the church believes that Jesus was raised from the dead and reigns as Victor over life and death, it also believes that historic destiny is neither the full scope of life nor the final determiner of life before God.

The **third sphere** of salvation language pertains to how we identify issues of *ultimate human destiny*. To ask about ultimate human destiny is to ask about the ultimate *end* of human life, meaning both end as *telos* or goal and end as *finis* or finality and conclusion. In discussing these issues we are

---

18. For a more complete discussion of the church and salvation see BCJC, chapter 4, "The Church as Ark of Salvation." While I would not recommend a theological perspective that would reduce the role of the church in salvation to being one among many instances of religious communities conveying salvation, it must be admitted that the work of the Spirit of Christ is not restricted to the church. How and where it might be at work is a profound theological question. See GCF, 497–501.

entering upon the doctrinal theme of *eschatology*: what is God's ultimate determination of the meaning, reality, and scope of human life, indeed of the life of the whole cosmos. Is death simply what is final about human life, and now death under the shadow of sin? Or are there *transhistorical* possibilities and realities? In traditional language, notions of heaven and hell emerge in this sphere.

The center of ultimate destiny language is the reality of the triune God: Creator, Reconciler, and Redeemer. We have affirmed that much pivots around what God did in Jesus Christ and its *benefits* for humanity. Not only does the incarnational narrative of Jesus' work include the cross as manifesting the vulnerable power of the divine Life in taking the destined consequences of sin upon and into God's Life and thereby depriving them of their power to be the *determiners of human destiny*, but the resurrection of Jesus is the gracious opening up of life beyond death. But for whom is this life beyond death—what I am calling *transhistorical life*—made possible? Only for those who have faithfully followed Jesus and thereby *earned* the right to dwell eternally in God's grace? Were this the logic of life beyond death, then only the faithful will be ultimately redeemed and the unfaithful will be absent, either in absolute annihilation in death or in being raised to an everlasting life in hell! Is it possible that the crucified Jesus descended into hell—as that stark and devastating extremity of human alienation from God—and thereby emptied hell as the ultimate destiny of any human being?[19]

I am proposing that the Life of the triune God with the world is from beginning to end—as the Alpha and Omega of life and being—the life of a gracious Creator in search of the redemption of rebellious creatures and therefore precisely as Omega has, is, and will be the *Ultimate Companion and Redeemer* of all creatures. Hence, rather than being saved by their merits or condemned by their demerits, in this sphere of ultimate destiny, all will finally be saved by the grace of God. Being raised to life beyond death is a gift of God and is neither a natural attribute of being human nor an earned reward for righteous life. Christians above all, not only know the grace of God, they also are keenly aware of the repetitious ways in which sin clings to their own acts and feelings. This awareness thus disabuses Christians of trusting that the presumed stalwartness and extent of their faithfulness could earn them such eternal life. Christians are those who deeply

---

19. On the status of hell, see Joe R. Jones, "Hell is Empty," *Disciples World*, vol. 3, issue 9 (November 2004), 13-15.

and passionately encounter death—their own and the deaths of the many others—as a dying unto the sheer gracious love of God. Bluntly, Christians trust and hope in the grace of God, not in their own presumed achieved righteousness! When all things are subjected to the work of Jesus Christ, they will be subjected by the transforming power of the triune God who incarnately and ultimately refuses to count the sins of the world against it and who graciously redeems all creatures. Joyfully, God's power and grace are the final and ultimate determiners of the meaning and destiny of human life. God speaks and enacts an unceasing triumphant *yes* to the world.

Yet God's ultimate redemption is not only the destiny of human life; it is also the destiny of the whole creation, including all creaturely beings and powers. Affirming that the created world as created is finite with a beginning—which is the beginning of time and temporality—the world also has an end, both as goal and conclusion. At some point in the future, God will consummate the whole creation as a redemptive kingdom in which nothing good is lost and all creatures cease conflict and rest in peace. It is the ultimate *yes* of God that subverts every doctrine that claims God will ultimately *destroy* the world in a final act of violence.

The church must never forget nor neglect the belief that the triune God, who lives in freedom and love, is the Alpha and the Omega—the beginning and the end—of all creatures and all principalities and powers.

5

Yoder and Stone-Campbellites

Sorting the Grammar of Radical Orthodoxy and Radical Discipleship

An essay written for a conference in 2009 on the theology of John Howard Yoder and the Stone-Campbell Movement and published in ed. John C. Nugent, Radical Ecumenicity: Pursuing Unity and Continuity after John Howard Yoder *(Abilene, TX: Abilene Christian University Press, 2010), 107–28.*

It is a great pleasure for me to participate in the coming together of sometime estranged friends from the Stone-Campbell Movement to discuss the work of John Howard Yoder, one of the most trenchant theologians of the twentieth century. While intending an irenic spirit, in his writings Yoder "took no prisoners": his analysis of issues bristled with such clarity that his patient readers were compelled *to think hard* about what he wrote and where they stood in relation to it. Yoder may not have answered every question we readers might have brought to the text, but he did speak directly and repeatedly to a decisive set of beliefs and practices that are at the heart of what it means to be a *disciple of Jesus and a member of his ecclesial body.*

In this presentation I do not promise any original contribution to the ongoing work of Yoder scholars.[1] But I do hope to consider the example of

---

1. I was a Johnny-come-lately to Yoder. I began seminary instruction in philosophical and systematic theology in 1965. I did not purchase Yoder's *The Politics of Jesus* until 1985, and it was only in the late 1980s and the early 90s that Mark Thiessen Nation, then a bright and engaging student of mine at Christian Theological Seminary, insisted that I read Yoder since he thought Yoder and I shared a host of theological convictions. I owe

Yoder to help us think about what I regard as the Achilles Heel of the Stone-Campbell Movement. In short, I intend to explore the Movement's hesitation—in all three of its branches—to wrestle with trinitarian orthodoxy and its connection to a more radical understanding of the Christian life and the church in relation to whatever world it might find itself. It is, of course, not the case that other church traditions that claimed trinitarian orthodoxy did in fact obviously succeed in being the community of radical disciples. Yet, neither is it so—given the theological baggage we toted around—that many Stone-Campbellites were able consistently to be a people of radical discipleship.

The nub of the problem, it seems to me, is that the Stone-Campbell Movement's intent to recover the New Testament church and bypass the orthodox-creating creeds of Nicaea and Chalcedon left the Movement utterly exposed to the political world in which it was being born—namely, the rise of American-style democracy and its need for civil religious rationale and support. As a peculiar and self-consciously American movement openly embracing its free-church, non-established status, the Stone-Campbell Movement (hereinafter referred to as SCM) simply could not resist being co-opted by the needs of American sectionalism and nationalism and their politics. It might be helpful to see this continual and differentiated co-opting as a facsimile of what Yoder has called the "Constantinianization" of the church.[2] And Yoder is exactly right: a Constantinian church finds radical discipleship *practically* impossible.

My aim is not to provide all the historical documentation of just how it was that all three branches of the SCM—in their differing ways—were simply overwhelmed by American politics, principalities, and powers. Rather, my aim is fourfold: 1) to provide some diagnostic comments about orthodoxy and orthopraxis within the SCM, especially in its first century; 2) to propose an understanding of "radical orthodoxy" as trinitarian in character and radical in relation to any and every world in which it might exist; 3) to explore some central convictions of Yoder regarding Christology and ecclesiology pertaining to radical orthodoxy and radical discipleship; and 4) to engage Yoder and the SCM by constructing a brief *theological imaginary*

Mark much gratitude for pushing me into having Yoder as a conversation partner, which also opened the door to re-engaging a graduate school colleague of mine from Yale days, Stanley Hauerwas.

2. A theme much articulated by Yoder and much discussed by others. See Yoder, *The Priestly Kingdom: Social Ethics as Gospel* (Notre Dame, IN: University of Notre Dame Press, 1984), esp. 135–47.

PART ONE—Ecumenical Theologizing with Ecclesial Friends

of trinitarian orthodoxy and radical discipleship.[3] Hence, by examining how certain trinitarian theological convictions and practices conceptually interpenetrate, I hope it is clearer how radical discipleship might be kept more keenly on the minds and hearts of the Movement's pastors, teachers, and laity.[4]

Orthodoxy and Orthopraxis in the Stone-Campbell Movement

I have argued elsewhere that any Christian ecclesial tradition simply cannot avoid questions of orthodoxy (right belief) and of orthopraxis (right practice).[5] Such questions are *practically unavoidable* insofar as any ecclesial body cannot persist without identifying in its *actual discourses* those beliefs and practices considered essential to its own self-identity as an ongoing Christian tradition. *Essential* here means those actual *identity markers* the tradition repeatedly returns to and acknowledges as minimally constitutive of its own self-understanding and in the absence of which it would become confused about its own identity and persons outside the tradition would be confused about what it would mean to become an active member. How

---

3. The expression *imaginary* comes to me by way of its use by Sheldon S. Wolin and Charles Taylor, and I have found it a rich way of talking about the deep interrelation between discourses and practices as construals of the social worlds in the church as well as in other social relationships. See Wolin, *Democracy Incorporated: Managed Democracy and the Specter of Inverted Totalitarianism* (Princeton: Princeton University Press, 2008), 17–40, for "political imaginary" and Taylor's *Modern Social Imaginaries* (Durham, NC: Duke University Press, 2004), 23–30, for "social imaginary," a concept that he also used extensively in his recent work, *A Secular Age* (Cambridge, MA: Harvard University Press, 2007).

4. I have enjoyed two previous opportunities to work with SCM theologians. See my contribution, "On Being the Church of Jesus Christ," in a special issue of *Leaven* on "The Church's One Foundation," 15, no. 1 (First Quarter, 2007) 6–11. See also "Spiritual Formation and Christian Discourse: The Shaping Power of Christian Discourse," in *Spiritual Formation and the Future of Stone-Campbell Churches* (Bloomington, IN: Ketch Publications, 2008), 1–20; also reprinted in *Encounter* 69, no. 2 (2008) 29–44. Also included in this volume.

5. Put succinctly, pertaining to the church's witness, I distinguish between 1) questions of orthodoxy and orthopraxis: what must *always* be said and done; 2) questions of heresy and heretical praxis: what must *never* be said or done; and 3) questions of permissible and nonschismatic disagreement and diversity. See Joe R. Jones, *A Grammar of Christian Faith: Systematic Explorations in Christian Life and Doctrine*, 2 vols. (Lanham, MD: Rowman & Littlefield, 2002), 40–43. Hereinafter this work will be referred to as GCF.

to decide these matters is, of course, difficult and contentious, and in good Calvinist practice I contend that, however questions of orthodoxy and orthopraxis might be answered, they are always *reformable*.

Surely members of the SCM are keenly aware that in our tradition there was from the start a competing worldly creed: "Nobody can tell me what I ought to believe; it is my own private decision." I would, however, propose that the SCM from the beginning intended to make the confession of "Jesus Christ is my/our Lord and Savior" as the minimal heart of church belief. Yet all three branches choked at developing any binding or guiding understanding of what it meant to say "Lord" and "Savior" about Jesus and see therein any strong implication about the reality of "the Father" and even less about "the Holy Spirit."[6] It is sufficient for my purposes to note that the anti-creedal disposition of all three branches repeatedly obscured from themselves what right beliefs and practices they did have and thereby prevented the communal identification and clarification of theological convictions that might have been beneficial to our ecclesial faithfulness. Further, according to the way in which I am using the term "orthodoxy," it should not be assumed that all orthodoxies get expressed as "creeds," though ecclesially they are cousins.

So, in the first century of their lives, what might it have meant in the SCM branches to have even talked about "right belief" and/or "right practice"? In a way that might offend many in all three traditions—to which I apologize now—I would suggest something close to the following is what counted as orthodox within the earlier and common years of the Movement.

1. Orthodoxy was the right belief that the New Testament alone was sufficient for identifying those beliefs and practices that are essential to the church and the Christian life.

2. Orthodoxy was the right belief that Jesus Christ is my/our Lord and Savior.

3. Orthodoxy was the right belief that "where the Scriptures speak we speak and where the Scriptures are silent we are silent."[7]

---

6. In ways I seek to justify in GCF, 158–66 ("Patriarchy and 'Father' Language"), for particular purposes I will use *Father* as an appropriate—but not the only—way of referring to the First Person of the Trinity.

7. This belief often became the practice that if a belief could be found in the "plain sense" of the New Testament, then it was "right to believe it." How else might we explain the Movement's continual obfuscating of differences within the New Testament, especially on large issues such as slavery and the status of women?

Part One—Ecumenical Theologizing with Ecclesial Friends

4. Orthodoxy was the right belief that the church is comprised of baptized believers only, whereby baptism is by immersion for the remission of sins.

5. Orthodoxy was the right belief that issues of church governance could be settled by reference to the singularly clear pattern of governance of the church in the New Testament.

6. Orthodoxy was the right belief that creeds are human artifices stultifying to Christian understanding and commitment.

7. Orthodoxy was the right belief that the church of the New Testament is more nearly a *movement* among local congregations than what can be called *denominations*, with their defining creeds.

8. Orthodoxy was the right belief that only a *movement* of Christian congregations could achieve genuine Christian unity.

9. Orthodoxy was the right belief that the United States of America, as a democratic republic, was a God-ordained nation important in God's providential governance of the world, however true it might also be that many Americans lived perversely in sin.

10. Orthopraxis was the right practice of observing the Lord's Supper whenever the faithful gather for worship, independent of ordained priests, apostolic or otherwise.

11. Orthopraxis was the right practice of baptizing by immersion only adult or near-adult persons who have confessed that Jesus Christ is their Lord and Savior.

Each of us could extend or contract this list according to our own experience and historical judgment.[8] The point of my list is that, in spite of our resistance to orthodox confessions or creedal statements, the SCM was literally and continually awash in orthodoxies, but few were willing to name and defend the orthodoxies as orthodoxies. Of course, the twentieth century saw the SCM breaking apart as de facto issues of orthodoxy and orthopraxis began rendering the branches unintelligible and opaque to each other. So the question never should have been whether there are

---

8. Folk from the Churches of Christ might also identify a cappella worship as orthopraxis supported by the orthodox right belief that worship without musical instruments is commanded by God.

orthodoxies or not, but *which orthodoxy and which orthopraxis?* And, *why that orthodoxy and that orthopraxis and not another?*[9]

We are now in a position to recognize that none of the branches ever developed any consensus about trinitarian orthodoxy nor about any orthopraxis of discipleship such as, for example, refusing to return evil for evil, turning the other cheek when injured, being a slave to Christ, loving the stranger and the enemy, forgiving those who wrongly use and abuse you, refusing to use violence against another, and the making of peace. Surely these practices that Jesus taught in the New Testament might have been foundational of any orthodoxy and orthopraxis in a movement publicly putting the emphasis on being *disciples of Christ*.

Toward a Trinitarian Radical Orthodoxy

What might it mean to talk of "radical orthodoxy"? A contemporary movement calls itself "Radical Orthodoxy," with such prominent and interesting theologians as John Milbank, Catherine Pickstock, and Graham Ward.[10] While I admire the aim of this movement to critique the way modern political liberalism, secularism, and capitalist culture co-opted much of Protestant Liberal Christianity, in this essay I am not interested in exploring and critiquing its arresting proposals. I simply mention this movement because it has promoted a verbal expression—*radical orthodoxy*—important to me in my early years of teaching in those notoriously conflictual times of the late 1960s and the early 70s. My use of "radical orthodoxy" intends no explicit or extended continuity with this current movement.

I wrote my dissertation on Karl Barth, and it was Barth who was pulling me away from my previous Tillichian and Reinhold Niebuhrian inclinations in theology and political ethics. With war raging in Vietnam and

---

9. The SCM never reached real agreement about *how* it is that Jesus *saves us*, but neither Nicaea nor Chalcedon elaborated on salvation.

10. See John Milbank, *Theology and Social Theory: Beyond Secular Reason* (Cambridge, MA: Blackwell, 1990); *Being Reconciled: Ontology and Pardon* (London: Routledge, 2003); *The Future of Love: Essays in Political* Theology (Eugene, OR: Cascade, 2009). For a useful introduction to and exploration of Radical Orthodoxy, see James K. A. Smith, *Introducing Radical Orthodoxy: Mapping a Post-secular Theology* (Grand Rapids: Baker Academic, 2004). I think the movement falters in openly espousing a more Platonic or Neo-Platonic frame of metaphysics. Such metaphysics, in spite of the admirable attempts by these theologians, can never adequately develop much sense for the agency of God.

PART ONE—Ecumenical Theologizing with Ecclesial Friends

in the streets, amidst racism shattering society and churches and political assassinations devastating to political hope, almost every traditional societal pillar was coming under attack: education, religion, economics, politics, and government. It was common for protesters and revolutionaries, inside and outside the church, to blame and dismiss traditional orthodox Christian beliefs as wooden, heavy, and incapacitated to deal with the modern world. In particular, this question loomed heavy and threatening: how could so many American church traditions have ever supported racism and going-to-war in such seemingly unjust ways?

I found it helpful during this turmoil to inform students that it was one of the great curiosities—indeed scandals—of church history that traditions self-identified as orthodox had repeatedly gone to war so easily in the name of king and nation, had repeatedly absorbed the ethos and politics of the particular nation or culture in which it was located, and had repeatedly identified the purposes of God with the political aspirations and causes of its nation, class, or ethnic group.[11] In spite of the accusation that the church's orthodoxy repeatedly succumbed to the ruling principalities and powers and that such orthodoxy was the root of the church's dreadful subservience to the powers, I averred in return that the problem was more nearly that *the church was not radically orthodox enough*. Were the church truly and radically orthodox, I argued, then it would consistently be clear to the church that it serves God first and that God's reality and will is known in the compelling contours of the life, death, and resurrection of Jesus Christ, very God and very human. Only by bearing this in mind could the church refuse to identify God's will with the arrangements of power and politics in any particular human government and culture. Hence, it was precisely a Chalcedonian Christology and clear trinitarian beliefs—not succumbing to a presumably natural theology that any rational person should properly believe—that would be the radical orthodoxy and radical orthopraxis that

---

11. For a less tendentious historical account of orthodox political theologies, see Oliver O'Donovan, *The Desire of the Nations: Rediscovering the Roots of Political Theology* (Cambridge, UK: Cambridge University Press, 1996); *The Ways of Judgment* (Grand Rapids: Eerdmans, 2005); with Joan Lockwood O'Donovan, *Bonds of Imperfection: Christian Politics, Past and Present* (Grand Rapids: Eerdmans, 2004); and Oliver O'Donovan and Joan Lockwood O'Donovan, eds., *From Irenaeus to Grotius: A Sourcebook of Christian Political Thought 110-1625* (Grand Rapids: Eerdmans, 1999). On the other hand, see Joerg Rieger, *Christ and Empire: From Paul to Postcolonial Times* (Minneapolis: Fortress Press, 2007); and Kwok Pui-lan, Don H. Compiers, and Joerg Rieger, eds., *Empire and the Christian Tradition: New Readings in Classical Theologians* (Minneapolis: Fortress, 2007).

had the power and authority to critique the variety of human political loyalties, governments, and social arrangements.

It was this sort of theologizing by Barth that had also empowered and authorized his critique of and nonviolent resistance to the Nazi overpowering of the German church traditions. Once we state firmly that God as revealed in Jesus of Nazareth is sovereign and *not* Hitler, we can all play out the logic or grammar of this tenacious, radically orthodox belief. This sort of Barth-like radical orthodoxy should be a theological prophylactic to the church's inclination to serve the reigning lords in whatever political and cultural arrangement it might find itself. Yet it was only in my later encounter with Yoder that the orthopraxis of nonviolence emerged as important to that theological prophylactic.[12]

The orthodox creeds of Nicaea (325 CE) and Chalcedon (451 CE) intended to clarify the reality of Jesus' life, death, and resurrection and the reality of the God of Israel, the Creator of the world.[13] If Jesus is where God's sovereignty, will, and purpose are truly and decisively manifest—having become incarnate—then this is the understanding of divinity that critiques all other appeals to divine sanction. Trinitarian belief is not about how three-in-one are magically important; it is about clarifying the divinity of Jesus, how he might be understood as the Lord of all things, and how that Lord is at work in the world. The ruling belief of a genuinely radical orthodoxy is that God is incarnate in Jesus the Jew from Nazareth at a particular time and geography, that this Jesus' life and teaching, his death and resurrection convey an identifiable pattern of beliefs and practices. People who confess this and who thereby follow Jesus are a peculiar people who live differently and serve a Lord different from the various lords and powers found in human societies.

---

12. Concerning The Barmen Declaration of 1934, see John H. Leith, ed., *Creeds of the Church*, 3rd ed. (Louisville: John Knox, 1982), 517–22. Among many books on Barth and the subjects in this essay is the spirited book by Timothy J. Gorringe, *Karl Barth: Against Hegemony* (Oxford: Oxford University Press, 1999). See also George Hunsinger, ed. and trans., *Karl Barth and Radical Politics* (Philadelphia: Westminster, 1976). Yoder was a careful student of Barth's theology, writing an early essay on Barth and war in 1954, which was published in an expanded version as *Karl Barth and the Problem of War* (Nashville: Abingdon, 1970) and republished along with some other Yoder essays on Barth as *Karl Barth and the Problem of War and Other Essays on Barth*, Mark Thiessen Nation, ed. with a foreword by (Eugene, OR: Cascade, 2003).

13. For the texts of the Nicene and Chalcedonian creeds, see Leith, *Creeds of the Church*, 28–36.

PART ONE—Ecumenical Theologizing with Ecclesial Friends

In making this case about the church and radical orthodoxy, I also formulated my first version of the nature and mission of the church, later formulated as:

> The church is that liberative and redemptive
> community of persons
> called into being
> by the Gospel of Jesus Christ
> through the Holy Spirit
> to witness in word and deed
> to the living triune God
> for the benefit of the world
> to the glory of God.

Hence, in those uproarious and uprooting times, if the church were truly radically orthodox it would have a more radical sense for what it might mean to be disciples of Jesus prepared to love in odd ways and suffer for such loving. Such discipleship—as radical orthopraxis and radical orthodoxy—is neither complacent about the reigning political lords nor incessantly seeking ways to overthrow those lords, whether by violence or nonviolence, in order to become the *dominant* power in the world. As might now be apparent, it was Yoder who helped me clarify and develop these concerns further. Even so, my definition emphatically affirms that the church exists to witness in word and deed *for the benefit of the world*. It is the world, with all of its sinful violence and conflict, that God loves and is intent on redeeming! Hence, the abiding issue is how to be *for* the world without being for the world on the terms determined acceptable by and subservient to the world.

Considering Yoder's Contributions

Salutary Traits of Yoder's Work

You may be reading this because in some way or another you have found the work of John Howard Yoder particularly challenging and illuminating and perhaps provocatively disturbing. Some of you have also spent more effort than I trying to interpret Yoder to an increasingly larger ecclesial and political audience. I applaud those efforts: Yoder is a gift to the Christian church and every encounter we might have with his works should be an encounter that is spiritually athletic and theologically stringent. Allow me now to identify some of the salutary traits of Yoder's work as I see them.

Yoder and Stone-Campbellites

First, Yoder is continually striving for clarity in his writings: it is more important to him most of the time to be searchingly clear about the subject matter under discussion than to be consoling and encouraging. Of course, the primary clarity he seeks has to do with Jesus of Nazareth and the biblical testimony to him. A great bulk of his writings are about or pivot about who this Jesus is—what sort of life he lived and what sort of teachings he conveyed and embodied in his life and in his death on the cross, and what it would mean to regard him as Lord and Savior of one's life and to be a member of a people who live their lives as his body and his disciples. It is from this centering on Jesus that issues about pacifism, politics, and ecclesiology emerge. If he is wrong about Jesus, then in his own mind he is wrong about pacifism, politics, and ecclesiology. It is not that Yoder thinks what he writes is authoritative because of his own authority as scholar; rather it is Jesus and the New Testament witness to him that is authoritative, and Yoder is the earnest student-scholar intending to understand the nature and content of that authority.

Second, there is amazing complexity as well as simplicity in Yoder as he explores what is involved in being a follower of Jesus. He does surprise us from time to time, refusing to say what we think he should have said or saying what we thought he would never have said.[14] Let me give a couple of examples of his refusal to elaborate, as it might also clarify some of my use of Yoder.

I think Yoder is profoundly trinitarian in his theological understanding, though only in a few instances does he discuss some of the theological issues at stake at Nicaea and Chalcedon.[15] But he never wavers in his belief

---

14. While it is unquestionable that Yoder and Stanley Hauerwas were good friends, with Hauerwas being one of the compelling champions of Yoder's work, it at least brings a smile to see the title of Yoder's 1997 book, *For the Nations: Essays Evangelical and Public* (Grand Rapids: Eerdmans, 1997) in contrast to Hauerwas's *Against the Nations: War and Survival in a Liberal Society* (Minneapolis: Winston, 1985). Perhaps the difference is more tone than substance, with Hauerwas battling liberal theology and ethics in the high precincts and cathedrals of Protestant theological education. But, as mentioned above, I have long favored an understanding of the nature and mission of the church closer to Yoder's phrasing—"for the benefit of the world"; see GCF, 25–29, 609–17. Cf. Yoder, "See How They Go with Their Face to the Sun," in *For the Nations*, ch. 3, for a surprising and powerful meditation on Jeremiah, Judaism, and the ecclesial power to endure foreign residency without hostility or obsequiousness.

15. Sometime in the early 1990s Mark Thiessen Nation indicated to me the existence of mimeographed notes of Yoder's lectures in systematic theology at the Associated Mennonite Biblical Seminaries in Elkhart, Indiana, delivered over several years from the mid-1960s to about 1980. I bought the lecture notes, gave them a quick scan, and placed them

PART ONE—Ecumenical Theologizing with Ecclesial Friends

that Jesus is the revelation of the God of Israel and that his life, death, and resurrection incarnates God's presence in the world. Jesus is the Lamb of God revealing the "grain of the cosmos."[16] In the same connection Yoder claims that Jesus is the beginning of a new eon, a new creation, and that eschatology is decisive for Jesus' preaching and way of life. But I am not aware that Yoder gives any extended attention to such traditional eschatological themes as the status of death and life-beyond-death and salvation eschatologically understood. Though he does not systematically address these topics, it would be wrong to conclude that he did not think them worthy of a disciple's concern. I have wondered whether Yoder ever gave a funeral homily or even commented on death and churchly grieving and hope. Other issues such as justification and grace, the work of the Holy Spirit, the relationship of God to those who do not confess Christ—which is not the same question as their relation to God—and whether God suffers are left unexplored.[17]

I make these comments about Yoder in order to suggest that Yoder does not write in order to satisfy all our theological concerns and questions. I say this also in order that we not prematurely conclude that if Yoder did not explicitly and fully explore a particular issue or question then it must not have been important to him and therefore need not be important to us.

---

in a Yoder file. It was heartening to see these lectures newly edited and introduced by Stanley Hauerwas and Alex Sider, published in 2002 as *Preface to Theology: Christology and Theological Method* (Grand Rapids: Brazos). In preparation for writing this essay, I read this later text with some care. I am impressed with Yoder's fair and probing discussion of issues at stake in Nicaea and Chalcedon. While he never quite recommended trinitarian constructions, he did not dismiss them either, clearly recognizing that the creedal controversies were addressing the genuinely serious question of how to explain the divinity of Jesus.

16. As in the title, *The Politics of Jesus: Vicit Agnus Noster* (*Behold the Lamb! Our Victorious Lamb*), 2nd rev. ed. (Grand Rapids: Eerdmans, 1994), esp. 246–47.

17. Yes, I know Yoder discusses Paul on "justification by grace through faith" in *Politics of Jesus*, 212–27. Without nitpicking what he says about Paul, it is important to understand Paul's language of "justification" and "reconciliation" as involving a *family of uses* that do not yield a precise definition that covers all the uses. But I am concerned that Yoder and a host of recent Pauline scholars neglect a fundamental Pauline conviction, namely, *that something happened in Christ Jesus that affects the universal human situation before God and is prior to any person's acceptance of Jesus as Lord*. That is the priority of God's grace, which it appears to me Yoder systematically underplays. Perhaps this is the Barth side of me, but it affects how issues of salvation can be analyzed and understood. See GCF, 503–9 and 513–19.

Radical Orthodoxy and Radical Discipleship in Yoder

I turn now to identify those aspects of Yoder's theologizing that warrant my identifying him in terms of radical orthodoxy and radical discipleship.[18] First, Yoder's pivotal concerns are Christological and ecclesiological: Jesus of Nazareth, a Jew, is the very revelation and incarnation of the God of Israel; and in his life, death, and resurrection, Jesus teaches, exemplifies, and conveys a way of life that summons persons to follow him by becoming gathered into a community of belief and practice that is an alternative way of life to the ways of life that seem so evident in the human social and political worlds. It is in the work of Jesus that God is bringing forth a new creation—a new aeon—and thereby revealing the meaning and goal of human history. It is this eschatological claim about Jesus and his work—and therefore about his reality and being—that is at the center of that *ekklesia* of folk summoned into a new way of life.

We should note that these basic claims about Jesus, God, and the new ecclesial community and its way of life are never proposed from any other perspective than as *confessional*.[19] He is, of course, interpreting the New Testament and in that way interpreting Jesus and stands ready to discuss whether he has interpreted the New Testament and Jesus correctly. On a variety of grounds it can be debated whether Yoder has adequately interpreted the New Testament in its testimony to Jesus. But he does not discuss whether anyone should believe these big claims about Jesus by way of arguments independent of scripture that would corroborate that Jesus is indeed truly God, for example. There is no retreat to an independent metaphysics or social ethics to confirm that Jesus is Lord. In these respects Yoder is akin to Barth.

Second, if the above is an accurate representation of Yoder, for the purposes of discussing Yoder in the context of the SCM branches, what might we construct as *orthodox* for Yoder? I propose the following theses for our consideration:

18. In this section I understand myself as doing no more than identifying convictions and arguments that are so common in Yoder and among Yoderian scholars that I am forgoing the tedious need to footnote all the major points.

19. As I recall, in the early 1990s one of the reasons Mark Thiessen Nation thought I would enjoy reading more of Yoder was because of my radically confessional understanding of theology. At that time Mark was keen on issues arising in philosophical and theological circles concerning "anti-foundationalism" and was convinced Yoder also was anti-foundationalist. See my discussions of some of these issues in GCF, 17–19, 24–25, 70–79, 101–9, and 141–47.

Part One—Ecumenical Theologizing with Ecclesial Friends

1. That Jesus, the Jew from Nazareth, is the very revelation of the reality and will of the God of Israel, the Creator of the world, and as such, Jesus is divine.

2. That Jesus' life, death, and resurrection reveal a new way of being the people of God, though such a way is a congruent development within the life of Israel.

3. That Jesus proclaimed that the kingdom God is bringing in a new social/political/ethical way of life that centers on love of neighbor, stranger, and enemy, on the refusal to return evil for evil, and on the refusal to use violence and to seek to rule the world through domination and coercion.

4. That Jesus called into being a new community of persons to be his disciples, to follow his path of servanthood, and to practice the new politics among themselves and in relation to the world, and that by so doing this new community will be an alternative community in relation to the other communities/cultures/nations/peoples that presume to give order to their worlds.

5. That this new community—the new ecclesia—will struggle to maintain its identity as a community of disciples of Jesus in a variety of ways in relation to the world, intending to be for the world without being so on the world's own terms.

6. That this new ecclesia, as the body of Christ in the world, confesses that God is in control of history and that such history has purpose and goal, and thereby the church gives up the belief or assumption common among various peoples that they are in charge of the world and it is their task to order the world and to do so by a 'justifiable use of violence.'

As should be obvious, this delineation of Yoder's orthodoxy is also a delineation of orthopraxis: these beliefs must be believed and these practices must be lived.

What is not included in Yoder's orthodoxy? While Yoder insists that Jesus is divine and acknowledges that this belief is the occasion for trinitarian thinking—that is, trinitarian thinking only arises because of the apostolic claims about Jesus' divinity—Yoder does not seem willing to make trinitarian beliefs essential to the beliefs of the church. Optional, yes, but not essential. Yoder does not include the belief in an inerrant

New Testament—though certainly an authoritative New Testament—and thereby he keeps the focus of the church on Jesus and his commandments and promises rather than on each and every sentence in the New Testament as having equal authority. Yoder does not include the belief that the reality of the church is dependent on the presence of "apostolic successors" as an unbroken line of leaders ordained by God.

In what sense, then, might it be illuminating to understand Yoder as embracing *radical orthodoxy* and *radical discipleship*? What is it in Yoder's work that would justify applying radical orthodoxy to him in differentiation from just the traditional orthodoxies of the church? I suggest that the radical orthodoxy of Yoder consists in his tying two elements inseparably together: 1) the belief in a divine Jesus who summons into being a new community of voluntary disciples defined by their confession of his Lordship, and 2) the community's practices of forgiveness; of loving neighbors, strangers, and enemies; of making peace and refusing to use violence for presumably justified ends; and of refusing to seek coercive domination of the world. The church's Lord is Jesus, the church's way of life is discipleship to Jesus, and the church, as an alternative community, lives differently from the ways of the world. This sort of *radical orthodoxy is inseparable from radical discipleship*, and without the practices of radical discipleship, the church becomes dominated and formed by the principalities and powers of the worlds in which it lives.[20]

A Theological Imaginary Engaging Yoder and the Stone-Campbell Movement

A Grammar of Radical Orthodoxy as Trinitarian

As I mentioned in my earlier brief discussion of "radical orthodoxy," I am gripped by the conviction that the church must be clear about its identity if it is not to be repeatedly overwhelmed by and conformed to the worlds in

---

20. In the language of the New Testament and the church, the uses of the word "world" are varied but interrelated. I have tried to sort out some of the differences and their interrelation in GCF, 47–52, under the heading of "The Dialectic between Church and World." In short, I distinguish among the following uses of *world*: 1) the world as the cosmos of creatures created by God; 2) the world as any human culture/society with its given structures and relations of order; and 3) the world as any human culture/society infected and skewed by sin. *The church is in the world in all three senses and the world is in the church in all three senses*. Hence, there arises a profound and ineradicable dialectic between the church and the world.

PART ONE—Ecumenical Theologizing with Ecclesial Friends

which it exists. I am gripped even more by the conviction that *the church's most basic identity is irrevocably tethered to the identity of God*, or as I have put it, by the radical grammar of the word "God" in the church's life. Precisely because there are many uses historically of "God"—and therefore many gods seductively hiding under the word "God"—the church cannot maintain a faithful identity in its life through the centuries without an ongoing and relentless conversation about the identity of God. It is in answering this question that the church must confront issues of orthodoxy, and it is in answering this question that the historic traditions of the church laboriously—and often languidly—developed and embraced trinitarian language.

I want now to engage Yoder—and therewith also the SCM—in the question of why trinitarian language is intelligible but only optional. *Why isn't trinitarian language essential to answering the questions of the identity of God and the identity of the church?*

It is beyond question that for Yoder it is essential to Christian understanding that Jesus is Lord and therefore Jesus is divine. And Yoder has acknowledged that the great trinitarian theologizing in the early church was a search for the proper and adequate Christian understanding of God. It is obvious that in the New Testament the names "Father," "Son," and "Spirit/Holy Spirit" are used as though they are *distinct*—e.g., the Father did not die on the cross—and yet fundamentally *one*. But do we have a grammar here that would fit well within the polytheistic possibilities of Greco-Roman philosophical and religious life? Supposing now you are an elder in a congregation in Asia Minor engaged in teaching the faith to new converts or would-be converts and one of them asks, "How it is that Jesus is divine and our Savior but this affirmation is not polytheistic?" What do you say? Trinitarian conversation and the creeds of Nicaea and Chalcedon are attempts by the church to put some exclusionary brackets on some ways of construing God the Father and Jesus of Nazareth. Nicaea confirmed that the Father and Jesus are one basic divine reality. Chalcedon confirmed that Jesus is both divine and human, and any attempt to deny either is to undermine the capacity to call Jesus Lord and Savior. These decisions are basic grammar for the church, even though there is much more to be said.

Now when some other ecclesial tradition, like the SCM, says we need neither Nicaea nor Chalcedon—we just need the real, human Jesus—the question looms as to how this real, human Jesus is our Savior. In what way is Jesus Savior and what does he save us from? Aside from the important sense in which Jesus summons persons to a new way of life, it must be admitted that Yoder tarries not over further questions about the meaning of salvation. He refuses to stress anything like an *experience* of being converted by Jesus, though there are such experiences and they were bread and butter for much of the SCM. And Yoder is certainly wary of developing atonement theories and he hesitates to clarify any imaginary of ultimate salvation.[21]

Suppose now some tradition goes on to say it is *inappropriate* for the church to attempt to answer these questions in some definitive way and that it must be left up to each individual to answer the questions for herself. The identity of God is left up to the individual to determine for herself, as though the church—as a community of engaging theological conversation—is incapacitated to distinguish between its own common teachings and the predictable struggles individuals might have in understanding, accepting, and appropriating those teachings. Isn't that a recipe for unremitting conflict, confusion, illusion, and despair?

Suppose one then says, as does Yoder, that *God is in control of history and the world process*. What sort of *control* are we talking about, such that earnest would-be believers might know how to conform to and pray to God? As for Yoder, I think he answers this by referring to the life, death, and resurrection of Jesus: God has power sufficient to bring God's kingdom to culminating presence in the world and yet God rules in the way Jesus rules as the Lamb of God slain for the redemption of the world. Yoder avers that trinitarian language arises from these concerns and intends to render these questions intelligible to the church, but he makes no further attempt to explore and construct such trinitarian understanding as though it is crucial to the church's understanding of God and therefore also the church's understanding of itself.

I believe that the creedal conversations and rule-making of Nicaea and Chalcedon are theologically crucial to the life of the church, even though I admit some of the church's use of the creeds has been confusing. In these creedal conversations, the church assumed that the identity of the Father—as the God of Israel and Creator of the world—was clear and non-controversial. Using some metaphysical concepts at hand, the Father was assumed to be immutable, impassible, infinite, all-powerful, and simple. The theological problem was getting Jesus—the Jewish human being who

---

21. See GCF, 503–9, for some brief diagnostic comments on the various meanings of "salvation" language.

suffered and was crucified—understood in relation to the divinity of the Father. However, at various points in the church's life it was able to *reformulate the question to become: how does the divinity of Jesus, given his life, death, and resurrection, affect and modify our understanding of the divinity of the Father?*

I think Yoder saw the radical character of this way of putting the question of the identity and divinity of God, perhaps under the influence of Barth. But he abstained—or thought irrelevant to his concerns—from making further inroads on trinitarian conversation. My concern is that in the absence of such further work, it is virtually unintelligible why anyone should suppose Jesus is Lord and humans are summoned to be his body in the world. Put another way, to say "Jesus is Lord" is to say more than "Jesus is the Lord of *my life*"; it is also to say "Jesus is Lord of the whole creation, whether anyone believes it or not." Jesus' Lordship does not depend on our believing, even though it is important that the disciples believe he is Lord. Isn't this why the church cannot confess the Lordship of Jesus without moving into trinitarian language about the reality of God and what God has done on behalf of human salvation?

Further, had Yoder pushed more firmly into trinitarian elaboration, he would have had to confront issues concerning the status of the Holy Spirit. Yet in this regard, Yoder is akin to the SCM with its almost complete neglect of the Holy Spirit. Such neglect poses sharply the question of how the language of the divinity of Jesus as Lord and Savior can be sustained and intelligible to the church without a trinitarian understanding of the unity and the complexity *within* the Divine Life. Furthermore, *it is trinitarian grammar that empowers the church to understand the life, death, and resurrection of Jesus as not only a historical series of events but also as salvific events internal to the complex Life of God on behalf of the salvation of the world.*

I invite you to look further at my *Grammar* book to see the virtues, as well as the truthfulness, of a trinitarian understanding of God. It capacitates the church's discourses to think of God as dynamically both one and complex in which there is real otherness, movement, and relationships within God's Life and in God's free and loving interaction with the world for the redemption of the world. The incarnational narrative about Jesus in the New Testament will surely fall into disarray in the absence of a robust trinitarian understanding of God. Hence, the radical orthodoxy I propose is one in which the divinity of Jesus reshapes and deepens the church's own life.[22]

A Grammar of Radical Discipleship and Ecclesial Identity

I have claimed that it is helpful to understand that issues of radical orthodoxy and radical discipleship are the deep grammar of the church's construal of the *identity of God and the identity of the church*. I remind you that I am also concerned with the perennial problem of the church's relation to the worlds in which it invariably exists and how the church is empowered to maintain a self-understanding that clarifies its ongoing and unavoidable being-in-the-world. What sort of identity must the church have if it is to be *for* the world without being *of* the world or being the vassal of the world? It is herein that I think Yoder's claims about radical discipleship will be helpful for us to examine further.

Radical discipleship is, of course, discipleship to Jesus as Lord and Savior. It is Jesus' life, death, and resurrection that summon the church into existence as the community of persons who live a distinctive way of life. While I think there is more to say about that distinctive way of life than Yoder emphasizes, nevertheless he is right to place discipleship to Jesus as central in the church's life. To drop out or minimize this discipleship and aim to locate the identity of the church by some other conceptual means is for Yoder to cease being the church of Jesus Christ. *The church exists, wherever it exists, only in the form of discipleship.*

How then does Yoder give definiteness to this alternative community's life of discipleship? That way of life includes: confessing sins and repenting; accepting sins as forgiven by God and learning thereby how to forgive others; seeking the good of the neighbor, the stranger, and the enemy and refusing to take the life of another; refusing to use violence against another; refusing to seek retaliation for wrongs done to oneself or to another; refusing to put limits on forgiveness; making peace with others; refusing to rule others as the Gentiles rule by lording over them; and more. These practices are clearly identified throughout the New Testament, and, as practices summoned by Jesus, it would be absurd to say Jesus did not really mean to so summon and form the church as his body.

---

22. See GCF, 149–232, for a full discussion of the case for trinitarian grammar, while at the same time adjusting the way some parts of the traditions have talked about God.

Part One—Ecumenical Theologizing with Ecclesial Friends

But! But what?

To understand this ever recurring *but* in the historical lives of the churches, let us focus on the disarming title of one of Yoder's most important books: *The Politics of Jesus*. Why the use of this word *politics*? Yoder tells us that he is aiming to question and counter a typical way in which many liberal Protestant theologians/ethicists have argued that the ethics of Jesus, which we have identified above, are irrelevant to the political realities of the world. They claim that the ethics or politics of Jesus are a useful *norm* but are not a useable *guide* to the church's concrete witness to and life in the world. If Christians really care about the world and its infelicitous conflicts and wars—so a non-Yoderian might argue—then the church must have a social ethics or a politics amenable to the politics of the world. Yoder's counter to this is to claim that Jesus provides an actual politics—a social ethics—that in fact bears upon and interacts with the world's politics. The way of Jesus is also the way of the cross and may include cross-bearing suffering as a consequence of discipleship to Jesus. Hence, the church properly, as the body of Christ in the world, lives an alternative way of life to the ways of life the world promotes and demands. To live in conformity to Jesus' way of life is the basic calling of the church.

Yet, have not even the various church traditions thought they were living differently from the world, even if they lived often in some *partial conformity* to the world's politics? How then is such done? Perhaps it might be argued that at the heart of the church are the practices of neighbor love—agapic love—in which the Christian and the church seek the good of the neighbor, even the stranger and the enemy as in the category of the *neighbor*. Might it happen, then, that the church so seeks the good of its many neighbors that it takes up—or is willing to endorse and support the taking up of—the sword to protect the neighbor in peril? Ah, there is the rub: the willingness to use violence against another in order to protect oneself or another from violence. For Yoder, that simple allowance of violence in the name of the world's various political orders is the source of *how* the church itself loses its own identity and becomes the vassal of the larger political world in which it exists. When the church sanctions the use of violence in the environing politics of the world, then, according to Yoder, it has forfeited its summons to radical discipleship and will thereby lose its distinctive way of life and perhaps its deepest theological identity.

Critics of Yoder are right to see that Yoder tethers the church's identity to radical discipleship to Jesus as that is also tethered to agapic love and agapic love to nonviolence. And yet they criticize Yoder for tethering all these together to comprise the identity of the church. They want a church that can also engage the interests of the worlds' politics on the worlds' own terms. But how is that done? It is done by appealing to some other set of principles that will endorse the use of restrained and justified violence in the political orders of the world in order to control violence and disorder. What principles? Consider how *natural law* can come into play or principles of *political realism*. The church comes to grips with two orders: its own internal order of love, forgiveness, and nonviolence, and the order to the world's various dependencies on violence in the name of peace and protection from harm.

Lest his critics or his followers think Yoder has erected pacifism into an independent principle that is in general persuasive to thoughtful folk, Yoder writes another book, *Nevertheless: Varieties of Religious Pacifism,* aiming to distinguish the church's radical discipleship as Messianic Pacifism from a host of other pacifisms with different rationales. Hence, it is not any sort of political pacifism that Yoder is endorsing; it is the pacifism of radical discipleship to Jesus.[23] It is extremely important to note, however, that Yoder is arguing that nonviolence is essential to the church and its radical discipleship, but he is *not* arguing that the politics of the states and nations could be better organized were they to adopt policies of nonviolence. Yet it is certainly clear that Yoder is harsh with Christians who would recommend state violence by reference to the New Testament or the teachings of Jesus. The politics of Jesus are not the politics of the state; the state—in its more or less liberal democratic rationale and form—is of necessity committed to the principled use of violence in order to control random violence and disorder, and whatever role the church might have in stately politics, it would only be to ameliorate specific practices of state violence.[24]

---

23. Revised and expanded edition (Scottdale, PA: Herald, 1992).

24. It is generally conceded in all philosophical discussions of the politics of the nation-states these days that Hobbes is foundational: citizens concede a monopoly on violence to the state in order that the state will protect them from harm internally within the state and externally from harm by other states and powers. Yet the Yoderian/Mennonite advocacy of nonviolence has never quite clarified how the church might reckon with the "police" function of the state in which the issue is not whether to go to war but how might the church construe, accept, and participate in and limit this more modest use of force and coercion. These issues are thoughtfully explored in a recent book edited by a Yoder student and containing essays from some Mennonite and Roman Catholic thinkers: ed. Gerald W. Schlabach, *Just Policing, Not War: An Alternative Response to World Violence* (Collegeville, MN: Liturgical, 2007). The book advances the thesis that,

PART ONE—Ecumenical Theologizing with Ecclesial Friends

To put in clear focus the dilemma of church theology in relation to the use of violence by the nation-state, Yoder argues that Jesus Christ is at the heart of the church, radical discipleship is the form of the church, and such discipleship involves the refusal by the church and the disciple to use violence against another human for whatever urgent or long-term reasons. *A church that practices this sort of radical discipleship is a church that will never be in danger of having its identity given to it or overwhelmed by the world in which it lives. God, Jesus, church identity, discipleship, and nonviolence are tethered together as radical orthodoxy and radical orthopraxis.*

Hence, the real worry about the Constantinianization of the church is not primarily about the church being *established* and under the domain of the state; rather it prevails whenever the church loses it radical discipleship to the various ways in which the state or cultural powers prevail upon the disciples to conform to the state's or the society's endorsement and authority and relinquish the nonviolent character of discipleship.

Conclusion

So how did we Stone-Campbellites become so formed by our worldly circumstances that we—presuming to restore simple New Testament Christianity—stumbled along submitting ourselves variously to American individualism, Southern and Northern warring sentiments and animosities, trusting an inerrant Bible that reduced Jesus to every "jot and tittle" of the text, and casually supporting racism and violence toward women for decades? How did it come about that we fell into reducing discipleship to Jesus to discipleship to American democracy or to our local idiosyncrasies or to our devotion to free market capitalism or to our willingness to go to war to defend American "freedom" or to our passion for liberal politics or to a multi-culturalism that relativizes even Jesus? Might our branches have stayed together and been on target if we had hewed to a radical orthodoxy *and* radical discipleship? Is it not even now the case that each of the branches has its own way of characterizing the other branches as folk who have forsaken the original dynamism of the SCM?

---

in light of the "fact" that modern war is beyond any serious ethical justification, neither just war theories nor complete nonviolence can seriously come to grips with the need to control violence in the world and to engage in active peacemaking.

Speaking boldy—as if for the first time?—are there even the theological resources, commitments, and appetites remaining in our various branches to engage robustly the sort of radical orthodoxy and radical discipleship Yoder seems to envisage and which I have pushed even further? Or in what respects would any of us, standing within our SCM tradition, find good theological reasons for questioning or even rejecting the basic outlines of Yoder's vision?

I have my own demurs from Yoder, but I like the stringency of his understanding of church and discipleship. Yet I do not think a simple affirmation of the divinity of Jesus is sufficient without a richer exploration of what Jesus' divinity means for our identification of who God is, and I do not see how the identification of God can finally avoid or walk away from trinitarian articulation. I have tried elsewhere to outline a trinitarian orthodoxy that is compatible with much of Yoder, but also more than Yoder. I am skeptical there can be a real "reformation" of the church in the absence of a profound principle of identity and critique that reminds the church in all of its life that it has a Lord—Jesus Christ—who summons it to radical discipleship as a radical alternative community to whatever world in which the church lives. In the absence of that reforming principle of identity and critique, the struggling body of the church will inevitably but variably submit to and rejoice in being the chaplain—or perhaps even a cranky prophet—of the various politics and economics of its world's dominant principalities and powers.

For my own branch of the SCM, the Christian Church (Disciples of Christ), it is hardly imaginable what it would mean to be radical disciples of Jesus in Yoder's sense. But then, whatever could it mean to call ourselves Disciples of Christ? Yet I also must admit that my own Christian pilgrimage is deeply rooted in that loose-jointed heritage, even though it is also the case that most of my lifetime of theological work and writings are hardly legible, much less acceptable, to my tradition's present discourses and practices in their utter disarray. That surely makes me sad, but Paul repeatedly reminds me that we have *these treasures in earthen vessels* that are always in need of reform.

I conclude these reflections on Yoder and us Stone-Campbellites with the question of whether there is even that solicitous and convicting *theological imaginary* among us of a proper radical orthodoxy centered on trinitarian discourses arising from the divinity of Jesus and a proper radical discipleship that comprises the church as a genuinely alternative community—a community neither simply *at war with* nor *in bed with* the various nations and communities of the world, but also *for the world* as those creaturely arrangements of power and goods that need radical redemption.

6

World Communion Sunday: Why?

A sermon preached on October 7, 2012 at Southern Hills Christian Church in Edmond, Oklahoma in celebration of World Communion Sunday. The scripture was Luke 22:15–27.

As you have noticed in the sermon title, I have put an emphatic *Why?* At least the why is there to encourage us to ask why we are celebrating something called "World Communion Sunday." The first step toward an answer to the why is simply to note that in the largely Protestant Ecumenical Movement in 1940 it was proposed that the first Sunday in October in each year be an occasion in which churches from around the world not only *celebrate Holy Communion* on that day but *search for a sense of what it is in that celebration that binds Christians around the world together as One body.*

Not only were leaders of the Disciples of Christ involved in this initial proposal, but we have been known as that Christian tradition that places emphasis on celebrating what we call the Lord's Supper as essential to our worship services. If Disciples are going to congregate for worship, then they will set and serve the Lord's Supper. When asked why we celebrate the Supper so often, we have answered because it focuses on the centrality of the life, death, and resurrection of Jesus Christ for our self-understanding as an ecclesial community and as individual followers of Jesus. Hence, the common name "Disciples of Christ."

Accordingly, it is a matter of faithfulness and honesty for us Disciples, gathered here this morning on this particular day of ecumenical celebration, to inquire carefully about *what we are doing* and *why we are doing it*

Part One—Ecumenical Theologizing with Ecclesial Friends

when we celebrate the Lord's Supper this Sunday and every Sunday. And in doing what we do in the Supper, how does that convey our sense of solidarity with other Christians?

To launch this inquiry of *faith seeking understanding*, I want us to acknowledge that the celebration of the Lord's Supper is a *practice* of the church. The concept of practice of course is not unique to the church, but plays an important role in analyzing social contexts, agreements, and interconnections. And, while it may seem initially dubious to you, it is impossible to perform a practice without a language describing and prescribing what the practice is and what it is for. Hence, I propose that a practice is an action or a set of interconnected actions that can be repeated—or performed—and that can be identified in language.

Consider how we speak of practice in the context of sports. If a person wants to play baseball, for example, he or she needs to be taught in language what it means to play baseball. There are objects called baseballs and they are hard and can be thrown or hit with a bat. If a person wants to learn how to use a baseball bat to hit a baseball well, he will have to practice hitting the ball with bat. Hence, to play baseball requires practice playing baseball, and it may take a long time—perhaps years—to learn *how* to play baseball well. Even more, practicing in order to play baseball well is not yet actually playing a baseball game. The activities of playing a baseball game are themselves dependent on the *rules* of the game and such rules are invariably expressed in language.

To call the celebration of the Lord's Supper a *practice* should helpfully throw into relief how the theological description of the practice is not a mere add-on but is in actual practice the heart of the matter. No theological language, no practice of the Lord's Supper. Drinking the cup is something anyone can do with any cup. To drink the cup of the Lord's Supper is something one has to *learn how to do*. Notice I said *how* to do it. And you cannot learn how to receive and drink the communion cup as an act of faith without learning the theological language of the church.

Notice the difference in possible responses of Fred when we ask him what he is doing when he is drinking the cup of juice that has been passed to him in the pew: he might say "I am drinking this grape juice" or he might say "I am drinking this juice to acknowledge Jesus Christ as my Lord and Savior." Might this provide us an insight into how deeply intentions are woven into our actions and thereby into our practices? Theological language is not an add-on or mere superficiality; it is the heart of the matter! At least the theological language *trains* us in how to perform the practice of receiving the bread and cup as signs of Jesus presence among us and with us.

I am proposing that we will continually miss the point of the practice of celebrating the Lord's Supper if we forget or deny that its theological center and rationale is the salvific significance of the life, death, and resurrection of Jesus of Nazareth, very God and very human. Drop out that theological meaning of the event and practice of the Lord's Supper, and we might inadvertently be reducing the celebration to being no more than a reminder of the need to be friendly and welcoming.

On the hunch that what I have just said might be puzzling to us, I want to make some remarks about the history of the church's celebration of the Lord's Supper.

First, aside from the agreement that the practice can be traced back to Jesus' last supper with his disciples, tensions and disagreements emerge quickly as to exactly what the practice is and what it means. Paul is wrestling in his first letter to the church in Corinth about what the practice is and what it means to perform it. Apparently some in Corinth thought it was primarily a time to eat a meal and to bring their own food. Paul calls this practice into question by rooting it back in the inauguration by Jesus with his disciples "on the night in which he was betrayed …" (1 Cor 11:23–26).

Second, within a couple of centuries or so, the practice is characterized as a 'sacrament' by the rising Roman tradition of the church, and became a *practice* that could only be performed properly when presided over by an ordained male priest. During this time we see the emergence of the practice of naming the celebration the "Eucharist" emphasizing thereby a practice of thanksgiving for the *gifts* of the life, death, and resurrection of Jesus Christ.

Third, over the succeeding centuries, it seemed a common assumption that the bread and wine are, when consecrated by a priest, really transformed into being the very real presence of the body and blood of Jesus himself. When stated as a theory about the elements, it came to be called "transubstantiation." From my vantage point today, this awkward language was aiming to affirm that in the partaking of the bread and the drinking of the wine the faithful were experiencing the real presence of Christ the Savior, and not just remembering him.

Fourth, during Reformation times, the left wing, which includes many of the predecessors of our Stone-Campbell traditions, decided that the priest was unimportant to the reality of the practice and that the transubstantiation issues were misleading. Partly due to its strong anti-Catholic

PART ONE—Ecumenical Theologizing with Ecclesial Friends

bias, this tradition tended more and more to regard the celebration as a 'remembering of Jesus' and thereby, almost inadvertently, de-emphasizing the real presence of Jesus Christ in the bread and cup. The communion table could no longer be regarded as an 'altar' upon which the sacrifice of Jesus' death could be re-enacted. So, why not just pass the bread and wine to believers as they sat in their pews?

Fifth, since the Reformation, most Protestant traditions have agreed that it is essential to a theological definition of the church that it is that unique community in which the sacraments are celebrated and the Word is preached. Herein the sacraments being referred to are baptism and Holy Communion.

Sixth, in our own time, I might add, it can sometimes appear in the language used in the enactment of the practice that its primary purpose is to be a warm, welcoming, and reassuring event. The Lord's Supper might then be seen as a means to the end of our feeling better about ourselves.

Having rehearsed some of the differences in the practices of the Lord's Supper or Holy Communion or Eucharist or Mass, we might be wondering whether we Christians can be theologically intelligible to each other.

These are real issues and I could mention that I have spent an adult lifetime searching through the various ramifications of how the discourses and practices of the church are by their very nature *theological in character* and that such is a language that needs to be *learned* in the discourses and practices of worship and everyday conduct.

Those words may seem a bit heavy to us, so let me pause to share some memories of my encounters with the celebrations of the Lord's Supper.

You may not know that I was raised here in Oklahoma City and attended Pennsylvania Avenue Christian Church. That congregation recently ceased existence, but I can assure you that for much of its lifetime during the fifties and sixties it sent more of its young people on paths toward ministerial leadership and Christian service than any other Disciples congregation in Oklahoma. Of course we celebrated the Lord's Supper every Sunday during morning worship. I was the youngest of four children and my family always sat on the back row of the left side of sanctuary.

As with most Disciples congregations, there was a table below the pulpit upon which the trays of grape juice cups and the trays of small cracker-type squares were stacked. The pastor might say something from the pulpit before we sang the communion hymn, but the two male laymen called 'elders' on the sides of the table said a few words and then each prayed, one for the bread and one for the cup. They then passed the trays to the 'deacons' who then distributed them to the gathered folk, aisle by aisle, with each person consuming the elements as they were passed. That scenario was pretty common for Disciples congregations in those days.

Of course, in my congregation, as was common in Disciples congregations, only persons baptized—meaning 'adult baptism'—were permitted to partake of the bread and cup. Baptism was never performed before the eleventh year of the person's life. I confess to you now that that exclusion did not strike me as odd or unwarranted or discriminatory. I felt no exclusion or neglect. It seemed evident to me that I was more nearly a spectator of the practice and the sort of life of discipleship that seemed connected to it.

Yet in those pre-baptism days I was a regular observer about how, seated a few rows in front of us, Mrs. Hempstead received the elements. She was a woman of substantial proportions and graced with a full head of brilliant red hair. I knew she was leader in the church and had a son going into ministry. But I was gripped by the unvarying drama that Mrs. Hempstead *wept* every time she received and partook of the bread and cup. To my immature mind, something really important but mysterious and deep was happening right there amidst Mrs. Hempstead's sobs and her partaking of the Lord's Supper. I was never quite sure whether her weeping was one of sadness or one of gratitude and thanksgiving.

When I was finally baptized as a rite of passage and was welcomed to the table, I confess that my first participation in the event did not seem to move me in quite the way it did for Mrs. Hempstead, but it occurred to me that that was my loss. But surely a loss worth thinking about.

Well, somehow I made my way through college, then to seminary, and then to a doctoral work in theology. My first professorial appointment was to Perkins School of Theology at Southern Methodist University in Dallas. As you can guess, it was a Methodist seminary with a robust and intellectually commanding faculty. I thought myself especially privileged to be chosen to be a member of the Perkins faculty. Among all the formative moments for me, in addition to the wonders of teaching students, was my participation in the worship life of the seminary. Chapel services were daily through the weekly classes and Holy Communion was celebrated once a week.

Two aspects of how Holy Communion was celebrated made a permanent impression on me. First, in preparation for receiving the bread and

Part One—Ecumenical Theologizing with Ecclesial Friends

wine, there were long recitations of the language of the faith in scripture and tradition. Jesus was firmly rooted in Israel and the narrative of his significance could not omit those roots. But it was especially gripping for me that we regularly sang the chant: *O Lamb of God, that takest away the sins of the world, have mercy upon us*. The chant being sung by all, of course, was ancient in origin, coming into the Methodist tradition from its Anglican roots. But that chanting seemed to me to convey wistfully the wonder of our being sinners for whom Jesus—the Lamb of God—took away from us our sins and, indeed, the sins of the whole world.

Second, we received the bread and wine individually from the ordained clergy at the front of the chapel kneeling at the communion rail with hands extended and open. There we were on our knees—needy supplicants neither proud nor triumphantly righteous. Frankly, something happened in that celebration of the Lord's Supper that simply became a permanent dimension of my experience of the communion. I could easily imagine Mrs. Hempstead on her knees at the rail with hands extended, weeping as she received forgiveness and hope and perhaps my reaching over to help her up from the rail.

While I taught at Perkins, we were members of our local Disciples church in Richardson, a suburb of Dallas. It was a wonderfully resilient and devout congregation, but we still received the bread and cup sitting in our pews. Even so, I found myself often moved by the solemn earnestness with which we prayed and received the elements. But it was still easier to imagine that we were *remembering ole Jesus*—still dead in that remote and dusty past—and not really present right here in this practice and in our lives.

In 2000 Sarah and I moved to live in a cabin on Fort Gibson Lake in eastern Oklahoma. It had been in the family since 1970 and we had gradually expanded it until it seemed commodious enough for all of our family to gather often. But we lived about equidistant from Muskogee and Tahlequah and Wagoner. Some untoward developments were happening in the Disciples churches in those towns, so we ended up attending a Methodist church in Muskogee, at that time pastored by a former student of mine at Perkins. But alas, Methodists vary greatly among congregations as to the times and the patterns by which they celebrate Holy Communion. Quarterly celebrations, not weekly, are common.

Shortly after our becoming members, the pastor was transferred to another congregation. His successor became a very dear friend and pastor to us. But, I share that we celebrated Holy Communion only quarterly and

World Communion Sunday: Why?

then with some urgency at the end of the Sunday service. That urgency is not an uncommon situation among Disciples. I was occasionally asked to help serve the supplicants at the rail and was moved again and again at their devout demeanor as they received the elements. But, my pastor friend worried that time was pressing, and he often rushed through the language of the service as though he was reading a ticker tape of the market. Just sounds, not quite words full of hope. The Great Thanksgiving of God's work in Israel and in Jesus of Nazareth's life, death, and resurrection receded into mere words, bereft of passion and faithful witness. And we never took the time to sing thrice: "*O Lamb of God, that takest away the sins of the world, have mercy upon us.*"

Finally, gently as you can imagine, I dared to urge the pastor to slow down, say the words as though they are rich and powerful in meaning—words that we the congregation also need to learn how to say and mean.

Sometimes, dear friends, I fear that many of us ordained persons think we have to reinvent the Gospel and faith in language that fits the contemporary folk and their moods. But I propose here today, that the precious words of the church and its Gospel are intended to *form us to fit the language*, rather than *form the language to fit we congregants in our worldly dispositions*. We need the liturgical rehearsals of the narratives of the faith to teach us *how* we might construe God and our human neighbors and even our enemies. And miraculously we might grasp what it is to receive grace and forgiveness and how appropriate it might be to weep in gratitude for such blessings.

So, today we Disciples of Christ acknowledge that many are they in other Christian traditions who are celebrating our common practice and confession that we not only remember Jesus but we reckon with the theological fact that in receiving the bread of his broken body and the cup of his risen life, we are not alone. Not only is Christ with us, but millions of other Christian friends are receiving the gifts of the Lord's Supper and will depart from their gathering together with a new and vivid sense that they have the gift of life from the grace of God. Not a gift we have earned and now deserve. The Lord's Supper is sheer gift. Jesus Christ is Lord and Savior of the world; the church knows that and is witness to the world now on this World Communion Sunday.

Might I conclude this meditation on the Lord's Supper in the hope that it might never occur to us to say or even to feel like saying: "Mrs. Hempstead, please refrain from weeping. Just pass the trays and let us get

Part One—Ecumenical Theologizing with Ecclesial Friends

this ancient ritual over without too much fuss. We really need to get out in time to beat the lunch crowd."

All this dear friends in Christ, I have dared to preach in the name of the Father, and of the Son, and of the Holy Spirit, One God, and Mother of us all. Amen.

Part Two

On Being Mugged by Politics
but Lifted by Gospel Hope

7

Venturing into Blogging

Friends:

As I venture into blogging for the first time, let me lay out some fundamental issues and discussion points that I hope will emerge again and again in my blogging and perhaps in the readers' responses.

First, I propose that it is theologically self-contradictory to claim to be a member of the church of Jesus Christ and also regard your national or ethnic or economic identity to be more fundamental to your self-understanding than being a disciple of Jesus. Yes, I know, the very way in which I have proposed this might seem prejudicial and misleading. And I will grant that the church of Jesus Christ has existed in fragmented forms here and there throughout what might be called 'church history.'

But I am proposing that a church tradition—and the individuals who comprise that tradition—that weds its Christian identity to its national, ethnic, or economic identity has already assured that the Christian identity will in fact be subordinate to that other identity. By *subordinate* I mean that the way in which the church and the members of the church put their lives together in concrete, day to day living, will inevitably subordinate prime Christian convictions and practices to those other principalities and powers that confer identity and vocation on a people.

I am not denying that the church always exist somewhere in some world under given conditions of political, economic, and social arrangements and configurations. The crucial question, however, is '*how* ought the church and the Christian so live in those circumstances?'

Second, I want to propose that the church theologically understood, wherever it exists, has as its primary and focus-giving mission: *to witness in word and deed to the triune God for the benefit of the world.* Hold steady right here: it really matters how the church understands who God is—how it identifies who God is—considering that there are many pretenders to deity and many acolytes claiming to do the will of that deity.

If we are not careful, the identity of God will be shackled to the identity and cause of the nation or the ethnic group or the rich or poor economically, for example. When America is adorned with the mantle of being a 'Christian nation,' deity becomes the endorser of the nation's values and conduct—or of the values of the powers in control of the nation. It is sobering to realize that the southern Confederacy invoked Jesus Christ in its new constitution and therewith was implicitly claiming that *states' rights*—in particular that state right to determine the 'legality' of chattel slavery for the blacks—was Christianly defensible!

Yet, however true it may be that the church through the ages has often been tethered to a nation or a people or an ethnicity, when I propose that the church must understand itself as theologically differentiated from the particularities of such social identities, I am not supposing that the church exists primarily to oppose or subjugate these other identities. Transforms them, yes, but by way of peacemaking. It has happened that such transformative peacemaking has not always been regarded by ruling powers of the world as that sort of benefit they find desirable and acceptable. Indeed, it can appear that such transformative benefits feel unattractive, intrusive, and repugnant to the world.

Put sharply, the church properly intends the benefit of practicing and witnessing to the way God bestows the *benefits* of reconciliation among people at war and consumed by fear, hatred, and enmity, the *benefits* of refusing to endorse and perpetuate the scapegoating of *strangers* and *enemies* the worldly powers have identified as a threat to internal solidarity and security.

These benefits the church intends for the worlds are rooted quite simply in the identity of God radically disclosed in the life, the crucified death, and the resurrection of Jesus Christ—the one the church confesses is the divine Logos. Surely it is immediately obvious that it is *not* the God-given logos of the world that human peace and safety and flourishing can *only* be obtained and secured through the powers of the sword, the gun, the cannon, the bomb, the prison, the occupying army, or the threat of overwhelming force.

So, the church exists and has as its non-forfeitable mission and purpose to witness to the triune God for the benefit of the world.

[Posted 10/13/12]

8

Following Jesus and Worshipping Jesus in Rivalrous Times

Friends:

It arises from time to time that some folk propose a strong distinction between 'following Jesus' and 'worshipping Jesus.' It is a distinction I find extremely unhappy and misleading and grammatically gross!

It seems to me that there are several matters in that grammar that are highly infelicitous for the church and the living of the Christian life. It would make it *appear* that there are some who simply worship and adore Jesus but ignore his summons to the way of discipleship. But that appearance simply hides the subterfuge that Jesus can properly be adored and worshipped without also following him. Or, that one can properly follow Jesus without also worshipping him—Jesus the prophet teaching the true moral law.

But when we—the church, Christians—hammer folk for only admiring Jesus but not following him, we must not slip into the other peril of supposing that it is *easy* to follow Jesus, *if we just try harder*. Trying harder can fall into the peril of trying to be and do what Jesus was and did. Yet, might it be possible that Jesus does something that we—whoever and wherever—cannot do for ourselves?

Perhaps we should change the language here thus: might there be a distinction appropriate to the church between 'following Jesus *Christ*' and 'worshipping Jesus *Christ*'? The addition of the title and office 'Christ' should remind Christians that following Jesus is following the One who comes to us as the Word of God and that worshipping Jesus is worshipping the One whose life, death, and resurrection convey God's grace and forgiveness that no amount of obedient following could ever earn or achieve.

I think the mainline grammar of the church has always intended to say that the way of Jesus' own life, death, and resurrection is at one and the same time God's incarnate coming into the world to disarm the desperate rivalries, conflicts, and violence that stalk human life and society. And Jesus—though murdered by those sinful and violent rivalries who seek domination through death and the threat of death—is that strange human who nevertheless refuses to perpetuate such rivalry and death-dealing, who refuses to summon his beleaguered followers to gather up their arms and make the crucifiers pay—as though the followers *owe* it to Jesus to destroy the crucifiers.

In good depth grammar, I urge folk to grasp in their living, speaking, and dying that it is impossible to follow Jesus truly without also worshipping Jesus, and it is impossible to worship Jesus truly without following him. Rough facsimiles to either temptation will, of course, emerge from time to time. But the very deep being of the church is dependent on not forgetting who Jesus Christ is and why he is Lord and why the sort of following he summons is rooted in the sort of forgiving grace he extends to all.

These matters are another reminder of why the church is not a nation nor in subjugation to a nation. But the church can be the church of Jesus Christ in whatever nation it might be located, and its being the church of Jesus Christ is not contingent on its being affirmed or endorsed by the nation or the surrounding culture. Even so, the church in obedience to Jesus Christ exists for the *benefit* of the world. God loves this world, which is not to say God approves of the ways the world creates and settles conflicts by rivalries, falsehoods, and violence. But God's judgment of the world does not require God to be the ultimate and violent destroyer of the world. It is God's love in Christ Jesus that is the final redeeming judge of the world.

For many of my friends who might read this blog, we live in a nation that is going berserk with electioneering rhetoric inflaming rivalries and fear. There is no reason why Christians should think that it is good to live, think, and speak that way. Yet how might Christian followers of Jesus Christ live and speak in the midst of such rhetorical mayhem? Might we simply engage the mayhem with as much truth-telling that we can discern and muster and do so without mimicking the rivalries?

[Posted 10/21/10]

9

Capitalism, Democracy, and Health Care

A Response to Family and Friends

Friends:
Jon Rex is a cousin dear and close in age to me. We shared wonderful times as youthful hunters and college fraternity brothers, remaining in close touch over all these intervening years. He is an enormously successful energy entrepreneur and a generous philanthropist for higher education and the church. Tom is a childhood friend from the neighborhood with whom I played baseball from grade school through high school, and talked endlessly about our sports heroes we were anxious to emulate. We haven't corresponded much since, but Tom had a distinguished career in the Air Force and is now retired.

Jon Rex:
I want to address your concern that my writings do not seem to be sufficiently celebrative of capitalism. In reply, here are some points of consideration:

1. If we draw a common theoretical distinction between a *capitalist economy* primarily dependent on entrepreneurial enterprise/private ownership to produce and distribute goods and a *command economy* primarily dependent on governmental ownership and/or control of the means of production *and* the distribution of goods—sometimes called 'communism'—there are few in Western democracies today who would not support entrepreneurial

capitalism as the most effective process for the production of goods and jobs. I include myself in that company. It should also be acknowledged that many are the capitalists that have been grand and generous philanthropists for hundreds of thousands of the private and public institutions of our nation.[1]

2. There are, however, several perils that historically have haunted capitalist economies: (i) that it is of the nature of the competitive impulse of capitalism to destroy other enterprises as much as it is to produce goods—history is littered with such destruction, that often have deleterious effects on social order; (ii) as we can historically observe, capitalism inevitably results in huge concentrations of wealth in the hands of the few; (iii) in so far as capitalism emphasizes free markets, it also in practice, without outside intervention, inevitably seeks to eliminate competitors, thus diminishing the freedom of the market itself; (iv) capitalism inevitably draws a distinction between the owners/shareholders and the workers/laborers, without which the enterprise cannot be pursued, resulting in the owners contending with the workers in order to increase or preserve the owners' self-determined profits; (v) the animus between capital and labor can be seen in capitalism's historic and incessant demonizing of workers and labor unions, with capitalists bringing great political pressure on government to diminish labor union bargaining; (vi) capitalism's capacity in recent times to move capital around the world in search of cheaper labor also produces great social adjustments, dislocations, and unemployment.

3. While it has been repeatedly claimed that capitalism—with its purported dependence on the power of markets to reward and to punish—is

---

1. Some readers have wondered why I did not also call a command economy 'socialist.' While there are some historical questions here, the word 'socialist' has many uses, many of which might apply to states that have a 'mixed' economy: some production of goods are under the control of the government, but not all, and the exact proportion of which is quite variable. Unfortunately, some persons on the 'free enterprise' right seem to argue that government should have no role in the production and distribution of goods, and that any state which has some governmental control over such—e.g., energy industries, transportation, military—is a socialist government. Hence, these folk would conclude that medical care and services should be left up to market forces and that the new health care bill is 'socialist.' But this use of 'socialist' completely obscures the actual fact that all the western democracies are variously mixed economies in which a central role of government is the *regulation* of capitalist enterprises. Of course, 'government' herein means more than simply the 'executive' branch; there are also the courts/judiciary and the legislative functions.

a self-correcting system, such claims, of course, have been continually debated in western democracies. Hence, it has been an inevitable outcome that the democracies have determined that capitalism needs governmental regulations in order to increase fairness in the production and distribution of goods and to limit or hedge in the inherent tendency to destructive consequences for the larger civil order. Surely our present 'deep recession' is rooted in business excesses made possible by recent reduction of federal regulations over the economic conduct of banks and other financial/investment corporations.

4. The continuing controversies over what sort of regulations of capitalism are good for the larger society simply points to the *political context* in terms of which capitalism exists for the sake of a larger and more just social order. Note: it is seldom argued by serious political theorists that capitalism is an end in itself; rather, it is defended as the most effective economic process for the pursuit of a *shared public good*. When Ayn Rand celebrates the capitalist hero, she does so in the name of a freedom from the socio/political needs of the hoi polloi, the herd of humanity. Is it too obvious to say that presumptive democracies can ill afford to ridicule the common folk to whom they are presumably accountable? It is also true that democracies become imperiled when the common people refuse literate and informed discussions of issues of their common and public welfare. And even further, democracies become imperiled when the wealthy control the vast instruments of modern communications and their power to form public impressions and opinions.

Briefly, then without in any way advocating an elimination of capitalistic enterprises, I have the following concerns as a Christian who lives in the midst of this particular world:

1. The politics of democracies, if they are not to dissolve into oligarchies of wealth and power, must continually keep alive the conversation about the *common good* of the people who comprise the economic/political life of the society. It is simply naïve and impossible in actual practice to suppose that the economic production and distribution of goods is a self-contained and self-correcting social system just of itself. There are moral issues of justice, difficult to discuss, that are embedded in our political life in this nation.

Part Two—On Being Mugged by Politics but Lifted by Gospel Hope

2. The concentration of wealth in the largest corporations and enterprises does empower them to use that wealth to influence political elections and institutions to achieve ends primarily consistent with their unregulated productivity and profits. Could any previous generation of political theorists have really anticipated the utterly new bestowal of power on corporations granted by "Citizens United"?

3. Christianity has a non-forfeitable obligation to see to the good of the least of these in the world, to those at the margins of the political/economic order. Hence, for Christian theologizing, capitalism is not an end in itself but a means, always existing amidst critical dialogue and regulation, for the pursuit of a common good. That is, *capitalism in theory and practice is not simply as such the common good of a democracy accountable to all the people.*

4. Any Christian with concerns about the common good must also worry about the inevitable consequence of capitalism's inherent tendency to reduce social value questions to monetary criteria.

And yes, there is more on this about Christians and the church, but that is enough for now.

Tom:
With the above remarks in the background, let us turn to your concerns for healthcare in general and the recent healthcare legislation just passed by Democrats. You have contended that 'Obamacare' will bankrupt the nation and bring havoc in its wake. I admit that it is indeed a complex piece of legislation, difficult to understand in its myriad of details and regulations.

But it seems to me that how one assesses our situation depends on how one answers a basic political question unavoidable in contemporary democracies:

Is the receipt of health care to be regarded as:

i. *a privilege dependent on one's financial capacity to pay for the care?*
or,
ii. *a basic human right in a just, democratic society?*[2]

---

2. Of course, in putting the issue this way I am forcing Tom and the reader to confront the issues of common goods not reducible to monetarization. 'Rights' language does, however, contain real tensions within it that are not easily resolved. But rights language and theory has always been controversial in particulars. We hardly know how to discuss a right to any and every sort of health care options. Yet, putting it in terms of rights also throws into relief the absurdity in a democracy that health care will be

I assume that we both can agree that that question has never been squarely faced in our present socio/economic/political system. In the earliest history of this nation, actual resources for health care were so sparse and scattered, it was a non-issue politically, except that it was assumed that private charities could help in extreme cases. In the twentieth century all of this changed as huge medical enterprises emerged to meet the health needs of a rapidly growing population. Just note the following indisputable historical social developments: 1) wars result in wounded who need health care provided by governments; 2) workers cannot be dependable if their work is continually interrupted by health problems; 3) state governments begin to discern that they need to fund medical schools to produce doctors and nurses to meet growing health care needs in their communities; 4) the federal government begins to invest huge amounts of money in all phases of scientific research into the causes and care of human diseases and physical deformities; 5) governments at all levels became interested in facilitating the production of medical and food products for a healthy citizenry. All of this was happening under the take-for-granted umbrella of the common good, and taxes—local, state, and federal—were used to pay for most of it!

Now suppose that someone were to say in the midst of all these developments that government of whatever level should not be spending money in these ventures; that it should all be left to private enterprises operating under the principal of profitability and to individual financial means to pay for such insurance and/or care. Do you really think that would have been politically possible—wherein we mean what the voting populace did want for themselves, which is not reducible simply to what the rich want?

Our brewing national double-mindedness about these issues reached crunch-time during the Great Depression of the 1930s. Simply put: it was politically decided that in extremis care for the poor might be undertaken by federal and local governments in limited ways, but that the bulk of health care expenses would come under the economic management of the insurance industries and that the costs of such insurance would be paid basically by employers. Consider the consequences of that decision: 1) health care expenses would be met by private enterprise insurance companies who also had the economic need to turn a profit for shareholders; and 2) other private enterprises would be saddled with paying most of the costs for such insurance. In the long run, we all know that those other private enterprises

provided only to those who can pay for the service. And those who can pay more will get more health care?

Part Two—On Being Mugged by Politics but Lifted by Gospel Hope

came to regard the mandate to pay such insurance for their employees as a burden, almost as a tax! And we know that insurance companies instituted systematic practices limiting whom and under what conditions persons might be insurable, always bearing in mind their own need for profitability.

So, what has happened? First, in spite of your warning that health expenses will grow out of hand under 'Obamacare,' the plain fact is that health expenses are already assuming an astonishingly large role in the national economy both as expenses and as productive of income. Second, in spite of all these huge medical care expenditures, more than thirty million citizens deal with life and health without health care insurance. Suppose you say, as I have heard some conservative politicians say, that most of these thirty million are getting their care in indirect ways from charities and hospitals, but who pays for that and what about those who, in their poverty, simply refuse to seek health care and suffer and die miserably?

I am further under the impression that many of my friends and acquaintances that are against 'Obamacare' have never been in a position of not having health care insurance and/or not having the financial means to afford health care expenses. Until our present 'deep recession' that sits so heavily on homeowners and their bankruptcies, it was common knowledge in recent decades that most individual bankruptcies were the result of persons burdened with exorbitant but uninsured or underinsured health care expenses.

Leaving aside for the moment the complexities and sausage-grinder character of 'Obamacare' as legislation—who doesn't cringe at the name of Max Baucus?—and who doesn't know that all Republican legislators just said 'no'—how would you, Tom, answer my first question about whether health care is only for those who can pay or is for all as a human right?

Just theoretically entertain the possibility that health care would become a single-payer system. What would happen? Might the following be the case: 1) private businesses would no longer bear the burden of paying health insurance for employees, though they would surely be taxed in some amount; 2) the single-payer would be relieved of the need to produce a profit for shareholders, the shareholders now being citizens paying for and receiving health care. As regards the distribution, expense, and regulation of such a single-payer system, it seems at least possible that it would be no more expensive than the present system and good reason to believe it would be considerably less.

Capitalism, Democracy, and Health Care

Suppose now, Tom, that you fear government bureaucracy. Consider this: in the complex world we live in now, bureaucracy is everywhere, in private enterprises and public governments. When I have an issue with my private secondary health insurance, I call and enter into the realm of bureaucracy. In fact, modern capitalism is itself dependent on the development of its own bureaucracies to handle the complexities of its business enterprises. Have you called the phone companies recently? From my experience the bureaucracies of Medicare and Social Security are much more efficient and responsive than my private secondary health insurer's bureaucracy. It is just a howler of extraordinary proportions that some politicians continually deride 'bureaucracy' as though it was peculiar to government, always inept, and easily replaced.

Two personal anecdotes: When I was president of Phillips University, the negotiation for health care insurance for employees was a nightmare. If among our 200 or so employees, one or two were to have a prolonged high-cost medical expenses, I could be assured that that our insurer would be raising our insurance costs the next year or sometimes simply refusing to insure us again. I did not expect them to do anymore than protect their own profitability, but that entrepreneurial need continually raised the cost of health insurance. Of course, the dangling issue in the background was how much profitability is enough?

When my middle daughter, a lawyer, had a rare spinal cord stroke in her mid-thirties, she was paralyzed from the chest down and required several months of care in a rehabilitation hospital that came to over $200,000, mostly covered by health insurance through her employer. She did manage to walk haltingly out of that hospital a few months later. But when she returned to work at her small social service company, she was fired on the excuse of cutbacks in their staff, in spite of the fact that she was their top attorney. You and I know that her company had been told by its health care insurer that they would no longer cover them if my daughter remained employed and bearing the need for further medical care. Her struggle since to find affordable health insurance is so disheartening that my family can easily imagine how many millions of persons each year are suddenly stricken with diseases or conditions that finally render them uninsurable and without health care and unavoidably falling into despair and thrust into poverty.

Hence, Tom, 'Obamacare' might be a messy proposition to implement and it might require further legislation to perfect it, but I hope you have the intellectual courage to ask what alternative there might be that does not

Part Two—On Being Mugged by Politics but Lifted by Gospel Hope

render 30 million or more of our citizens without health care and desperate. Suppose the right-wing succeeds in reversing 'Obamacare,' then what? Do you suppose that the train wreck already facing the nation will not happen? Surely you know better.

Well, Jon Rex and Tom, there's something of a response to the tough questions I understood you two to be raising. You did me a great honor in reading my blogs and taking them with intellectual and moral seriousness. I hope it is also apparent to you that my response did not just suddenly spring out of my momentary imagination.

[Posted 11/1/10, slightly edited later]

10

Narratives

Sociopolitical, Personal, Perhaps Theological

Friends:

In the last third of the twentieth century much discussion arose in academic circles concerning the nature and function of narratives in human societies and individual lives. Certainly the concept of narrative seemed immediately relevant for Christian understanding, given its inescapable emphasis on the revelatory character of God's work in the history of Israel, in Jesus Christ, and in the rise of the church.

Of course, the word 'narrative'—often a synonym for 'story' or an account or recital of some happening or recital of some facts about a sequence of events—has enjoyed a long history of usage. It was already common among historians to think their craft involved developing a plausible narrative account of the primary agents and causes in a previous sequence of events.

In addition to this use of narrative by historians, it also proved helpful in other humanistic disciplines to use the concept of narrative as a diagnostic tool for understanding how societies and individuals construct their own sense of identity and destiny. Hence, in this sense of narrative or story, what really matters is *how* such constructions of origins and the sequences of events embodying common actions and purposes, knit together a sense of identity—who are *we* and where did *we* come from and who are the *not-we's*, the *others* with whom *we* have to contend, subdue, defeat, or convert. Obviously, this large sense of narrative has a wide application to how societies create and implement such narratives in their sociopolitical life together.

Part Two—On Being Mugged by Politics but Lifted by Gospel Hope

Hence, we can see that the narratives people tell about themselves are essential to their self-understanding, or to put it another way, the narrative they adopt is *how* they have a world and a sense of origins, common values, and purposes. Identifying and analyzing the narratives societies and individuals tell about themselves can provide an amazing insight into who they think they are and who we—the diagnosticians and analyzers—think they are.

Without supposing that all narratives are neat and precise, I think we can abstractly note some of the ingredients in a compelling narrative that gets a grip on the lives of persons and societies:

1. At the heart of a narrative is a *we* and the *we* usually has a *not-we* or those *others* that comprise an ongoing struggle internal to the narrative. Thus, a narrative answers the question: who are *we* in distinction from some *others*?

2. A narrative conveys some sense of a common origin—where did we come from or where have we been?

3. A narrative conveys as well as sense of destiny or purpose—where are we going?

4. A narrative conveys a sense of 'how do we get there?' and 'what do we have to do to get there?' Hence, a narrative identifies the nature and scope of the struggle that is internal to the *we* for whom it is *their* narrative.

5. The more powerful a narrative is for some social group, the more coherent its own sense of identity and cohesion. And too, when a social group internally struggles with competing narratives, the less cohesion it has.

6. Certainly, then, the narrative itself must be repeated, told, developed in sub-narratives and stories, if it is to maintain a grip on the group for whom it is *their* narrative.

Notice now the following issues that emerge in human history. In order for a narrative to maintain a grip on folk it must be spoken, repeated, narrated, performed, heard. Words and gestures! So too, drawings, paintings, pictures, and then texts, printed books and newspapers, photos, movies, video, and so on. As the available media have historically multiplied, the struggle to maintain coherence and continuity in the narrative intensifies. And a narrative's power depends on the grip it can maintain on the identity of the *we* for whom it is *their* narrative.

Narratives

Born in Oklahoma in 1936, I grew up amidst the huge terrestrial upheaval and conflict known as the Second World War. A compelling narrative was repeated every day in ways small and large: *we* were attacked by *enemies*—Japs and Nazis—who wanted to conquer and enslave us. Our *freedom* was at stake, and we all had to pull together in order to defeat these vicious warriors. We were democrats and they were fascists; we were good and they were evil; we were honest and moral, they were sneaky and immoral; we worshipped God and they worshipped idols.

Yet in addition to this large sociopolitical narrative, there was also a personal narrative emerging of a Joe Jones who was part of a particular family with particular siblings, in a neighborhood with particular neighbors about whom many intriguing stories could be told. This Joe attended a church, had idiosyncratic fears and hopes, talents and attachments, and some exceptional physical abilities. No need to carry this story further, except to remind us of the inevitable but complex phenomena of how persons gather a sense of self on both a large sociopolitical scale and a small, local, familial and neighborhood scale. Yet, with my wooden machine gun I killed many an imagined Jap hiding threateningly in the bushes and creek in the neighborhood.

Today in the 'Western world'—another identity marker—the media by way of which narratives of nations, states, towns, persons get formed are so multiple, complex, and conflictual that the struggle for identity, for origins, for goals, for hopes, for a sense of community is overwhelmingly exhausting.

Perhaps these few remarks about narrative can throw some light on how wrenching the differences might be between persons who imbibe the narrative of Fox News, *The Wall Street Journal*, and *The Washington Times* about 'America' and its enemies and persons who pick around in *The New York Times*, *The New Republic*, *The New York Review of Books*, and PBS/NPR. Or, the narratives between the ardent capitalist pushing for greater profits and less governmental regulation and the union laborer striking for security, greater pay, and assured medical care. And we are all invited to ask 'which powers are in control behind the scenes of all our various narratives?' Whose interests are being served by which narrative?

And how messy have the churches become: their own discourses and practices are in shambles, lacking coherence in narrative. Presumably born of a vivid narrative of what God had graciously done in Israel and in Jesus Christ and was summoning the church to become, the churches' narratives

Part Two—On Being Mugged by Politics but Lifted by Gospel Hope

in our time have become no more than mirror images of these large, contentious political/media principalities and powers. Under the grip of what narrative do folk go to church and read the Bible and vote? Whose servant have the churches inadvertently lapsed into becoming? Has anyone recently heard a compelling sermon about the narratives that have ingressed into the hearts and souls of *we* listeners sitting unexpectfully in the pews?

Narratives do matter! Is it possible that the church's narrative might chasten and critique the political and national narratives that produce wars and conflicts? But, then, it also matters which church narrative is invoked.

In this same line of thought, there is a set of issues that many Christians and non-Christians often misconstrue and confuse. That is, it is assumed that the stronger and more distinctive the Christian narrative is so too the more it marginalizes persons in other religious traditions. I once read a prominent theologian averring that you could not even enter into serious conversation with persons of other religious traditions until you were willing to suspend intellectually your own prime religious convictions. While it was obvious that his remarks were primarily aimed at what he thought of as 'dogmatic' Christians, those remarks also entailed that the 'others' in the conversation—presumably Jews, Muslims, Hindus, Buddhists—were also to enter the conversation having suspended their own firm identity precisely as a Jew, a Muslim, a Hindu, a Buddhist. So, what were they expected to be or become when they went to the table of conversation? Saints who had transcended the niggardliness of their previous convictions? I would prefer that folks in such conversations simply confess their religious identities and get on with learning more about each other's lives, beliefs, and practices—about their respective narratives.

I propose that a strong Christian narrative pivots around the givenness that those in 'other' religious traditions are 'neighbors' created and loved by God and to be loved and engaged and listened to by the Christian. Yes, there may be respectful disagreements and arguments not easily resolved, but surely there will be greater understanding of each other's differences and they can be friends.

But alas, it is painful to reckon with the fact that there are already 'other' Christian narratives that more nearly identify those in other religions as the ones who are virtual enemies of God and needing conversion or prison or death. And the sad part is that too many of the laity and ministers in churches today in America are themselves incapacitated to identify and teach a Christian narrative that is *not* basically also about America as a 'light to the nations.'

Ponder this: when the Nazis hijacked the German/Lutheran/Reformed Christian narrative they literally dismantled and dismembered that narrative, rendering it unrecognizable. Today the church in Germany, in putting itself back together in some faithful form and narrative now some two-thirds of a century later, is forced to re-educate lay and clerical alike in what it means to be a disciple of Jesus Christ quite apart from what it means to be a postmodern German.

Isn't there something close to this that is beckoning the few and faithful in the churches in America to think non-American? To think non-American is not necessarily to loath America or even to judge that the radical right in America is the 'false' America. Rather, it is fundamentally to subordinate, in discourses and practices, all narratives of America to the prime Christian narrative. And how long will that take? Only God knows, but it is likely to take a long, long time. Really good news, Gospel news, is exceedingly demanding but surprisingly joyful to appropriate.

Is there not a profound sadness and darkness that engulfs the church in America when that prime Christian narrative of what God has done in Israel and in Jesus Christ for the world is continually subordinated to a narrative about 'righteous and democratic America' in a war on terror, about the freedom to be capitalists and escape the dependencies of 'self-imposed poverty' and government handouts, about the evils of Islam, about the evils of divorce and homosexuals?

Another apparent narrative today—in supposed distinction from 'righteous America as a light to the world'—is America the 'consumer nation' in which each person must invent his or her own narrative and satisfy his or her own palate of tastes and dispositions. Invent yourself and prescind from all previous commitments and narratives—just be yourself; be authentic. Get out of my face and leave me alone!

It can be excruciating for the churches and its members to ask 'who are we and what is our real narrative?'

[Posted 2/22, 25/11]

11

How Might We Get On with Politics —but Who Are We?

Friends:

While the national political scene, with its government deadlock, might make us gag now and then, I assume all of 'us'—the 'we' who might chance upon reading this blog and exploring this website—will *get on* somehow. That *somehow*, however, might be exceedingly various and perhaps threatening. Some of us might vomit, or we might cuss, or we might watch another movie or play another CD, or have another sip of inebriating spirits, or unpack and brandish our firearms, or some might suffer great deprivations, or, perhaps, a few might pray that something approaching sanity and justice could take the *we* of the nation by storm and render it governable, or almost governable.

I confess that I am seized with regular bouts of sadness, occasioned by a yearning for hopefulness when the justification for hopefulness seems dim and elusive. I am sad too because I fear the political train-wreck has, in a sense, already happened, already become the fate—the *moira*—of the nation. A deeply divided people cannot even share a narrative of what is happening and why. History itself has been hijacked by principalities and powers. Governing has been rendered ridiculously comic but verging on the tragic.

Who cares about governing when the only important political issue is who will be the next President? Yes, everything must be sacrificed for the sake of electing 'our' candidate as the one who will be invested with the imagined power to save the 'democracy,' but then he or she will be impaled on the drawn swords and firearms of our ungovernability.

Our historic Civil War befell the nation some 150 years ago, but with slight variations here and there, *civil war* remains the given statutory destiny of the nation. In our unrelieved xenophobia we might go to war against perceived foreign enemies, but we remain mired in incessant internal wars of xenophobia—some people among us are just not deserving of our 'rights' and 'freedoms.'

Sheldon Wolin, a prominent political philosopher, spoke to this incessant war among us. He traced it back to the *original constitution* that invested white male property owners with the power to determine the fate of the property-less—the impoverished—and the women and the slaves and the natives. "We the people" of the preamble became an abstraction, a non-redeemable linguistic gesture, occasionally invoked to keep the people well-ordered and dependent and even fleetingly hopeful that the vague premise might someday be a promise kept.[1]

While it has been a given that money always impacts and mostly determines national and local elections, the recent Supreme Court ruling—"Citizens United"—guarantees that corporate wealth will increasingly control outcomes, with the only interesting byplay being among the wealthy in the vagaries of their self-interests.

The most disheartening comment by Wolin—which all of 'us' already knew but preferred to ignore and suppress—was the extent to which 'free enterprise' marketing has engulfed us all, and we are left with the shattered and divisive self-images constructed *about* us and *for* us by the advertising and persuasion experts. These experts also aim to identify the presumptive *enemies* and prepare us for *war* against them. The real name for this culture-wide phenomena is *propaganda*.

During a surreal courtroom scene in James Baldwin's *Blues for Mister Charlie*, Meridian, a Black minister whose son has been murdered by a white man, pronounces the epitaph that still painfully reverberates in our time—"the truth cannot be heard in this dreadful place."[2] What sort of people do we have to become in order to learn how to care about the truth and seek it with patience and perseverance, ever mindful of its precious fragility?

---

1. See Sheldon S. Wolin, *Democracy Incorporated: Managed Democracy and the Specter of Inverted Totalitarianism* (Princeton, NJ: Princeton University Press, 2008).

2. New York: Dell Publishing, 1964, 138.

Part Two—On Being Mugged by Politics but Lifted by Gospel Hope

Perhaps in the midst of the politics of destruction and assignation that today reigns among and between us, there is the church of Jesus Christ that might be empowered, by virtue of its narrative of what God has done for us all and how we are called to live in hopeful truth—might be empowered to witness to a cross-bearing, forgiving, and resilient way of life. But is there such a 'church'? Where? What witness does it have? Is it even capacitated to speak the truth amidst lies and counter-lies, amidst indifference and boredom, amidst a despair that truth might be uttered and heard, amidst solemn assemblies that can neither weep in repentance nor rejoice in courage and hope?

Or, does whatever conjures up the name for itself of 'church' have any truth-telling courage in these days?

But note: I am not supposing the church of Jesus Christ is the real soul of this nation and its fumblings toward democracy. No, the church of Jesus Christ should indulge no such pretensions or aspirations. But might the church be sadden and distraught when it too, amidst its own internal multiplicities and contradictions, simply becomes a mirror image of the political conflicts of the nation?

To be sure, Wolin has no concern for the theological reality of the church of Jesus Christ, but he does remind us of how vulnerable to misuse church discourses and practices have become by the politics of the powerful, often invoking 'God' to sanctify and buttress the causes of the nation, or perhaps the cause of the self-appointed elite of the nation.

So, is this Nation-America a democracy or a republic? Is there a difference? What sort of difference, and does it matter, and to whom does it matter? Which 'we' are *we*?

Wolin speaks of a 'fugitive democracy' wherein real folk *practice* being equal and bearing witness to the mutuality of equality. That does dramatically pose the haunting question of who the 'we' are who might be such witnesses. Might a few of the 'we' find their succor in the church of Jesus Christ and practice a new politics of peace-making and hope?

Let us pray that it will be so.

[Posted 7/31/11]

12

A Letter to the Churches After 9/11/2011

Friends:

On September 24, 2001, I wrote "A Letter to the Churches After 9/11" that was widely circulated around the Internet, and later appeared in my book, *On Being the Church of Jesus Christ in Tumultuous Times*.[1] In the last couple of weeks, we—the people of Nation America—have staggered through the various solemn commemorations and ceremonies that testify to the continuing pathos of death, fear, loss, heroism, resolve, and hope that will not let us either forget or quite embrace the shattering effects of the events on September 11, 2001.

I would remind my friends that the letter was written for and to the 'churches' and not to the 'nation.' But there were here and there worrying comments about the nation and especially the likelihood of our going to a war that will reverberate with national and international consequences for decades or centuries long after the war might be declared concluded. Well, sadly the war goes on in Afghanistan and Iraq, though slowing down, we hope. But surely there is nary a person reading this blog who is suffering under the illusion that the nation—its government, its politics, its social fabric—is somehow better off since we decided to go to war. In Oklahoma, where a large number of reservists and guardsmen/women, as well active duty military, have been sent to war and have died, we repeatedly witness the painful funerals groping to affirm that the dead have died 'so that we

1. Eugene, OR: Cascade, 2006, 3–9.

PART TWO—On Being Mugged by Politics but Lifted by Gospel Hope

may be free.' Do not tell these weeping families that these wars might not have been necessary nor that the 'freedom' for which their loved ones were presumed to have died seems so elusive either of definition or realization. The rhetoric of war—any war—must wrap itself in ideals of kinship, justice, and peace, with such wrapping obscuring the naked need to exert power over others deemed enemies and evil.

Did the 'terrorists' succeed in their apparent purpose of inflicting severe and self-perpetuating devastation and disarray on America? In spite of all the amazing heroism of the few, is it not clear to the sober eye that they succeeded beyond even their most hallucinatory aspirations: today, a nation economically and politically confused, scared, angry, divided, looking for scapegoats? But did the terrorists truly grasp what they might achieve or did they in their own hatred unwittingly exacerbate a divided people already wandering in the wilderness of greed and class and racial insularity? No, I am not suggesting we 'deserved' what happened—the sufferings of the many are simply too vast. But the effects of the planes' destruction on the national psyche found resonance in pre-existing fears and animosities. The narrative construction of the myth of the Muslim as universally a hateful terrorist intent on destroying the 'Christian' west was already festering before 9/11. But after 9/11 the myth burgeoned everywhere in digital media and print and ingressed deeply into the imaginations of the many.

Alas, my words to the churches was the reminder that they are neither first nor last simply Americans waving flags of solidarity against enemies near and far. Rather, I was hoping and urging the churches, clearheaded in their own Christian identity, to be empowered to ask difficult questions. In particular I wanted the churches to be that sort of communities empowered to ask: 1) what is it about American conduct and character that had the power to so incite the terrorists acts of destruction? It seemed obvious to me that Osama bin Laden was himself clear about the rationales for the attacks. Is Christian America simply innocent of aggression abroad in Muslim countries? Yes, answering such a question is complex and disturbing.

And the other question: 2) how can we—Christians—become better acquainted with the history of Islam and the differences within it? I assumed that gross ignorance of Islam was virtually definitive of ordinary congregational life. By the same token, it seems obvious that many Christians simply thought all Muslims are exact replicas of the terrorists, just as many Muslims suppose Christians are undiversified replicas of America's capitalistic and imperial aggressions abroad.

A Letter to the Churches After 9/11/2011

It has been pleasing to see some church traditions and some congregations engaging in deliberate and systematic study of the history of Islam and its various contemporary expressions and differences. It is also good that some churches have developed confessional documents exploring ways in which inter-religious dialogue might take place. It was at least conceivable that such studies might reveal an obdurate kinship between Christianity and Islam: both have historical trajectories within them advocating a divine behest to 'convert' or 'conquer' the 'infidel,' wherein the infidel is all those who are other than themselves. However much each religious tradition has had earnest advocates of peace among them, the more militant have terrifyingly resorted to much violence in the name their god. But this use of militant violence in the name of a god is just as often the pursuit of some political cause or quest by the powerful to control land, people, and economic goods.

I do not mean to suggest hereby that there is a theological equivalency between Christianity and Islam. I am simply pointing out what is obvious to thoughtful people: not all persons who call themselves 'Christian' nor all who call themselves 'Muslim' bear identical traits of belief and ethics. Any thoughtful church person in America must wince daily at the ways in which the media use 'church' and 'Christian' as though they are naming a group of folk with obvious and clear identity markers. Yet, the words 'Christian' and 'Muslim' are in linguistic fact contested concepts hidden from view by common words. This in no way implies that it is invalid for individuals and groups to call themselves by these names, but it does mean that they should expect to be asked by others to explain just where they stand relative to other concepts, beliefs, and activities.

In daring to write to the 'churches,' albeit American churches, I had discerned that, as the leaders of Nation America were proceeding to wage war under the banner of a "War on Terrorism," with few exceptions, churches as congregations would fall in behind the leaders and their wars. Many church-folk would work in the factories and industries essential for warfare and many church-folk would actually fight and die in the fighting. The radical right in the churches, never the clear majority, remained stout in their support of the Bush regime. It was they that further identified the war as a theological battle—perhaps Armageddon—between Christian American and infidel, terrorist Islam. As the horrors of the wars unfolded in video, photo, and print and it became our young men and women who were dying, some of the churches I was hoping to reach did lift voices of protest.

Part Two—On Being Mugged by Politics but Lifted by Gospel Hope

Perhaps some among my friends will feel as though I have 'blamed' America for the destruction of the Towers and the Pentagon—as though we 'deserved' it. Yet for anyone to say we deserved it, they would have to mount a moral argument in support of the terrorists and their self-proclaimed cause and its justification. There is no such moral argument available to me; the acts were, without reservations, cruel and vicious and immoral. But then what moral arguments can be advanced by faithful church-folk, invoking theological concepts, about our American destruction of people and habitats in Afghanistan and Iraq? I do not think there any such sound arguments, but then I am not writing as a 'political realist' calculating outcomes in a world bereft of moral structures and commands. Of course, I think otherwise; this world is the Triune God's world, replete with moral structures, commands, and consequences.

So, to the churches, I pray we will neither annually nor decadally participate in the virtual pagan idolatry of converting the death, suffering, and destruction of 9/11 into a holy time and space resonant with our national imperative to defend ourselves against an evil enemy. Remember, Nation America is not the church of Jesus Christ, and that church has a non-forfeitable calling to witness to a Gospel in which the way of God's peace is not the way of the gun or the bomb, but sometimes the way of the cross. We are not summoned to be rulers over others, but servants who empty the trash that clutters the life of the world, to utter 'peace' when the crowd utters 'war—let us wage war on the enemy and then we will have peace.' I do not expect any nation to be the church, and I pray that no church will succumb to being no more than a chaplain to a nation.

And yet, it is inescapable that Christians should weep when they recall the sheer sudden brutality of planes crashing into buildings, skyscrapers and fortresses collapsing, creating horror for people helpless and trapped and unprepared for death and for folk unprepared for their loved ones' deaths. But in our Christian weeping might it be an act of faithful solidarity to invite our Muslim friends to weep with us? Or should we make sure they dare not come near the sacred ground of the towers of death? But then, who are 'we' anyhow?

Yes, methinks Reinhold Niebuhr—under whose inspiration I thought I would be a good soldier in the war against evil, willing to do what is realistically necessary to delay or postpone or limit evil as it inevitably raises its ugly head—might that Niebuhr be in despair over what I have written here, or, as we might put it in Oklahoma, 'turning over in his grave'?

[Posted 9/25/11]

13

Troublings

Campaign Rhetoric, Voting, Democracy, and Truth

Friends:

I assume that anyone who might read this website's various writings is in a state of profound 'troublings' about what is happening before our eyes and seems destined to produce even more troublings in the future, regardless of who 'wins.' I cannot imagine anyone, either on the right or the left, thinking the election will produce some startling new policies and styles of political exchange and debate. We are in a headlock-deadlock! I assume that most of us agree that whoever might win the presidency will not face a compliant congress, and without a will to govern democratically for the common good, congress will remain in ideological chains.

But even as we troubled souls feel the deathlock of disagreements profound and if we can avoid sheer cynicism, it seems almost impossible to retain clarity about fundamental principles and diagnostic politics. Even if we can get beyond Romney's continual charade of self-indulgent and duplicitous mind-changes and Obama's deeply hesitant appetite for intellectual and practical political leadership, the socio-political-economic cards are stacked against whoever becomes president.

It is in this connection that it is astonishing that neither Romney nor Obama has urged voters in the various congressional elections to support him by supporting the party's candidates. It is as if both know that the various congressional candidates are themselves reluctant to come out swinging for either presidential candidate, except in districts considered really 'safe.'

PART TWO—On Being Mugged by Politics but Lifted by Gospel Hope

And how might we escape the gnawing conviction that the great American public is having difficulty putting three consecutive thoughts together about their own self-diagnosis of what ails them?

In previous writings, I have attempted to say something insightful about our political past and prospects as a nation and somewhere in that to talk theologically about limits, pitfalls, illusions, and lies that stalk both nation and church. And it is impossible to forget the frightful consequences unleashed in this election by the Supreme Court ruling in "Citizens United" in 2010, confirming we are in the midst of the specter of inverted totalitarianism of oligarchies of wealth.

Yes, I will vote for Obama for a plethora of relative obvious reasons, not the least of which is to prevent Romney and the Tea Party Republicans from attempting to impose their ideology on the whole nation. I am not distressed with Obama for 'not doing more to make the economy hum.' I think his hands were tied by the immediate and long-term economic collapse under Bush's policies and perpetuated by a House imprisoned by the Tea Party and a Senate filibustered to triviality! But I do believe that Obama reneged on the fundamental responsibility of a president to be an educational leader continually speaking to the nation and listening to the complaints and addressing them.

If Obama is re-elected, I recommend that he hold press conferences at least bi-weekly and let the press ask all their tough and often asinine questions and reply directly and forcefully and clearly to them. Public discourse has become captive to special interests and a president cannot afford the luxury simply observing from afar the harsh criticisms that are aimed at presidential leadership. In short, Obama, in a way that has not really emerged in this campaign and was mostly absent during his presidency, must regain rhetorical and intellectual influence over the continual criticism that emerges in a democratic polity. Let Fox News and whoever have a go at the president and let him have a go at them in the fragile hope that a nation might hear some truth-telling and sustained arguments beyond sound bites.

But two questions remain: 1) does Obama have an appetite for such engagement? and 2) would such straightforward speaking itself become vulnerable to the press's inclination to forget context and take words completely out of context? But if press conferences were done regularly, might that at least limit the press's penchant for distortion? And one reminder is scorching: we do not have and do not want a sovereign presidency but neither do we want a sovereign press.

Troubled, yes, but I will forgo my newly conferred right in Oklahoma to buckle my pistol on my belt and carry it with me wherever. Not every 'right' granted is morally right!

[Posted 10/22/12]

May 2013 addendum: Obama has certainly had more press conferences since the election. But they seem more wistful and lamely winsome than vigorous, forthright, and engaging the issues. The severity of the continuing legislative gridlock has its own paralyzing effect on the fulfillment of hopes for our governability; ungovernability sits astride the nation and therewith suffocates hope.

14

Our American Agony

Friends:

Fifty years ago Kennedy was assassinated in Dallas and it seemed immediately credible to almost everyone, including Dallasites, that it was done by 'one of our own.' But there was a cosmic sigh of relief when it seemed that an interloper, an outsider, a Communist was the assassin: not *us* but one of *them*! But, then, who are 'we'?

We *Americans*—a.k.a. folks living in the boundaries of the United States of America and sometimes called *citizens*—have been stalked from the colonial days by the quest for a just and peaceful *we* that remains contested to this very day. At times the *we* seems powerful and obvious, especially when *we* go to war against an *other* who is not *us*: wars with armies and weapons seem to galvanize the natives and lure them into laying aside their own agonisms. Hence, within the boundaries of an assertive *we*, it can seem opaque that this *we* is riven with internal rivalries and warfare. This *we* turns out to be a *multitude* bound together by an *agonistic* sociopolitics that incessantly divides us, in which there must be *winners* and *losers*. And the question remains: is there anything else that binds *Americans* together that is other than the rivalries themselves and the quest for power and domination and victory?

It might sometimes appear that America is itself the crown jewel of *free enterprise capitalism*: competition is that primitive instinct in which life is simply a matter of sorting out *winners* and *losers*, by whatever means available and defensible by law, but now the *law* itself as something decided by the winners. And the winners, in order to be winners, must have deep

Our American Agony

pockets, and deep pockets elect legislators and executives and actually the judiciary as well.

So it turns out there is no commanding ideal—either *republicanism* or *democracy*—understood historically or practically. Is it then really true that America has always been a *civil war* among presumed *citizens* as to who are the winners and losers? For more than a century if you were black or red, female, and poor, you were a *loser*. If you were male, white, and rich, you were, in one way or another, a *winner* demanding respect and power.

Of course, from time to time, amidst multi-dimensional *agonistic and civil warfare*, there were occasional voices proclaiming an *equality* among persons rooted in something variously called *theological* or *metaphysical*. There are still rumors flitting around about these odd and apparently impractical notions of equality. Lip-service is everywhere, however, but nobody pays any real attention to it. It doesn't seem to have any real cash value, and of course, the market is the great judge of winners in the warfare called competition.

I write these thoughts not because I was a devotee of Kennedy and want to enshrine his name in metaphysical glory. Actually, there are only two results that Kennedy brought about that put him dramatically on the plus-side of American politics. First, there was his soaring political rhetoric that in fact seemed to inspire a whole generation of folk roughly my age to either undertake a career in elective politics or simply become a local person-of-interest aiming at something called *justice*. Second, there were those electrifying press conferences in which he met his adversaries with that forthright sound and fury of superior intelligence and intimidating presence that could smile through it all. No president since has even come close to matching the brilliance of his performance in those televised press conferences and other occasions as well.

Yes, there are some dreadful life-style moral lapses that emerged post-mortem that at least ought to make Kennedy's admirers shudder in dismay and regret. And it cannot be overlooked that Kennedy was himself a product of free-enterprise-upper-class-America. No struggling Massachusetts working class here, rising in politics by virtue of sheer intelligence, hard work, and moral resolve.

And yes, I do think of myself as a Democrat, but I weep a lot. Clinton's utter idiosyncratic betrayals are simply indigestible morally and they opened the way for Bush to sneak into the presidency under the cover of a Supreme Court gone-rogue. And then Bush repealed taxes on the rich, undermined the presumably balanced budget Clinton seemed to have left behind, and then took us into a terribly stupid war bringing chaos to us and to the Middle East.

And now I weep a lot about and for Obama, caught up in the promise of a post-racial nation but subverted from his first day by a latent but festering American racism that seems to have captured the Republican Party. The presumably party-of-Lincoln begins inflaming racial hatred and flagrantly appealing to class warfare of that free-enterprise sense of justice. And Obama seems himself to be stumbling in disarray. I do not blame him; what can a divided nation expect when an African-American rises to the presidency of a people long nurtured by *racial hatreds that cut both ways* and that justify a suspicion of those who are *other*, even when the criteria for who the *other* are remain cloaked in the rhetoric of *justice* and *rights*. Yes, it seems as though America is almost ungovernable, lacking any consensus about justice and rights.

This agonistic disposition has for centuries bred the suspicion and the practice that *freedom, justice, rights* are deservedly *ours* but not quite appropriate for *them*.

Sometimes the spectre of Eisenhower lurks at the edges of my mind, warning us once again of the military-industrial complex and its incessant urgency to identify enemies—near and far—and the need to prepare for war and to go to war. An agonistic people? Without enemies to defeat and profits to make, without winners and losers, life would surely seem boringly peaceful. But who really wants peace when there are competitive contests to be won or lost?

Peace, Joe

[Posted 11/22/13]

Part Three

Fragments from Times Past
and Emerging Hopes

15

Spiritual Notes on Growing Up in Oklahoma

These notes were started in 1998 in preparation for a faculty retreat at Christian Theological Seminary. It was my turn to provide reflections on my own spiritual development. It turned out that I had time only for early years in Oklahoma. In the late winter of 2013 I began adding more material to the notes, but haven't been able to get beyond my arrival at Yale Divinity School in 1958. Yet, having ventured these reflections, I am clearer about the vagueness of the distinction between something called 'spiritual reflections' and simple, straightforward autobiography. When I read back over what I have written, I am acutely aware of the tension between a simple autobiographical record of events and experiences, especially in details of friendships and sports events, and a reflective probing of what seems important to me now in this present moment of memory and spiritual narration. I remain somewhat uneasy as to how well I have recorded and remembered profound indebtedness to formative family and friends in my youth.

I realize that I have lived a rich and variegated life that exceeds my capacity to convey in precise and insightful representations. Knowing oneself well and profoundly is itself a spiritual achievement of rare occurrence, and I have no reason for supposing my self-knowledge is exceptional. But I have been asked by the Faculty Committee to share something of my life spiritually understood. And I assume this request has not been made because I am spiritually translucent or transparent or because I am a model of sanctified development. So, with some considerable misgivings and no small bewilderment, I offer a few remembrances of my life in the hope that they will

PART THREE—Fragments from Times Past and Emerging Hopes

be neither boring nor self-indulgent and might be interesting and perhaps upbuilding for some others.

What should be included under the concept of spirituality and where do we draw some lines? When I am doing systematic theology I understand spirituality to include the whole of one's life in relation to God and to the many neighbors that comprise one's social worlds. Using a concept of Kierkegaard's, a person's spirituality is the *how* of his or her life: *how a person puts together in characteristic decisions and passions the many relations of his or her life, including the relation to God*. For some of us this *how* has really been many *hows* over various periods of our lives. For a few, the *how* has been relatively constant and discernible. I assume that Christian faith aims at persons coming to have a distinctively *Christian how* that includes faithfulness and gratitude to God, love of God, and love of the neighbors as central virtues of living a sanctified life. No part of one's life can be considered as falling outside the scope of these dimensions of how one lives.

I am not confident I can give an account of the many *hows* of my life's journey over my twenty-one years of growing up in Oklahoma. I will try to highlight and explain some of the events, influences, persons, and attitudes that have given shape to my life. It is inevitable that these notes will pivot around family, sports, school, church, friends and important events.

I am the youngest of four children born of the marriage of Idabel Augusta Seitz to Dick Sterling Jones on June 6, 1927. I was born on September 18, 1936 in Oklahoma City at St. Anthony's Hospital. My family was living in Okemah at the time, but because of the severe heat wave setting records across the state, in August my mother was brought to St. Anthony's as a safer and cooler place in which to give birth to her fourth child!

What is now called the State of Oklahoma was a virtual no-man's land in much of the nineteenth century. In the 1830s, under the Indian Removal Act of 1830 during the presidency of Andrew Jackson, the Native American tribes of Cherokee, Choctaw, Creek, Seminole, and Chickasaw located in the mid-Southern and Southeastern states, were to be forcibly removed under military control to land in the eastern half of what later became the State of Oklahoma. The obvious horrors of the round-up and removal of the tribes became known as "The Trail of Tears." The lands occupied by the tribes, under military supervision, became known as Indian Territory, while the lands to the west eventually became known as Oklahoma Territory. It was only on November 16, 1907 that these two territories were joined together to form the State of Oklahoma.

Spiritual Notes on Growing Up in Oklahoma

The pre-history of this state and its rivalrous, even riotous, first half-century of statehood are deep and dynamic factors presupposed in this narrative of my reflections on life and spirit in growing up in Oklahoma.

My mother, born January 13, 1904, was raised on the farm in Noble County near Billings that my grandfather homesteaded during the Cherokee Strip Land Run of 1893 in Oklahoma Territory. I never knew this grandfather, Charles Seitz; he died from pneumonia in 1927, just after my father and mother married. But consider this: from the border of Kansas, he made the run on a horse—reputed to be a white horse—to stake his claim; rode into Enid to file his claim on the 160 acres—a quarter section; returned to Missouri to get his young bride; came back to the claim, built a sod house and began farming. He and my grandma proceeded to have five children, all of whom were to receive college degrees.

My father was born in Pealed Chestnut, Tennessee in 1905, and in that same year his family—included Joneses and McMahans—moved to a new town in Indian Territory named "Okemah"—Creek for "Town on a Hill." His father was Redman Brown Jones, known as "R. B." but of obvious Cherokee descent, though never entering the rolls of the Cherokee Nation. Okemah would become somewhat famous later as the birthplace of Woody Guthrie, a matter about which my father was reticent. Except for his years at the University of Oklahoma—where he earned his law degree, received the Letzeiser Medal as the Outstanding Senior Man, and met, courted, and married my mother, Idabel Seitz, in 1927—Okemah was home until we moved to Oklahoma City in 1939.

In returning to live and work in Okemah, my father became an important figure in the town and county. In retrospect we must remember that the Great Depression started in 1929 and had a continuing impact on my father and mother and their families well into 1950s. In 1928 my father was elected Okfuskee County Attorney as a Republican and served as such for four years. Bank robberies were common during the 1930s and the banks of Okfuskee County were hit hard and often, and my father was on many occasions involved in actual pursuits and arrests of such robbers. It is also amazing that he coached the Okemah American Legion Junior baseball team into national playoffs in 1937 and 1938! Small town life could be full of excitement, as father often regaled us with these stories of life in Okemah.

In Oklahoma City we moved into a red-brick house on NW 24th Street, just north across the street from Cleveland Elementary School and two blocks east of Taft Junior High School. The house seemed commodious to me, but was probably about 1300 square feet: a compact three bedrooms,

PART THREE—Fragments from Times Past and Emerging Hopes

1 and ½ bathrooms, a small living room, dining room and breakfast room adjoining a kitchen, and a basement converted into a bedroom and laundry room. The distance between houses on our block was never more than thirteen feet. In the twelve-square block area in which we lived, our house was about average: some a bit larger and some a bit smaller. It accommodated six of us handily, we thought: four children and two adults. Yet, in those occasional drive-bys over the years since, it looks really small! Completely unavailable to me or our family conversation at the time, was the fact that we lived amidst a middle-class stronghold, devoid of dramatic socioeconomic differences.

Soon after our move to Oklahoma City, my father was appointed to the State Criminal Court of Appeals to fill a vacated position as one of three judges. Oklahoma is one of a handful of states that has a dual appellate court system: a Supreme Court for civil and constitutional cases and a Criminal Court of Appeals as the supreme court for criminal cases. My father was the youngest person to sit on the court up to that time and served for seventeen years. With a quickness and brilliance that was widely acknowledged, my father proceeded in a few years to remove almost single-handedly the court's substantial backlog of cases. While I knew he was a legal genius, it was only later in life that I discovered how diligently his opinions were respected and studied at the University of Oklahoma Law School as a model of analytic clarity, directness, and succinctness. I remember well my father's silent brooding at the dinner table when a particularly vexatious case was before the court for review. But I can never recall having a conversation with him on the meaning of justice, a lack that has been acutely felt over the years. My father was a strong advocate of the death penalty and many times upheld such death sentences as the lower courts had directed. While I felt no deep misgivings about this matter in my early years, it was to become a troubling issue in later years.

Father was an avid sportsman and it was around sports that much of his life pivoted. A star baseball player at the University of Oklahoma, he raised his sons, of which there were three, to be enthusiasts for sports as well. He also loved hunting and fishing, spending at least two or three days a week pursuing these sports seasonally throughout the year. So too I was early exposed to the rigors of paddling a boat while dad and others fished, of participating in organized baseball and basketball by age seven, and of hunting with my own automatic Remington twenty-gauge shotgun by age nine. There is much to be explored in the sporting activities and

Spiritual Notes on Growing Up in Oklahoma

dynamics of my family, but let it suffice for summary here to note that my father played and coached sports to win and fished and hunted to be the most skilled and productive. We never went fishing or hunting that he did not keep score on how many each of us caught or shot. My father meant to win, and he never spoke of fairness or the sheer joy of play as such. It was only in later years did it become utterly clear to me just how extraordinary these traits, attitudes, and practices were. Yet, we never thought of our guns as necessary for our self-defense or protection from the intruder or from the government!

In his late seventies my father decided to write his autobiography, which was published in 1983 by the Oklahoma Historical Society under the title *The Life of Judge Dick Jones: From Okemah to the State Court of Criminal Appeals*. It is a fascinating read, full of many details that could only be available through memory—and my father's memory was astounding right up to his death in 1996.

A graduate of the University of Oklahoma also, my mother was a woman of extraordinary strength of character and will. She was herself a star on the OU women's basketball team. I never doubted her loving affection for me, even though her straightforward words sometimes sobered my dilatory soul. She was decisively the anchor of the family, and fully dedicated her whole life to the care and service of her family; loyalty to her family was the first commandment, and not without a twinge of idolatry. As one of the hardest working persons I have known, my mother never held a paying job. Immorality and laziness were never accommodated, though she would tear out her own heart before she would ever cut off one of her children from her evident and unceasing love. Her judgments of folk could sear to the bone, but Mother could always be counted on to be fair and staunchly herself; fickleness was an impossible possibility for her. She expected much from her children, but I can never recall her rubbing salt in the wound when one of us had obviously committed serious misbehavior. She did not hide from the flux and flow of life around her or evade a counsel sought. Mother read her Bible diligently, but seldom talked piously or quoted biblical passages, yet it was taken for granted by all of us that her faith in God ran deep and shaped the foundations of her life.

It was not uncommon that my siblings would say or imply that I, as the youngest in the family, was surely spoiled and allowed privileges denied them. There might have been some truth in that. It remains an odd but perhaps easily analyzed fact that I would not allow my mother to come to any of my athletic events until my high school days. And it is true that I unselfconsciously enjoyed those four years as the only child in the home before I went away to college!

Let this image of my mother suffice for now. From about age seven, even with two older brothers, it fell my lot to mow the grass and keep the lawn. This I did until I went away to college in 1954. At that point my mother began taking up the yard work. In 1959 my folks moved to a larger home with about an acre of lawn and many shrubs, trees, and gardens. She was in her element, and some of our fondest memories are of mother behind the power lawn mower (not a riding lawn mower!) in the heat of the day, marching determinedly back and forth across her lawn, often with a grandchild tagging along behind. This she did in a dress and stiff girdle and did so until a broken back in her early-eighties slowed and sapped her energy. The harsh early life on the frontier farm indelibly marked my dear mother. My father never gave a second thought to the care of the lawn.

June sixth was a milestone date in our family's life: my folks were married on June 6, 1927; middle brother Sterling was born on June 6, 1932, and my mother died on June 6, 1994 at the age of 91, having spent the last few years of her life on a hospital bed in her living room, under constant medical care and suffering from diabetes, two broken backs, and Parkinson's disease.

A few words of orientation are now in order about my siblings—two brothers and a sister. My oldest brother was eight years older than I, my sister seven years older, and my middle brother four years older. Charles, the oldest brother, was the least athletic of us brothers, but walked away with academic honors in high school, college, and law school. He was the 'brains' in the family. Much later in life he and I were to have the closest of relationship among the siblings, but until I was well into graduate school, he hardly noticed that I existed. After a distinguished career as a lawyer, he was appointed Federal Magistrate and was the designer of the school-desegregation scheme for Oklahoma City. He loved to read and talk theology with me, and there was more *simpatico* between us on religious and political issues than with anyone else in my family. He was such a formative influence in his local Disciples congregation that the pastor began taping his Elder's prayers and talks in the church; these tapes were passed on to me by the pastor after Charles' untimely death from pancreatic cancer at age fifty-one. His last two years of life were intensely permeated and gnarled by the suicide of his only son, a tragic victim of the rampant drug culture that was devastating college youth in the 1970s. In the face of overwhelming grief, he never lost faith, and it was in faith that he faced his own excruciating death. In these many years since his death, I have had innumerable occasions to weep bitterly my loss of his presence and wise counsel and encouragement.

Sister Carolyn suffered the inevitable slights that come from being the only girl in a family of three brothers dominated by competitive sports and hunting and fishing. She abstained from it all. Her angle was mathematics, and she pursued briefly a career in math until her marriage. Since the marriage she has been, like her mother, the central caregiver in her family of four children and a husband. Her closest relationship among us siblings was with Charles, their being only one year apart. With political and social views antipathetic to my own, my relations with her husband and her over the years have been sometimes strained and a bit antagonistic. There was a long period of time in which to her and my middle brother, Sterling, I have been the 'brat who got spoiled by Yale.'

Sterling was my father's favorite, his constant hunting and fishing companion, and a stellar athlete. A near All-Stater in basketball and baseball in high school, he went on to be a starter at the University of Oklahoma in both these sports. He became a skilled 'fly-tier'—a person who ties those artificial flies we use in casting for trout, and sometimes bass. His skills enhanced our family enjoyments of traveling to western Colorado in August for a few weeks to fish for trout at Mesa Lakes Resort on top of Grand Mesa.

Being nearest me in age, we shared a bedroom in the basement, and in all candor he was an intimidating brother who demanded compliant behavior from me. To smart off to him was to guarantee instant retaliation. I was pummeled often but just as often he had my back as I could threaten older bullies that 'Sterling will get you.' On the diamond and the court he was a fierce competitor, playing rough and tumble in any way that might assure victory. More than once I was embarrassed by his sports behavior, but I ached bodily when he was occasionally criticized by the fans for his rough play. As an Air Force ROTC graduate, he enjoyed several years in the Air Force, much of it being spent playing competitive basketball, about which he developed a strong reputation. Since then he has had a variegated career as a geologist/deal-maker in the oil and gas industry.

The religious and political differences were most pronounced between Sterling and me, as indicated by his early membership in the John Birch Society. I know he has often regarded me as an 'arrogant pseudo-intellectual'

PART THREE—Fragments from Times Past and Emerging Hopes

who doesn't know anything about anything important. At the time of my mother's death in 1994, as we three children sat around with our father and the pastor trying to plan her funeral, his fury at the definiteness of my convictions about the place of a sermon in a Christian funeral exploded in his shoving me half way across the room! I share the blame for that disheartening event—perhaps little-brother-the-theologian is not yet entitled to such definite opinions—and for the unhappy state of our relationship over many years. To this day I am wary of his clenched fist ready to strike.

Of course, I am writing these notes many years later and with a wiser demeanor and patience. Hence, having identified those strains of conflict within the family, from time to time we are all three aware of a tender pathos and grace that remain inviolable in our relationships. We are, after all, family: she's *my* sister, and he's *my* brother! And it is in that spirit that in 2005 I dedicated my second book to this extraordinary *family of origin*.

As should be obvious by now, I was born and raised in a self-identified Christian home. Having moved from Okemah to Oklahoma City in 1939, my family attended Pennsylvania Avenue Christian Church throughout my youth, and my mother and father were to be members until their deaths. The church was located at twelfth Street and Pennsylvania Avenue, about a mile south and a mile east of where we lived. It was a congregation primarily of working middle class folk, in which my father and mother stood out with respect to education, social position, and personal bearing.

Brother Roy Harp was our first pastor, an imposing man with a volcanic voice and a fondness for smoking cigars and fishing. Though I don't remember any of the theological content of his sermons or conversations, I do recall the enormous respect and affection my folks had for him. In fact my father revered few people in his life, and none compares to the awe in which he held Brother Harp. Even so, Brother Harp did not arouse in me any inclinations to imitate him or his vocation.

I enjoyed attending Sunday school and church, but was lax about Sunday evening Christian Endeavor, and I never attended summer church camps. While loving to talk about God and Jesus in the church, I never experienced the congregation as a warm and safe cocoon. My baptism by immersion occurred around my eleventh year, and while exciting at the time with its ticket to participate in Lord's Supper or Holy Communion, I don't recall much impact. Having been long fascinated by observing Mrs. Hempstead weeping quietly during every communion service, I did wonder whether I would ever find that event so emotionally compelling and profound. And for the benefit of those contemporaries who are worried that children will feel excluded from church if they are not allowed to participate in communion until after baptism, I can only laconically report that I never had any sense of being so excluded or that I wasn't truly a part of the congregation. I seemed to know that I was not prepared to participate in such a profound event, and that was all right.

In the late 1940s into the 1950s, our church called Donald W. McEvoy, a young recent graduate of Phillips University, to be our minister. Handsome, with an Irish sort of swarthiness and audacity, Reverend McEvoy—I could never then call him "Don"—brought liveliness and sex education to the delight of the youth and the dismay of our parents! Later in life, Don was to serve with distinction for several decades as an executive of the National Conference of Christians and Jews.

In retrospect I guess at least fifteen youths went on to college at Phillips University to pursue church-related vocations during the period in which I was growing up. Little did I see any handwriting on the wall that would suggest I might later spend almost thirteen years giving leadership to Phillips, first as Dean of the Graduate Seminary and then as President of the university.

My father would end up teaching the Men's Bible Class for forty-plus years, while mother was loyal to the Golden Deeds Class. My father taught the men's class like a true frontier Lockean rationalist: the Bible and Jesus made good sense if you just understood and followed the teachings. Not much cross and grace in this milieu, though great faithfulness in teaching this class of men for so many years. My father was the only member of the class to have an advance degree and his social status as judge evoked much respect. The singing in the class was robust in Gospel hymns, but I can never recall seeing or hearing my father sing any sort of hymn anytime. On this front he simply abstained without explanation. Until the time of his death in 1996, my father still attended this class, which had dwindled from its glory years of more than seventy-five men to a mere five.

As a sad commentary on church life in this new twenty-first century, Pennsylvania Avenue Christian Church closed its doors in 2011 and sold its property to a congregation in another tradition.

There were some memorable experiences, surely spiritual in character, during my fourth and sixth years. At age four I was left home as one too young to manage going to the State Fair. For hours I sat in the bedroom of my folks in the front of the house, looking out the window hoping to see my mother and siblings returning from the fair. It was a devastating sense of 'being left behind.' A couple of years later, during a time of acute awareness of the spreading polio epidemic, I had walked the three blocks to the Saturday Kiddy Hour Cartoons at the Villa Theater. I had been there often, so it was not a new experience. But this time—described now in retrospect—as I sat down in my seat I felt a startling numbness surge through my right arm. I must have the polio! So up I jump and run back to the lobby, shouting/crying, "I have got the polio!" Some older girls, about junior high, comforted me and called my mother to come and pick me up. Of course, I did not have polio, but my good friend Lionel did have it, and I was fearfully anxious about that debilitating disease. It never dawned on me until later that I had just hit my elbow 'funny bone.' Along this same line of childhood fears, I remember riding in the back seat as my mother was driving up a state highway on our Memorial Day trip to the Billings cemetery. The wind was blowing strong from the southwest, thick dust was hurtling across the highway, and suddenly we could not see ten feet in front of the car! Stark and surreal images of twisted car fenders, broken glass, and suffocating dirt loomed in the imagination and scared my little soul severely and for a long time. Common childhood fears full of darkness and death!

My youth from grade school through high school was dominated by competitive athletics, mainly baseball and basketball. In Oklahoma City at this time, there was no organized football of any sort from grade school through junior high. Hence, for athletic experience, except for unsupervised football scrimmages at the parks, baseball and basketball teams were available with supervision from grade school and through junior high.

I was well coordinated, strong, game-smart, and typically one of the best athletes on my teams. A perfectionist who couldn't practice enough, I did not like losing, and I was wickedly self-condemning when I committed errors of performance. This self-condemnation and frustration were to stalk me throughout my athletic career and into my academic life. I could not be bullied or intimidated or unnerved by any sports opponent, except by myself and my bad temper. Yes, I was competitive and hated losing, but it was the galling disappointment in my errors and missed hits and shots that troubled me most.

But sports at this level meant neighborhood friends playing and growing up together. By age seven, I was playing summer baseball for the Cleveland Bulldogs, and would do so throughout grade school. Jim Belcher, Tom

Spiritual Notes on Growing Up in Oklahoma

Spear, Bob Murray, Billy Staples, Sherrill Hudman, Bob Tracy, Jim Barnett, and Don Wilson spent many a hot afternoon listening to what we thought were live broadcasts of major league baseball games. In junior high we became the Taft Exporters, and we were joined by Jimmy Cox, Bill Pinkerton, Jackie Byrum, and Paul McDaniel to comprise a formidable team empowered to win most games. Shortstop was my position, most of the time. Of course, we were together for three more years through high school and summer American Legion baseball.

At Classen High School, basketball was my stronger sport. I had a wonderful coach my sophomore year, and even played more than I thought I should. But he retired after the season and another competent new coach arrived. In my senior year we were the pre-season favorite in Class A—the highest class—to win the state championship. The starting lineup included Bill Pinkerton, George Susens, Bill Blackwell, Phil Lee, and me. It is some indication of our team talent that Pinkerton and I would both go to the University of Oklahoma on basketball scholarships. But, the season was a bit up and down and in the first game of the state playoffs we lost to a modest team; hopes crushed! It was one of those games not too uncommon in sports in which a clearly superior team suddenly collapses, is all thumbs, out-of-synch, and gets humiliated by an inferior team. Would not have happened the next night, but it did that night! It was a colossal disappointment, and I can still feel it in my bones when I see it happening to other teams these days of incessant TV sports coverage. All those hundreds of hours shooting baskets at the goal on the backboard bolted to the garage; perhaps college will be better!

Athletics did not leave much time for religion, and religion then meant church attendance, Bible reading, and prayer. But in junior high I developed the practice of praying nightly upon going to bed. My most fervent prayers asked Jesus—I prayed to Jesus a lot—to help me become a better athlete and to overcome my errors and temperamental outbursts of disappointment and self-anger. In praying for Jesus' help, I thought *life was in essence an accurate throw from shortstop!* Somehow during these early years I did come to the conviction that God was gracious and forgiving, but I did not think of myself as particularly obedient and morally admirable. My flaws were much too obvious to me. But surely I was searching for some peace and assurance. Putting this more sharply: it never occurred to me that God was the reality that should be doubted; I was the one about whom

PART THREE—Fragments from Times Past and Emerging Hopes

there should be much doubting. But I did not feel hard pressed to conjure and defend a stronger and more precise understanding of 'God.'

Sometime during junior high I undertook to read the Bible through completely, and this I did chapter by chapter two times before going to college. It was the discipline of reading every night before bed that was bracing to my soul, but I cannot recall now any particular impressions that have shaped me deeply from those readings of the biblical texts and stories. It was only in college in a course on the Bible as English Literature in my sophomore year that I encountered a coherent way in which to construe and connect the two Testaments and the distinctions among the various texts therein. Even so, I never entertained the thought that the Bible was in its totality a set of discrete truth-claiming sentences. That was not a conviction that in more mature years I would have to learn how to relinquish.

To be candid, in junior and senior high school, I had slight appetite for reading other books or even novels. My brother Charles managed to acquire a small record player and several records. What secret pleasure I enjoyed, sneaking into his room and listening to such magical and inspirational pieces such as *Bolero, 1812 Overture, Carmen,* and *Finlandia.* For me and my limited cultural sensibilities at that time, classical music was emotionally uplifting. In high school this appetite for classical music led Dr. Shorbe, the father of Janyce a classmate, to allow me access to his impressive den/studio full of the latest LPs, turntables, and speakers for a couple of hours of inspiration before going to school for basketball games my senior year. Not a refined connoisseur, it always seemed to me that louder was more aesthetically captivating and upbuilding. But enthralled by the passion of the music, in my imagination I never missed a basket nor lost a game!

As a youth I had an unusually deep and loud voice that would on occasion startle folk. In ways then opaque to me but perhaps foretelling future skills, I won the Kilpatrick Oratorical Contests for each grade at Taft Junior High. These awards happened to the chagrin of competitors who thought athletes weren't supposed to possess such refined and honed gestures and intonations. Interestingly, during my years at Classen High School I completely abstained from any school activities related to the arts.

In high school much of my religious reflection was stimulated by regular conversations with two fellow athletes, one, Joe Mosley, a staunch Southern Baptist headed for a career in ministry, and the other, Clark McPhail, a Nazarene, since become an agnostic distinguished professor of sociology at the University of Illinois, Champaign. Our arguments were vigorous, and for the first time I came to understand myself as a 'liberal.' Our conversations stand out for their intensity and honest good will, even though they were convinced I was going straight to hell, if I did not change my beliefs and my ways. Here it is important to recall what a later professorial colleague said to me: "those of us who were raised liberal spend the rest of our lives trying to prove that we are orthodox, and those who were raised fundamentalists, once our dam breaks, struggle desperately trying to find a liberal safe haven, though often without success as the faith just withers away." It is also important to note that these students remain close friends even to the present day.

Academically in high school I was a good student, but not remarkable or exceptional. A's and B's were satisfactory to me, since sports were the most important considerations. Now as a function of retrospection, I can confess that I did not regard myself as brilliant but I knew I would do much better in college, at which time it would be necessary to settle down to academic concentration. This in fact did happen when I went to the University of Oklahoma, albeit on a basketball and baseball full athletic scholarship. I had a simple confidence that I would academically hunker down when I went away to college. It would not, however, have seemed likely to a neutral observer that I would make Phi Beta Kappa at OU!

During my senior year in high school I met the person who has shaped and formed my life more than any other: Sarah Jane Jones, a beautiful, smart, all-miss-everything sophomore sensation. Yes, you read that correctly—she too was a Jones, but not kin! We began to date, fell desperately in love, and continued to date for four more years until our marriage in April of 1958 during the latter part of my last year in college. Our lives have been so intimately and lovingly intertwined for so long that even now it is thick and complex to track all the interactions and mutual influencing that have shaped us both. We helped each other grow up, is one way to put it, and we are each other's best friend. I should note here that Sarah's sincere, Methodist piety encouraged me to try to become a better person and even more religious.

Sarah's folks, Glenn and Peggy Jones, were co-owners of Crown Heights Drug Store with Ed and Naomi Belew, Naomi and Peggy being sisters. All four had migrated to Oklahoma from Tennessee in the 1930s. It is a winsome family story that Glenn had first refused to let his sophomore daughter date an older senior student unknown to him,

PART THREE—Fragments from Times Past and Emerging Hopes

even though family friend Hyla Hyde Harding had assured him that I was trustworthy. However, he was moved to change his mind when he overheard some other students at a restaurant speaking favorably of a mysterious 'Joe Jones.' It is a nice and memorable story, true or not. It also should be noted that the Belews, who were childless and considered Sarah and her brother as their own, in 1970 purchased a little cinder block cabin on Fort Gibson Lake in eastern Oklahoma that was to become a haven for our family over many years.

For the 1956-57 school year, Sarah's senior class was moved to a new school building and became Northwest Classen High School. She was elected by the students to be the first student body president of that school!

Now, some fifty-nine years later and fifty-five-plus years of married life together, it remains a sheer miracle that this astonishingly beautiful and brilliant woman would look upon me with tenderness and fidelity and a love rooted in *eros* and blossomed by *agape*. We were to have three exceptional daughters, and one of their favorite remarks to others over the years was "how remarkable it was to know that at any gathering their mother was the most beautiful woman there."

Being raised in a time of all encompassing segregation, I knew racism in society and within my own family from a very early age. In ways that I can only now consider providential and prevenient grace, segregation and its accompanying racial attitudes never seemed right to me. To nobody in the family's particular interest, in grade school I began to protest in the home the status and life of our maid, who lived under the bridge in 'shanty town.' I loved and was loved by Jo Ella with a tenderness and anguish that still remains vivid and provocative. We later communicated from time to time, and it is an unending pleasure to know that her children and many of her grandchildren have gone on to distinguished careers in medicine, law, education, and business. Over the ensuing years some of the harshest conflicts in my family have pivoted around matters of racial prejudice and justice. I should note that from grade school through high school the public schools in Oklahoma City were legally segregated. I do not recall that I did anything public to protest such; only a few rumblings and arguments in the family. But it is a plain and simple, however painful, fact that all through my schooling in Oklahoma City there were no African American students with whom to be friends.

Spiritual Notes on Growing Up in Oklahoma

It is a strange and enigmatic fact that my family's Native American roots seldom rose to conversational consciousness. My father never discussed these roots in his own autobiography previously mentioned. Of course, being raised in Oklahoma I knew friends who were Indians and many other persons of fame and infamy who were Indians. In fact my first year roommate in the athletic dorm at OU, Gary Lovett, was a 'full blood' Indian raised in a Cherokee school in Oaks. But I never thought of myself as being an Indian until much later in life. Somehow it was not a card that could be displayed readily and played to advantage, as has become the case in these later years in Oklahoma. Since returning to live in Oklahoma in 2000, we often joke with friends that I have more Native American 'blood' in me than many of the Cherokees on the rolls today. The reticence in my family to discuss our Native American heritage, at least to my ears, is regrettable. Yet, notice how even today we tread gingerly among the contested boundaries around 'Indian,' 'Native American,' 'Negro,' 'Black,' 'African American,' 'white,' 'American,' 'Caucasian,' 'European,' and 'Spanish/Hispanic/Latino,' all suffering severe grammatical mayhem?

It is also unnerving that in grade school during World War II, I killed many a "Jap" and "Nazi" with my wooden tommy gun amid the bushes and creeks of the neighborhood. And Paul S. was a Jew and a really good friend, who went on to become quite famous in the world of entertainment. But small and vulnerable Frank M., also a Jew, was on more than one occasion taunted by me with the snide question—actually an accusation—of 'where he went to church?' Childish and childhood meanness in the past might be forgiven and even produce healing, but it can never be undone. Such deep lesions on my soul are resistant to healing and forgetting. Those too are dimensions of my 'spiritual' past.

Off to the University of Oklahoma in 1954, with athletic scholarships in basketball and baseball, to play sports and get an education! Both of my parents and all three of my siblings also graduated from OU. At that particular time in NCAA rules, freshmen were ineligible for varsity sports. Freshman practiced only with freshman and did not play in varsity games. Such certainly made for dull workouts and a sense of ambiguity for the freshman and affected my relationship with both the basketball and baseball programs. Awkward is the word! But my freshman basketball class was regarded by sports observers as one of the strongest in recent years at OU. And my sophomore and junior years found me an on-and-off starter on the

Part Three—Fragments from Times Past and Emerging Hopes

basketball team, and lettering in baseball my sophomore year. I had hoped for a more rewarding and outstanding collegiate athletic career, but it was not to be. Unforeseen complications emerged for my sophomore year.

At the end of my freshman year, the basketball coach who had recruited me was summarily dismissed and replaced by a person who had been successful as coach at Oklahoma City University. I had known him previously and knew he was a severe tyrant confusing the incessant abuse of players with coaching. And sure enough, he so viciously and constantly harassed and berated us all that many scholarship players started bailing out, and I finally decided not to play my senior year. In retrospect my failure to be more outstanding in collegiate sports is painful. But the harassment was so intense that the game was no longer pleasurable but had become sheer misery. And to no players' surprise, we had wretched records in basketball. These conflicts also complicated my baseball hopes, then playing centerfielder. While lettering in the spring of 1956—sophomore year—as we won the Big Seven Conference title, the basketball dismay and the strain of the long basketball season intruding into the spring, led me to give up baseball in 1957.

Lanny Anderson from Wewoka was my sophomore year roommate in the athletic dorm and he departed the team at the end of that year. Lanny became a first-rate thoracic surgeon in Oklahoma City. He finally found some relief, as did I, in reading Pat Conroy's 2002 autobiographical novel *My Losing Season*, a compelling but painful story about a passion for basketball and team camaraderie become discombobulated by coaching malfeasance.

My coach would later be fired and drifted around for years searching for work. In the mid-1980s, while I was president of Phillips University, my secretary rang to say "a Mr. P." was at her desk and wanted to visit with me. He sat in my office with his head down and hands folded and in a low voice we exchanged some pleasantries. It was painfully clear that he was a defeated soul, now bereft of all that venom and bluster he had expressed for many years as coach. We both knew that he wanted to somehow express an apology or at least regrets about my experience at OU, but he could not utter any words approximating that. It seemed quite inappropriate to mention my anger and griefs and those of many other players in his past. To this day I am ambivalent and vexed as to whether I should have, nevertheless, *expressed* forgiveness; but how can you express forgiveness without mentioning the deeds being forgiven? Perhaps my simple hospitality conveyed some measure of personal respect and forgiveness. But have I forgiven him?

Spiritual Notes on Growing Up in Oklahoma

I pray I have, but I have not forgotten. As he left I thanked him for dropping by and wished him well in the days ahead.

I have on occasions been inclined to puke in protest when I hear glib comments by others, usually TV sports announcers, about the presumed beneficial effects of coaches' verbal harassments and physical abuses of their players.

But I did become academically competent, being the university athlete with the highest grade average all three of those years (1954-55, 55-56, 56-57). I am sure the dismay and disappointment in basketball pushed me to embrace my studies more earnestly. I studied hard, and played hard, getting about four to five hours of sleep a night. It was brutal on my body, but perhaps redemptive for my soul.

Hence, in juxtaposition to my basketball misery, at the beginning of my sophomore year I took my first philosophy course under Gustav Mueller, a world-renowned Hegelian scholar who was just then publishing in German his great study of Hegel. In this introductory course we read Mueller's book, *Dialectics*, a Hegelian introduction to philosophy, facts unknown to me at the time of enrolling in the course. The reading of the book and his barely understandable lectures strangely fascinated me: something important was going on here. The class of sixty had to write their first paper on a couple of the chapters of the book, and I delved in with great relish, handwriting a six-page paper. A few class sessions after the papers had been handed in, Professor Mueller paused before beginning his lecture, and, in barely audible and heavily accented English, asked if "Mr. Jones would come forward and read his paper." I was astonished and disbelieving, thinking surely there must be another Mr. Jones in the class. My cousin Jon Rex Jones was also in the class and sitting next to me; maybe it was he who was being asked to read. It turned out it was I who was being invited to read, which I surely did. Somehow I had gathered and conveyed some insight into his philosophizing, which he regarded as significant. It was the first time I-the-athlete had ever received real intellectual recognition, and I never turned back; in the ensuing college years I was to take over sixty hours of philosophy, including advanced seminars individually on Plato, Augustine, Kant, Hegel, Jonathan Edwards, and Tillich.

One experience, which I remember vividly as if it were yesterday, expresses some of the transformation that was shaking my life. I was in the library later that semester, waiting to go to basketball practice at 6:30 p.m.

PART THREE—Fragments from Times Past and Emerging Hopes

and reading the section on Spinoza in Will Durant's *The Story of Philosophy*. My eyes came upon the phrase "the intellectual love of God" and I became filled with a transcending and awesome ecstasy. In later studies I realized more clearly just what Spinoza had in mind, but to me then and there, this was a shatteringly revelatory thought, kept hidden from me and the world for far too long! Truly, at that moment the radical possibility began emerging that I could not pursue the career in law which had been set out for me: I must do whatever it took to continue to think and study such profound thoughts about the reality of God and human life. The idea that one might love God with the full vigor and rigor of the mind galvanized me into the passionate study of philosophy and theology. And yes, I know, Durant is no great philosopher among philosophers, but his book was just about my speed for that point in my life.

During the next semester I came under the wonderful and freeing influence of J. Clayton Feaver, a philosophy of religion professor regarded as the most stimulating professor on campus. He kindly took me under his wing and guided me through many courses in the philosophy of religion, encouraging me along the way to consider a career in teaching and ministry. He had a PhD from Yale University, and once I had bitten deeply on the apple of philosophy and theology, he pushed me gently in the direction of going to divinity school at Yale. He was to do the same thing for daughter Serene some twenty-plus years later. And it was he who gave the address at my departure banquet at Phillips in 1988. Dr. Feaver was the mentor who gave me an adult understanding of Christian faith and the confidence to think of myself as having a ministry in teaching.

It was also Feaver who introduced me to Paul Tillich's theology. While I had only heard Tillich's name mentioned in lectures, I knew little about his theology. During the 1956 Big Seven Christmas basketball tourney in Kansas City, I was browsing through Cokesbury Bookstore and came upon a book, *Love, Power, and Justice*, by Tillich. I bought it and rushed back to the hotel to devouringly read it. Probably I truly understood little, but I thought I understood much and felt compelled to travel down a road of reading everything I could get my hands on of Tillich's. In the summer of 1957 I took Tillich's just published volume two of his *Systematic Theology* to summer ROTC camp, and stayed up nights reading it, even forsaking the weekends off to stay in the barracks and read Tillich!

In later years as a graduate student I was to have a conversation with Tillich that confirmed the feelings I had during my last couple of years of college: he would allow no question or objection to defeat or fall outside his system; everything significant was interpretable within his categories. By that point in time I had become something of a critic of Tillich's, but his deft dialectical rhetoric reminded me of the supreme confidence I had in college. It had become so compellingly obvious to me in my collegiate study of Tillich and the greats of Western philosophy that God was unavoidably evident in the world and in experience, and that anyone intelligent enough to think fairly about these matters would be ineluctably led to encounter God and have that "faith in the God beyond gods" that was so persuasively and patently Tillichian. I was not very precise as to how I identified this god, though 'being-itself' seemed helpful. In those days I had a synthesizing plasticity that allowed me to turn every objection to faith into an affirmation. I was not developing, yet, a discriminating and critical mind that could see more deeply into objections to Christian faith. I was a breathing, walking, talking Tillichian, who knew Tillich's systematic thought like the back of my hand, and I arrogantly assumed that I was invulnerable to intelligent objection or refutation. I had much yet to learn, but I was off and running fast!

An event occurred during my third year in college that has assumed considerable importance to me over the years, though not so important at the time. I had moved into the Kappa Sigma fraternity house during that year, and my increasing preoccupation with philosophy and religion was strong and compelling. During one evening it was announced that some members of the Campus Crusade for Christ were available in the house parlor for anyone who might like to discuss religious issues. Knowing quite surely that they would earnestly be seeking the salvation of my soul, I went and had a lively and honest discussion with them. Near the end of the conversation their tone intensified by their incessant inquiry as to whether "I had been saved and, if so, when?" Of course, I knew that question was coming, and I knew they wanted a time-specific event in which I was "really saved." But I surprised myself when I uttered "I was saved at Golgotha!" They were stunned, almost speechless, but then they said "goodbye" and departed. That conversation still reverberates with meaning as I have been incessantly preoccupied over the years about the complex and interrelated meanings of Christian talk of salvation.

I should also mention that I actively attended Sunday evening meetings of the Methodist students at OU, as well as listening in on some strong Presbyterian preaching. Frankly the Disciples student group was weak and

PART THREE—Fragments from Times Past and Emerging Hopes

disappointing, though it had become robust by the time our oldest daughters went to OU. For the first time in my life I found myself participating in rigorous theological discussions with student friends, including two from Classen: Bob Webber, who would later get a PhD at Yale in New Testament, and Paul McDaniel, who would go off to Harvard Law School and become an internationally renown professor of tax law at Boston College Law School. Amazingly Paul remained an unrepentant Tillichian, and was an avuncular presence to our middle daughter, Kindy, as she studied at BC Law School.

Since I gave up varsity sports my senior year, I inquired of the Oklahoma Disciples office whether there was a church I might serve on weekends. To my surprise they recommended me to the Atoka First Christian Church. These were wonderfully kind and devout folk who listened patiently to my sermonic deliverances on the Gospel with a decidedly Tillichian flavor. They heard much about existential estrangement and the invitation of the New Being. In retrospect I think the Gospel did come through, however skewed it must have been by my callowness, naiveté, and intellectual presumptuousness. Sarah often traveled to Atoka with me, and they loved both of us with a generosity and authenticity that gave me some new glimpses of what the church might be and become in its deepest reality. Thirty years later we returned to Atoka for a glorious reunion and celebration with the folk. I mention this church experience to underscore that I never thought of my intellectual feats and life as in any way separate from the life of the church. I cannot recall that my philosophical studies in college led me then to hold the church in contempt or to diminish the significance of the God we know in Jesus Christ.

In the summer of 1956 my father was running for re-election to a third term on the Criminal Court of Appeals. The eastern third of Oklahoma was the region he represented. Giving up sandlot baseball for the summer, I traveled by myself all over the region making speeches at candidates' rallies, handing out brochures, and just meeting folk on the street and telling them of my father's outstanding work on the court. (During one speech-making rally, I met a young high school teacher from McAlester who was running for the state House of Representatives. His name was George Nigh, and later he was to become a two-term governor of Oklahoma. Our friendship led me to invite him, serving then as governor, to give the address at my inauguration as president of Phillips University in 1979.) Despite my 'heroic' efforts, my father went down to defeat at the hands of the most powerful senator in the state, who had decided he wanted to become a judge. This baptism into rough and tumble politics, heightened my political sensitivities, which had been rather dull, and it disclosed to me how different my politics were from my father's. During this summer of electioneering I made up my mind to give up the law career for one in teaching ministry. My father never tried to talk me out of that decision. In fact over many years he and mother provided continuing encouragement and financial support for us.

In light of the differences I was to have with my father, let me recount this memorable event. The election defeat was a devastating blow to my father, who had greatly enjoyed being "Judge Jones." But the morning after the election, after some expressions of misgivings about how we had run and financed the campaign, my father got in his car and went in search of a location in which to start up his new law practice. He did not moan and groan his loss but went straightforwardly into the future to meet its demands and possibilities. And he had no interest whatsoever of being part of a large corporate law firm. That determined resoluteness and refusal to weep over the losses of the past struck me forcefully at the time. It should not be surprising that I asked my father to be my "best man" at Sarah's and my wedding in April of 1958.

In looking back over my years growing up in Oklahoma, it is amazing that I was in fact so politically naïve in theory and practice, except for my campaigning for my father. Oklahoma politics were dominated by the Democratic Party, my father had become a Democrat, and I was simply by default. Certainly some political issues emerged in my readings in philosophy, but I refrained from campus politics. Of course there were many issues surrounding racial segregation, which I had long opposed, and I did greet happily both the passage of the Civil Rights Act of 1957 rendering segregation in public schools illegal and Eisenhower's intervention in Little Rock, Arkansas that same year. But I cannot recall any conversations with other students in which other political differences were hot and bothered. It was only at Yale, with the election of John F. Kennedy and the further harsh issues of racial justice front and center that I began to develop a defining political posture. In this same connection, I graduated from OU as a commissioned Infantry officer in the U.S. Army, under the lurking obligation to serve two years on active duty upon completion of my studies at Yale. Aside from the predictable pall of looming active duty, I had no disdain for the military. In fact I graduated as one of the top two students in the ROTC! There it is in its simple givenness.

Part Three—Fragments from Times Past and Emerging Hopes

I should also record that my summers in high school and college were variously spent doing really hard labor. First, as a member of the Hod-Carriers and Laborers Union I worked on the construction of the new Northwest Classen High School. Next, I dug ditches for the Oklahoma Natural Gas Company and played sandlot baseball on their team in the evenings, though ONG was not then nor was it ever to become a union company. Then as a member of the Steam-Fitters and Plumbers Union, I did construction labor for my cousin. I am not aware that any other member of my family had such experiences as part of labor unions, and it changed me forever about the place of labor unions for working folk. Actually, I joined the unions as a way of getting better pay and receiving some protection from the arbitrariness of construction superintendents and bosses. Yet, these summers as a laborer supported by labor unions predisposed me to labor union sympathies in politics that to this day remain vivid and strong.

In the fall of 1957 I did apply to Yale Divinity School for the three-year degree called Bachelor of Divinity (now referred to as Master of Divinity) and was admitted with substantial scholarship help. In the meantime Sarah and I made plans to marry on April 5, 1958. Being two years behind me in school, she would continue her education at New Haven State Teachers College. It is true on the mark to say that Sarah's encouragement and support of my pursuit of a graduate theological education was decisive for me, and, in some elusive respects, I think I was trying to live up to her love and piety.

My enthusiasm for going to Yale was intense and almost without doubt and hesitation, except the lurking thought that perhaps I might not be smart enough to do the work well. I was clear in my own mind that I wanted to go on to a doctoral degree, hopefully at Yale, and teach in a theological school. Teaching the faith was so firmly impressed on my consciousness that I imaginatively enacted it often and with verve. Was God calling me to this teaching vocation? I surely believe so in retrospect, but at the time I simply knew I had to pursue the study of the reality of God as far as I could, and in that sense I knew it was to be a lifetime vocation. However much I went to Yale aiming at a teaching career, I never thought parish ministry was a lesser calling and I remained open to that possibility.

Yale was more of a feast than my Oklahoma imagination might have conjured. Two impressions stood out in the first few weeks. First, all the other entering students seemed extraordinarily intelligent and of the Phi

Spiritual Notes on Growing Up in Oklahoma

Beta Kappa type, with a large number seemingly intent also going on for a Ph.D. at Yale. Second, I was astonished at the unapologetic piety of the faculty, who showed no hesitation about expressing their faith. I expected that reserved indirection that is the practice on a secular university campus. The obvious erudition of the faculty did not surprise me, and I fled into my course work with zestful delight, reading much more than my assignments. In the first year I took full year courses in Old Testament with Brevard Childs—this was Childs's first year at Yale—in New Testament with Paul Meyer, in Church History with Roland Bainton, and in Systematic Theology with Julian Hartt and Robert Calhoun.

I was warned that students should not take systematic theology until their second year, but I would hear nothing of it, confident as I was that Tillich would see me through. Indeed it was soon evident to me that my many hours of undergraduate philosophy courses and my careful absorption of Tillich were almost unrivaled preparation for divinity studies, even if I was coming to the Ivy League from a state university of modest reputation. But what did surprise me was the relative disinterest in Tillich's theology among faculty and students! My previous intellectual conceit was simple: if you are smart and thoughtful you will be persuaded that Tillich's type of theology is inescapably true. Well, here were all those smart professors, and many did not even understand Tillich as well as I, and they were not clutching Tillich's volumes to their breasts as the latest word from above!

It was a genuine existential shock to me when in systematics I read Karl Barth's recently translated *Church Dogmatics, II/1*. Not since my ecstatic reading of Spinoza had I encountered a text that was to have a permanent effect on me. While it may not have been 'the strange new world in the Bible,' it was the strange world of authentic Christian discourse that called into question virtually every easily believed conclusion of my previous study and reflection. To this day I regard that volume as one of the premier achievements of twentieth-century Christian theology. While I had been a bit quarrelsome with Tillich's Christology, Barth made Jesus Christ inescapably central in such a way that I was overwhelmed with the sheer energy and beauty of Barth's theology. I had never heard such traditional theological language used with such brilliance, passion, and persuasive power. My blessed world of philosophy, ontology, and natural theology took a drubbing from which it has never quite recovered.

Of course, I was soon to discover that H. Richard Niebuhr and Robert Calhoun, the reigning elder statesmen in theology at Yale, had a strong

PART THREE—Fragments from Times Past and Emerging Hopes

distaste for Barth. However, Julian Hartt, the instructor in the first semester of systematic theology, and Hans Frei, a young junior professor, had a keen openness to Barth that was encouraging to me. To use language common today, in reading Barth I was massively being deconstructed and reconstructed theologically. His theological texts interrogated and challenged many of my heretofore easy assumptions, and I had never heard such consistently powerful words of grace.

Now in June of 2013, as I put the final touches on these notes—that have almost doubled in size since their initial recording in the summer of 1998—I remain troubled both by what I have not covered and by some of what I have in fact written. My daughters have been insistent that I continue writing in these ways and produce perhaps a memoir of my life at Yale and beyond to the present day. Some of those years have been briefly covered in the following essay written for the fiftieth reunion of my 1961 B.D. class at Yale Divinity School. But for now I have no appetite for undertaking an even larger project. I do hope, however, these reflections by an elderly theologian might at least prove interesting to whoever might read them.

16

A YDS Reflection

Remembrance of Things Past and the Present Discontent

On October 10–12, 2011, my Yale Divinity School B.D. Class of 1961 met at Yale to celebrate our fiftieth year reunion. In preparation for the event, the Class Planning Committee decided to establish a website and invite all of our class to post reflections on 'how my mind has changed since then' in the interest of having a stimulating discussion among ourselves at the reunion. Recognizing the built-in limitations of space, I share here my posting for my class colleagues. I am sure there are matters discussed herein that are unknown to many of my friends. Text slightly edited.

Dear Colleagues of the YDS Class of 1961:

The invitation to members of the YDS Class of 1961 to post on this website some reflections about early 1960s aspirations in relation to the present situation—however we might define 'the present situation'—is a welcome and forbidding task. Not the least of the forbidding is that this site is unprepared for a book and my classmates are wisely uneager to read such and I am incapable of writing such. So, some notes on traversing from then to now.

Like many of my classmates, I arrived at Yale Divinity School under the impression that I was ascending into the ranks of the well-educated elite who were ready to consume whatever quasi-liberal YDS had to offer. I had graduated from the University of Oklahoma with over sixty hours of philosophy and considered myself well read in Western philosophy and embracing a Christianity heavily formed by Paul Tillich and Reinhold Niebuhr. It was crystal clear to me that my vocation was somehow teaching in higher education.

I had married my high school sweetheart, Sarah, in the preceding spring and we moved into Bellamy Hall of the new married student housing. I loved every minute of my life at YDS: the classes, the faculty, but also the unending conversations with other students, who seemed so 'smart' and committed. Chapel, common room coffee and conversations, basketball and volleyball in the gym, tennis on the new courts—what excesses of joy and learning! By the time I graduated from the B.D. program, Sarah and I had two children, completely unplanned, but then also bearers of previously unimagined and unfathomed blessings.

But a theological tornado struck me during my first year, and I must try briefly to state it clearly, considering that its aftermath would reverberate throughout my personal and professional life. Because of my background in philosophy as an undergraduate, I was allowed by my adviser to take the year-long course in systematic theology, being taught by Julian Hartt in the first semester and Robert Calhoun in the second. In that first semester Hartt required the class to read Karl Barth's *Church Dogmatics, Vol. II/1: The Doctrine of God* (Edinburgh: T. & T. Clark, 1957). Put in its simplest terms, Barth drew a prolonged and carefully examined contrast between two methods by way of which the church's theologians have defended or attempted to justify the church's knowledge of God—or in the way I would come to put it: ways in which the grammar of God might be constructed and elaborated. The first attempt has long been credible in traditions that assumed there was a basic rational or natural grammar available to anyone. Or, in the language of much Christian theologizing in the nineteenth and early twentieth century, the first task is locate God-talk on a spectrum of human epistemic and moral possibilities, and then symbolically construct what might be peculiar to the church. But Barth turned that grammar on its head, declaring that at the heart of the church's language has been the belief that God reveals Godself in Jesus Christ. Rather than trying to locate this possibility along the spectrum of inherent human possibilities, Barth proposes this self-revealing of God is what must be taken as *given*, from which we can then explore what sort of grammar is implicit in the claim that God is known as the One who reveals Godself in Jesus Christ. The first part of this volume then proceeds before our eyes to unfold how that sort of self-revelation is rooted in the divine life itself.

A YDS Reflection

Most of you know how that would further unfold, and I suspect many of my classmates have spent a lifetime simply dismissing Barth, but then struggling to find some presumably rational defense against the self-conscious atheistic philosophers of our time. Or simply giving up the hope that there is any case of whatever sort to be made in defense or explanation of prime Christian beliefs and practices. Well, reading Barth in that first semester turned my life around and gave me an agenda I sometimes wished I could cancel, but more often I feel blessed to have been so turned around or turned upside down!

In the fall of 1961 I entered the doctoral program at Yale in philosophical theology. By the time I had started in this program, Tillich had definitely faded from interest, Barth had become a challenging conversation-partner, Kierkegaard and Hegel had re-emerged, linguistic philosophy of all sorts, including Wittgenstein, moved front and center, with Paul Holmer kibitzing from the sidelines. I moved among Hartt, Holmer, Frei, Lindbeck, Gustafson, and Christian, and caught some last days of H. Richard Niebuhr and Robert Calhoun, and downtown in philosophy with Smith, Weiss, Brumbaugh, and Sellars. It was a treat!

My dissertation topic became issues surrounding the interpretation of Barth's understanding of divine revelation, now viewed through the lens and tools of 'analytic philosophy.' I left Yale in 1965, dissertation unfinished, to take a position in philosophical theology at Perkins School of Theology at Southern Methodist University in Dallas. (Kennedy had been shot in Dallas in 1963.) I considered the faculty at Perkins to be one of the best in the nation and was delighted to be invited to join them.

Interlude: when I entered OU in 1954, all male students were required to take two years of military training. To avoid being drafted, in 1956 I also entered the advanced Army ROTC, knowing that the cost of not being drafted was a commitment to serve two years in the Army as a commissioned officer. I graduated with high honors in 1958, had my pick of branches, and in good Niebuhrian style chose the Infantry. I knew by then that I would be deferred to go on to graduate school at Yale. Still, two years was out there in the future as a time of military service. On June 6, 1963, I was ordained in my tradition, the Christian Church (Disciples of Christ), and duly reported such to the Army in my annual request for another year of deferment to continue my studies at Yale. To my surprise, they wrote back inquiring whether I would like to transfer to the Chaplaincy, and I replied, in good tough liberal style, that I preferred staying in the Infantry.

Part Three—Fragments from Times Past and Emerging Hopes

And they would later inquire, without explanation, whether I would like to apply for an honorable discharge with no further military obligations. In utter surprise and astonishment at this offer, I said yes. It had never previously dawned on me that being ordained would complicate my military commitment, and to this day their offer of an honorable discharge only makes sense to me in terms of the Army's apparent unwillingness to have an ordained minister serving as a field officer in the Infantry.

Thus, the military obligation disappeared and my life could go on without serving the two years. Vietnam was beginning to heat up. It is a common belief in our family that I would not have survived what eventually became known as the Vietnam War; the lives of Infantry lieutenants in the field of combat were short. There it is in its utter bafflement. Many years later I would consider myself in league with Christian pacifists, but in 1963 I was not a pacifist and was still under the impression that our intervention in Vietnam was defensible in that rough and tumble way of Reinhold Niebuhr's strong reservations about communism and its various aggressions.

Arriving to teach at Perkins in the summer of 1965, we settled in Richardson, a northern suburb largely populated with Texas Instruments engineers and a brand of racist and fundamentalist churches exercising political control over the town. Even though President Johnson had signed the Civil Rights Act of 1964, resistant racism seemed everywhere in greater Dallas. Johnson would defeat Goldwater in 1964 under the impression that he alone would not mire the nation in a long war in Vietnam. Yet, by 1968 there were 542,000 American troops in Vietnam. The war itself was getting caught up in that huge cultural earthquake that would shake me and, I am sure, all of us who were 1961 YDS graduates, wherever we were. Martin Luther King would be assassinated on April 4, 1968, and on June 5th, Robert Kennedy, then a Democratic Party candidate for president, was assassinated. In November, Nixon—much despised by the left—defeated Hubert Humphrey—unsupported by the left—for president. After inflicting frightful causalities on the Vietnamese but unable to achieve military victory, in 1973 Nixon ordered a complete U.S. evacuation of Vietnam: a defeat leaving over 58,000 U.S. military dead and over 300,000 wounded, and an estimated 42,000 draft evaders living outside America, as well as over 1 million Vietnamese combatants and over 4 million non-combatants dead. It was defeat predictably indigestible to stalwart 'America-first' citizens that haunts and fractures U.S. politics right up the present day.

A YDS Reflection

As all of us also know, the sociopolitical fabric of American life was being comprehensively fragmented by protests of war, of the continuing entanglement of racism in all aspects of social life, protests for women's rights, gay rights, abortion rights—the list is long, but it is a list of the principalities and powers that were shaping all of us then and for years to come. And it would devastate much mainline church life: some theologians counseled that 'God is Dead,' others pronounced the end of the sermon, the patriotic right retreated to a new form of right-wing political fundamentalism, and the liberal left became skeptical whether it makes any intellectual and moral sense to be Christian in any traditional form. 'Secular Christianity' seemed attractive at first to many with its announcement of the demise of any defensible intellectual truth claims about God or Jesus. Is it any surprise that mainline graduate students in biblical studies would henceforth claim to be no more than historians of early Christianity?

Of course, I lectured continually in seminary and in churches about all these issues, yet I limped spiritually. But there were signals of grace all around me: 1) the faculty of Perkins were an amazingly robust and learned group daily embracing the stringent demands of intellectual conversation interacting with faithfulness; 2) our family began worshipping in a Disciples congregation in Richardson, Community Christian Church, that was blessed with an exceptionally energetic, fair-minded, earnest inquirers eager to worship God and to engage the larger social world in various political activities; 3) the discovery of friends in other traditions—Jewish, Roman Catholic, mainline folk, and struggling doubters—to form *ad hoc* social-action groups, such as CALL (Christian Action Laymen's League) and LEARN (League for Education Advancement Richardson Now); 4) a family of women—a devout wife unwaveringly committed to me and to our three young daughters, who were talky, indefatigable, clever, and blessed with attentive ears whenever adults gathered to talk politics, church, and the collapse of the old structure of social order.

But I experienced a vocational/intellectual/moral crisis—surely in all these ways a *spiritual crisis*—during the late 1960s at Perkins. I had become offended by some developments in church and the world. The careless ways in which many in theology were caving into revisionary ways of construing God-talk and the meaning of the church concerned me. While I too had my doubts about some theological beliefs, I became convinced that some of the proposals being advanced were not merely reformative of Christian theology, but were in fact the demise of anything bearing an identifiable relation

PART THREE—Fragments from Times Past and Emerging Hopes

to Christian traditions. A basic question of honesty was emerging for me: either stay in church and get serious theologically or leave church and give up any pretense that one is a Christian. For me the only theological substance worth saving was a Radical Orthodoxy with a substantive Christology and a Trinitarian heart, closer to Barth rather than the later Milbankian sort. Only a church with those theological linchpins could possibly have sufficient integrity and conviction to survive the overwhelming sociopolitical upheavals surging in America and be faithful to the Gospel of Jesus Christ.

My personal problem was that I was privately tortured as to whether I believed that sort of Radical Orthodoxy. And in the midst of that personal turmoil, my dissertation on Barth and the Concept of Revelation, languished in notes and imagined but unwritten pages. Perhaps I should just give up this project, forget the dissertation and the doctorate, resign from Perkins and find a teaching position in philosophy, or maybe go to law school. The depth of this struggle was not obvious to most colleagues and students, but at a pivotal point in the summer of 1969, Joe Quillian, the Perkins Dean, and Fred Carney, Professor of Christian Ethics, graciously intervened with wise counsel and devised a leave simply to finish the dissertation in utter seclusion during the upcoming fall semester. While it was never the dissertation I thought I would write, in three months time it was done and in January submitted to Yale.

In ways not easily summarized and encapsulated, I healed spiritually and became clearer about my vocation as a *church theologian*. While I have never retreated from strong opinions about the shape and politics of America, my own vocation was to help the church learn how to be the church in the midst of that rankling and social conflict that did then and has ever since dominated American political life.

It was, then, this train of thought that in 1975 led me to accept an invitation to become Dean of the Graduate Seminary at Phillips University in Enid, Oklahoma, the university being founded before statehood by the Disciples of Christ for the education of ministers and teachers for the church. This is not the place in which to celebrate and explore the wonders of that seminary and its distinguished faculty and then my acceptance of the invitation in 1979 to become President of the University. Essential to my undertaking these administrative tasks was a firm conviction that the university and the seminary had a purpose and character rooted in the church—not a church of a quasi-fundamentalist past, but a church with muscular convictions about the Gospel, the magnitude of God's grace, and the challenge of being Christ's church in relation to the world as we find it. It was at Phillips that I was able to clarify ecclesial convictions, percolating since Perkins, in this working definition of the church:

> The church is that liberative and redemptive
> community of persons
> called into being
> by the Gospel of Jesus Christ
> through the Holy Spirit
> to witness in word and deed
> to the living triune God
> for the benefit of the world
> to the glory of God.

The following statement of the Gospel emerged as well:

> The Gospel of Jesus Christ is the Good News
> that the God of Israel, the Creator of all creatures,
> has in freedom and love become incarnate
> in the life, death, and resurrection of Jesus of Nazareth
> to enact and reveal God's gracious reconciliation
> of humanity to Godself, and
> through the Holy Spirit calls and empowers human beings
> to participate in God's liberative and redemptive work by
> acknowledging God's gracious forgiveness in Jesus,
> repenting of human sin,
> receiving the gift of freedom, and
> embracing authentic community by
> loving the neighbor and the enemy,
> caring for the whole creation, and
> hoping for the final triumph of God's grace
> as the triune Ultimate Companion of all creatures.

This is not the appropriate place for that further reflection on my experiences as President of Phillips University from June 1979 to 1988, during which time Oklahoma and contiguous states experienced the collapse of its oil and gas economy, eventuating in a incapacity to raise funds and hastening the university's closing in 1998.

Deteriorating health—an incessant, harsh, and deep cough—led to my resignation from Phillips in 1988, assuming that I would need some time to diagnose and heal what only three years later would finally be diagnosed as sarcoidosis of the lungs. That resignation also opened up an invitation to join the faculty at Christian Theological Seminary in Indianapolis to teach theology and ethics and to be dean for four years. It was a gift that

CTS offered an opportunity to return to systematic theological reflection, including teaching a year-long course in systematic theology. It is the notes for this course that prepared the way for publishing, after my retirement in 2000, a two-volume work entitled, *A Grammar of Christian Faith: Systematic Explorations in Christian Life and Doctrine* (Lanham, MD: Rowman & Littlefield, 2002), which is still in print.

It was during those years at CTS that I entered into vigorous reading of the works of John Howard Yoder, then teaching at Notre Dame, and renewing conversation with Stanley Hauerwas, an old friend from YDS days and just a few years behind our 1961 class. Yoder and Hauerwas helped me clarify the complex relationships between the church and the world that can properly empower the church to retain an identity that is neither conferred nor authenticated by the powers of the world.

In 2000 I retired from CTS and Sarah and I moved to back to Oklahoma to take up residence in a cabin on Fort Gibson Lake that had been in the family since 1970 and had been the prime vacation spot for my family for all these years.

But the retirement here has been spiritually sobering. And I now get to a troubling point in these reflections: since my YDS days I have been teaching and administrating in church-related educational institutions and have received immeasurable joy in doing so. I was under the impression that such work would be strengthening to the integrity and truthfulness of the church's witness in a world that was becoming incessantly acrimonious in discourse and violent in action.

The church I was envisaging and teaching would eschew all efforts at a demonstrable epistemic superiority or presume that its grammar of divine revelation must be credible to all in some neutral epistemology. Hence, the church would become athletically *confessional* in word and deed for the sake of the world before God. Pastors, male and female, with acute intellectual and spiritual skill would steer deftly among that sort of Protestant fundamentalism and that sort of Roman infallibilism that seems to divide the world between the children of God and the children of the Devil and inclined to go to war against the demonic enemies, and that sort of vaguely secular spirituality, morally tolerant, easy-going, and comfortable in a multi-cultural, free-enterprise world. A radically orthodox confessional church might staunch that unhappy deterioration in which the churches are no more than mirror images of a politically conflictual American culture.

A YDS Reflection

But that church that I had hoped to help mold and in which to worship and be addressed Sunday after Sunday by a disarming and upbuilding Gospel—that hoped for ecclesial world is rapidly fading. Alas, there are some *fugitive* congregations here and there across denominations and traditions, and yet the supply of the hoped-for pastors blessed with such acute intellectual and spiritual skills dwindles as I write.

Yet I vacillate between understanding my sadness as a theological and existential disappointment or merely the disgruntlement of an aging former professor finding himself neglected and lonely in an ecclesial and secular world that has gone on a holiday. Might it seem odd that for all the years since YDS days I have been an unrepentant proclaimer of Universal Salvation—God's grace is the ultimate verdict on us all!

Dear YDS classmates, I know many of you have traversed routes quite different from mine and bear wounds and disappointments as well as joys as we have emerged into our seventies. My reflections herein have been aimed at the question raised by our planning committee: how have you and I changed from our time at YDS fifty years ago to our present conditions of spiritual habitation.

It should also be noted that Sarah, my high school sweetheart, and I have been married over fifty-three wonderful years and have brought three daughters into the world who are leading very interesting lives: Serene and Kindy were born during Yale days and Verity in Richardson. Serene Jones is now president of Union Theological Seminary in New York City and a distinguished theologian and author; Kindy Jones is Assistant Attorney General for the State of Oklahoma; Verity Jones, a former Disciples pastor and editor of *DisciplesWorld*, is now Executive Director of the Center for Pastoral Excellence at Christian Theological Seminary in Indianapolis. Alas, Serene and Verity also received several Yale degrees. Sarah is retired as a licensed psychotherapist.

I look forward to our Fiftieth Class Reunion in October and some engaging conversations as we remember where we have been and how we have travelled to get to these challenging times in which we now live.

Peace,

Joe

17

Spinoza, H. Richard Niebuhr, and Ben and Me

Friends:

Over the Christmas holidays, Ben—a native of Enid, Oklahoma, a student of mine during my brief tour at Yale Divinity School in 2005/06, and now a doctoral student under Stanley Hauerwas at Duke—dropped by for a brief overnight visit. In the course of cross-examining him about his upcoming doctoral exams and dissertation venture, I learned that a portion of his dissertation topic will involve an exploration in the philosophy of Baruch Spinoza. The very mention of Spinoza (1632-73) stirred some deep recollections that I shared with Ben and wish now to share here.

In 1954 I matriculated at the University of Oklahoma on an athletic scholarship for basketball and baseball and intending to prepare for a career in law. In the first semester of my sophomore year I took my first course in philosophy under Gustav Mueller, rightly famous as an authority on the philosophy of Hegel. That course excited me greatly and set me on an adventure that would lead me to take over sixty hours of philosophy while at OU.

Of course my excitement led me to reading widely in philosophical literature. I vividly recall that during that fall semester, as I was studying in the library awaiting going to the fieldhouse for basketball practice, I came upon a chapter on Spinoza in Will Durant's *The Story of Philosophy*. Yes, I know, scholars may scoff at Durant, but for me he was about my speed at that moment in time. In that chapter on Spinoza my eyes fell upon a famous

Spinoza, H. Richard Niebuhr, and Ben and Me

Spinoza remark: "the intellectual love of God." Those words sent an electric shock through me, and to this day I still suffer and rejoice under the power of that shock. To love God with one's mind—is it really permissible to think hard about God?

It turns out that Spinoza, a Jew whose family had fled Christian persecution in Spain to the relative safety of Amsterdam, became known as a *pantheist*, affirming that God and the world are two sides of the same reality: God the nontranscendable One of being and the world that One being in all its multiplicity. His critique of both Jewish and Christian forms of traditional or classical theism opened the path for some of the great German thinkers of the late eighteenth and early nineteenth centuries—Fichte, Schelling, Schleiermacher, Hegel. It should be no surprise that Spinoza, who ground lens for a living, was called an *atheist* by Christians and Jews of all stripes.

Today I do not count myself among the followers of Spinoza in the particulars of his metaphysics of God and the world, but I am grateful for that shocking phrase—*the intellectual love of God*—that made me want to keep reading philosophy and postpone going to basketball practice!

Now, about H. Richard Niebuhr: he was one of the 'great theologians' who put Yale Divinity School at the top of the heap in the decades after World War II. Upon arriving at YDS in 1958, I took several courses under Niebuhr, learned much, was absorbed by his wise but cranky demeanor, but did not quite think of myself as his follower or devotee. At that point in his career Niebuhr was becoming sharply critical of two movements of thought that were becoming important to me: the dogmatic theology of Karl Barth and the growing influence of so-called 'linguistic philosophy.'

In June of 1962, I had just completed my first year in the doctoral program at Yale in philosophical theology. Sometime in mid-June I went to the YDS quadrangle, quite abandoned during summer months, to check my mail at the mailboxes under the chapel. As I was retrieving my mail, Professor Niebuhr was retrieving his, and as the only persons there at the boxes, we naturally fell into conversation. He revealed that he was leaving soon for his summer retreat to their cottage in western Massachusetts.

But feisty, pushy students should never pass up the opportunity for some good conversation with a distinguished theologian, so I asked how his work was coming along. In the midst of his long response to my question he said: "I think I am really a Spinozist at heart." That comment was noteworthy—I had never heard others so characterize Niebuhr—but not surprising, as his recent book, *Radical Monotheism and Western Culture* (New York: Harper & Brothers, 1960), seemed to me to have come close to it.

In early July we learned of Niebuhr's sudden death at his cottage on July 5th.

The assumption of the traditional theism of Aquinas and others was that certain metaphysical propositions about God as Pure Act—immutable, impassible, simple and utterly self-sufficient—could be derived by reason alone without recourse to revelation. These metaphysical propositions came to be known as 'natural theology.' I think Spinoza pushed this conception of God as Pure Act so hard that the only candidate really remaining for him was the world itself in its non-derivable oneness: looked at one way the world just is immutable, impassible, simple, self-sufficient and not dependent on any other being; but looked at another way it is mutable, alive, and malleable. Both!

So, the passion of the intellectual love of God remains, but now also the urgent question is which 'God' or which use of the word 'God'? In the absence of the self-revelation of God in Jesus Christ, Spinoza and perhaps Niebuhr had it about right. But, then, there is that Jesus Christ confessed by the church as the Logos of all things and the beginning and the end of all being. For me, a trinitarian understanding of God trumps Spinoza and Aquinas.

Thanks, Ben, for being the occasion of such recollections! In fairness to Ben, though, he is not working on Spinoza's doctrine of God but some other insights into human being and political life. Let it also be said that Ben understands that the intellectual love of God for Christians is indissolubly linked to the daily practices of loving God in how we live and love in relation to our neighbors in the world.

Alas, when I ran this little narrative by my daughter Serene, she reminded me that we named our first cat 'Spinoza'! Go figure.

[Posted 1/4/11]

18

Owen Died, K. Died, Bodies Age, Madge Writes a Christmas Letter, and Life Lurches On

Dear Friends:

Sometime ago, Owen, a member of our Sunday school class, died. He was born the same year as I, 1936. I had only been acquainted with Owen for about eight years, but long enough to have observed sadly his decline in health. I make no claim to have known Owen well or to be in possession of any profound insights into his particular decline in health, except to say that most in the class were not surprised by his death. We all knew death would not be long delayed.

As to be expected, his funeral was held in our church sanctuary, was modestly attended, and was respectful, even though scant use was made of traditional funeral liturgies. But at one point a slideshow was presented displaying a host of photographs of Owen at various ages in his life and under many different circumstances. While I confess that such slideshows at past funerals have been generally burlesque and distasteful, this one overwhelmed me with an astonishing realization—the photos of Owen from his twenties to his fifties were of a man I did not recognize. That handsome, attractive, energetic, and engaging man was the same Owen I knew in his declining years? An Owen whose young bride was a woman of exceptional beauty.

PART THREE—Fragments from Times Past and Emerging Hopes

Obviously, I am writing this blog because Owen's death and funeral stirred an intense range of reflections and musings in me. Here are some further reflections.

Yes, most people under twenty-five know—in a vague sense—that it is inescapable that their bodies will decline as they age. Of course, persons under twenty-five have family and friends that die, but that they themselves are destined to age and to die, well, that lurks unnoticed in the peripheries of awareness. But for those of us blessed—yes, I wrote 'blessed'—to live well beyond that twenty-five or so years, our bodies have become something of a harsh reminder of our finitude, our redolent aches and pains, our mental declines, our mortalizing misgivings, and our search for a reposing wisdom.

Recently, K. died: a sudden and abrupt departure, without goodbyes, without hugs, and without prayers for healing and hope, alone. A robust male in his early twenties, funny, everybody's friend, always eager for a 'good time' in the youthful confidence that there will always be another day tomorrow in which to abbreviate, if not abrogate, dangerous patterns of behavior. There must still be future-time to settle down, finish school, get a job, etc., etc. This 'best friend' of my grandsons and an occasional visitor to our cabin on the lake, was found dead one morning in his sister's apartment. He was irretrievably gone. Disbelief and grief ricocheted through his family and friends, as though the death was an incomprehensible invasion of the sacred precincts of twenty-something males.

Yes, at the funeral—held in a vast theatre-space turned church sanctuary in an abandoned shopping center—there were indeed slides and videos of K. and an unending sequence of testimonies about the loss of their 'best friend.' As we neared the end of the 135-minute service, the fundamentalist minister assured us that K. had accepted Christ and had now 'graduated' to a higher life—a bit early to be sure—but we can also be sure that if he had not accepted Christ, then no graduation, only descent and fire. From his impassioned tongue, we—exactly who 'we' were remained understandably vague—were assured that only Christians will be saved.

The gathered energetically tried to 'celebrate' K.'s life as a beautiful life. Yet at the edges of our souls lurked the horror of his abrupt death and departure, but we could not quite express it—best just to celebrate. But we were all aware that there will be no future funeral for K. in which the gathered family and friends, young and old, will give thanks for a life grown old with bodily decline but having lived robustly for more than seven decades. K.'s recent death cancels any future death at an age-appropriate future-time.

Life Lurches On

Over Christmas, Sarah and I heard from Madge, a Muskogee friend who had moved to Tennessee after the death of her son a few years ago. Madge is an exceptional and admirable example of indefatigable living-life-to-the-fullest, wherein 'fullest' has a definite meaning of being one who survived breast-cancer surgery in her mid-nineties, has now lived beyond one hundred years, and still drives herself on weekly ventures to grocery shop and get her hair 'fixed.' Madge remains in secure possession of a mind and tongue of shocking acuity. With delicate and clear characters and steady strokes, she hand-wrote us a Christmas letter of warmth and concern and hope—hoping that we were 'doing well.' She is skilled at being a blessing to folk. It seems unlikely that we will learn of her death in time to be present for her funeral in Tennessee. But she will not mind our absence; she has never been one to fuss for attention and respect.

Christian faith must surely have at the core of its discourses and practices the intent to train us—a blessedly motley crew of individuals—in how to live as a body in an ever-changing space and time, yet destined to age and finally to die, with no further space and no more time. But Christians cultivate the hope that in death they and other humans will come face-to-face with a divine grace and love. Might it then be transparent to everyone that such graceful love is not a reward we have merited by good deeds or because 'we love Christ so much'? Of course, it is a calling for us all to do good deeds for others and to love Christ. But even for Christians living in time, we will still grimace with grief at the deaths, timely and untimely, of friends and family, and occasionally for those simply far away and vaguely known. Yes, bodies having lived tangled lives, but then maybe the hope for healing, spiritual bodies for all.

[Posted 2/18/12]

19

In Transition but Hopeful

Friends:

In a widely circulated Christmas letter, Sarah and I announced another big transition in our lives that might explain my absence from blogging since late September of 2011. Here is a portion of that letter:

> We greet you with that joy and thanksgiving that is rooted in an overflowing gratitude for the simple but profound gift of God's tabernacling among us in Christ Jesus and sanctifying thereby the gifts of life, of family, of friendships near and far, and of friendships from the distant past and friendships recent and ripe. In the flow of such gratitude, Joe plunged into 75 and Sarah glided into 73 this past year: older?—yes! wiser?—perhaps! robust of body?—perhaps not! robust of spirit?—a work in progress!
>
> In 2000 we retired to Anchor Point, our family cabin since 1970 right on the shore of Ft. Gibson Lake in eastern Oklahoma. Eagles often greet us in the large tree just 30 yards from our living room windows. Fish have been known to sometimes bite our lures, and foxes and deer sleep on our lawns. But we are remote from towns and medical institutions, and we spend much time traveling to shop and find medical care. And, as you might guess, the maintenance of such a place is constant and strenuous.
>
> Our immediate family typically gathers here on July 4th and Thanksgiving. This Thanksgiving time we engaged in a searching and honest discussion, and we all came to the reluctant, even sad, conclusion that Joe and Sarah—aka Dad and Mom, Grandsir and Nami—needed for reasons of health to move to smaller and safer lodgings in the Oklahoma City area and sell Anchor

In Transition but Hopeful

Point. Why OKC? We were both raised there and daughter Kindy and her family live there now. So, in the coming weeks we will start the search in OKC and seek to find a buyer of our beloved 'cabin'—yes, we confess, our 'cabin' is about 3900 square feet! Yet, as one friend opined: "you have been living the dream and now it is time to move on to other challenges and meeting other age-appropriate needs."

As most of you might remember, Sarah had hip-replacement surgery in the fall of 2006, and had two hip displacements in 2007 requiring emergency ambulance transport to the hospital in Muskogee, and in 2008 she had the hip-implant replaced in another surgery. All of that took a heavy physical and psychological toll on Sarah, and falls and the fear of falling have become all too common. And this past year the vision in her left eye was producing triple images and, after months of consultations with her befuddled eye doctors, she had surgery that seems to have restored almost normal vision. Yet, she remains persistently dizzy, the exact cause of which is still unknown, though medical testing continues. Regrettably, especially here at Christmas time, her handwriting is unsteady.

Over the years, many of you, dear distant family and friends near and far, have blessed us with your visits here at Anchor Point. We will miss those casual strolls along the roads, those lingering and relaxed conversations on the veranda overlooking the lake, and the cozy warmth of logs burning in the big fireplace. We may not have as much boarding room at our new home, but the excitement of serious conversation about world, nation, and church will still be available! Come and see us then.

Selling and leaving Anchor Point will not transpire with tranquility. But our anguish and sadness of what has brought us to this transition will not extinguish the wonderful memories we have of an 'anchored' life on the lake amidst family and friends and a plethora of animal companions. We will take Sadie with us! But the eagles and deer and foxes and squirrels and ticks and chiggers will have to remain behind.

Well, the two months since that letter have been hectic. The continuing search for medical solutions to Sarah's vision problems did clarify that there is no evidence now of any brain tumors or massive strokes, but she remains plagued with what we now call peripheral blurred/overlapping images. As I write now, we are still trying to find a path to more promising medical diagnoses and healing therapies.

PART THREE—Fragments from Times Past and Emerging Hopes

As also mentioned in the letter, we were planning on moving to the Oklahoma City area. Well, that destination has been secured with our closing on a cottage at the Epworth Villa Retirement complex in northwest Oklahoma City. We will move there by June, perhaps earlier if we can sell our beloved Anchor Point.

So our lives have been in transition and will be for some time to come. But there is so much of the 'world' transitioning through my mind that I aver now that I will re-engage my website with blogs and postings.

It is also the case that on Tuesday, a group of pastors and laity who have been meeting with me monthly for two years and reading through my *A Grammar of Christian Faith* will have its final session. It is of special note that we will be discussing the over-large but exacting final chapter of the *Grammar* on hope and eschatology. I will miss their acute questions and passions about being Christian in these troubling times. Their steady, insightful, and engaging conversations and their challenges and reports from the frontline have been a blessing to me.

Yes, in transition, but ready now to re-engage church and world through the means of this website. I hope there are some still there who might care to read some more of my critical encounters with church and world.

[Posted 2/13/12]

20

On Hearing a Sermon

Friends:

I confess that I am one of those ecclesial Neanderthals who still 'go to church'—that is, attend a worship service being performed by a group of folk who characterize themselves as in some sense 'Christian.' And my going to church is in part stimulated by my own need to 'hear' something I cannot say to myself. Yes, I say a bunch of things to myself day in and day out, and that can often be rather prideful and confusing. I go to church on the tentative assumption that the folk gathered there, more or less, acknowledge they are called there—called together—because they stand in a tradition that believes God has spoken to human beings in some way and in some form. I assume the folk there gathered are armed with Bibles, understood now as authoritative testimonies to God's speaking.

I go to church, therefore, in the ever-renewing hope that in that gathering of folk I will hear a sermon. I use 'sermon' here as a theological word, not simply a reference to any talk or speech that intends to lecture or tell or inform the audience of something interesting. In popular usage the word 'sermon' sometimes suggest 'preaching' as a form of address that is accusatory of the misdeeds or the misinformation of those gathered as the audience. Hence, in our presumably postmodern world, a sermon smells of moral arrogance and interference in our 'private' lives. Who wants to hear a sermon detailing one's missteps, misplaced affections, misdeeds, and misjudgments? Uplifting—that is what the folk want, but of course that sort of uplifting that feels good, at least for a few moments, perhaps lasting through lunch.

Part Three—Fragments from Times Past and Emerging Hopes

So let me own up to the following, which should be no surprise to the few who might read this small meandering blog. I was raised in a church-going family, hence in some sense I was raised in the church. My father taught a men's 'Bible Class' with faithfulness of preparation and presence; the class always sang the old hymns with gusto, but I never heard my father *sing*. My family—two older brothers, an older sister, and my parents—always sat on the back row during the worship service. In the tradition of the Disciples of Christ, we celebrated the Lord's Supper every Sunday, though I could not participate until I had been baptized. During the passing of the bread and cup down the rows, I always kept my eye on Mrs. Hempstead: an imposing woman of substantial proportions and startling red hair sitting alone a few rows in front of us. Invariably as she received the bread and cup she would weep; it was amazingly evident even to me that her weeping was exceptional but appropriate. Apart from that, Mrs. Hempstead never struck me as a sad woman. Might she be weeping the weep of overwhelming joy in the overcoming of some commanding sadness and despair? I wasn't sure, but I was sure that something really important was happening right there in that service in her soulful bodily movements and the passing of the bread and cup. And the sermons? Well, they happened too but seldom gathered my attention, though I never could rid myself of the thought that the sermons *should matter* to me. But I never blamed the preachers for my inattention. I had other things on my mind that seemed more interesting.

Yet somehow I got caught up in preparing for ministry as I skirted through college and then, surprising to everyone, got married and went off to seminary. Later, there came a career or vocation teaching theology to seminary students preparing for the ministry of the church. There is no need for further rehearsal of those matters, except to note that I always thought the church was itself a subject of great importance, but forever disappointing in its actual life—messy earthen vessels. But I have never been able to ignore the power of my conviction that the most important task any congregational pastor has to perform was that of preaching the Word. And yet over these several decades, apart from many incidents of being straightened, judged, and uplifted by a disarming sermon, I confess that my disappointments with pastors/preachers are numbing in retrospect and in fact. Yes, they are all-too-human, but might it be divinely possible that even a fragile and frightened human could muster the *savoir faire* and the humble courage to witness to a Gospel that he or she neither controls nor sanctifies?

On Hearing a Sermon

As my web friends might surmise, my seminary students over the years were exposed often to my tirades about ministers insufficient to their calling. Insofar as my students have also been exposed to my overly stringent inspection of *what* they say and *how* they say it in their essays, sermons, and conversations, they wonder aloud whether any of them could endure having me in the congregation, listening critically to their every word and gesture. They find me incredible—unbelievable—when I tell them how much I *need* to be addressed by the sermon, and be addressed time and again, without ceasing. None of us trained in ministry have either the wisdom or the truth-telling capacity to preach to ourselves, though many are we/they who seem to try. For most of the human race, the Word of judgment and grace needs to be spoken by another. But a sermon empty of theological insight and passion, thrown together at the last minute, largely ignorant of the scripture and bereft of a skillfully learned use of the English language— well is it really a *sermon* rooted in the revelatory summons of the God of Israel that we know in Jesus Christ through the Holy Spirit? Or is it a lazy, arrogant, and unrepentant blaspheming of the Spirit and to those gathered in the name of the Spirit?

Let me put a point on this: I want a preacher whose preaching conveys: 1) a sense of being well-grounded in the biblical testimony and capacitated to sort through the variations and even contradictions of its many verses; 2) a sense of being familiar with and capacitated to sort through the host of learned preachers and teachers—their discourses and practices—in the rich ecumenical traditions of the church; 3) a learned discernment, perhaps gathered by reading history, current news, and literature, of the present situation of the church in whatever local, regional, national, and international variation it is located; and 4) a profound and compassionate sense for the gnarled, broken ambiguity of the gathered folk, yearning for a good and truthful word of judgment, forgiveness, and hope. Well, put it sharply: might they have been yearning to hear the Gospel of Jesus Christ?

I do admit that from time to time I have been addressed and encouraged by some faithful preachers, but in these later years, amidst so much junk religiosity, hard-hearted fundamentalism, and scurrilous political rhetoric, I am yearning to *hear* a sermon faithful and discerning of a divine Gospel.

Sarah and I, especially since our recent move to Oklahoma City, have been in such a search for some time and there have been some bitter disappointments. Yet recently, by the grace of God, we heard a preacher speaking the Word, discerning and fetching, biblical and literate, with uncanny gestures, and kind, winsome tones. We did not have to preach to ourselves, and we were relieved of the burden of complaint about the nincompoop in the pulpit as we wended our way home after the service.

The preacher is Gary Byrkit, pastor of Southern Hills Christian Church in Edmond, Oklahoma. We have had no previous history of association and conversation, though his name had come up in other conversations and had been recommended by other friends. For more than twenty years, Reverend Byrkit has formed a congregation of surprisingly interesting folk passionate about God's work and summons right here in 'River City'—well if not River City, then here in the land of hysterical voices on the right, loud and supremely confident that god is on their side! In the midst of all that sound and fury, Sarah and I have been blessed to hear a Gospel of peace and good will in the name of Jesus Christ.

Yes, I *heard* a sermon and it made a difference! I needed it, and thankfully I have been deprived, for awhile, of my souring contempt for superficial church language and practice. Thanks be to God!

I hope my friends have heard a sermon recently that made a salvific difference. Perhaps some have recently preached such sermons redolent in the Spirit. I pray that it has been so.

And yes, some of my dearest friends are pastors, but their congregations are either far away or deposited in a forlorn past. And some of these dear friends have found their pastoring and preaching unwelcomed by the reigning self-interests of their congregations.

I thank God that there are some saints out there—known and unknown to me—who week after week labor over faithfulness in worship and preaching—*what* to say and *how* to say it—and stride hopeful into the pulpit armed with the Gospel of Jesus Christ.

[Posted 7/18/12]

Part Four

Sermons Ventured on Behalf of the
Witness of the Beloved Church

21

On Being Identified as Ambassadors for Christ

A sermon preached at the ordination of our youngest daughter, Verity Augusta Jones, at a joint service of the Christian Church (Disciples of Christ) and the United Church of Christ in Colchester, Connecticut on March 25, 1995. Verity is now Executive Director of the Center for Pastoral Excellence at Christian Theological Seminary in Indianapolis.

2 Corinthians 5:16-21

> From now on, therefore, we regard no one from a human point of view; even though we once knew Christ from a human point of view, we know him no longer in that way. So if anyone is in Christ, there is a new creation: everything old has passed away; see, everything has become new! All this is from God, who reconciled us to himself through Christ, and has given us the ministry of reconciliation; that is, in Christ God was reconciling the world to himself, not counting their trespasses against them, and entrusting the message of reconciliation to us. So we are ambassadors for Christ, since God is making his appeal through us; we entreat you on behalf of Christ, be reconciled to God. For our sake he made him to be sin who knew no sin, so that in him we might become the righteousness of God.

Part Four—Sermons Ventured on Behalf of the Witness

It is a wonderful occasion to participate in the ordaining of a person to Christian ministry. The wonder becomes even more intense and overwhelming when the person is your youngest daughter, grown now into competent and commanding adulthood. Many of you know Verity as just this confident, intelligent, and astute friend, pastor, or colleague. You probably don't have packet full of 'little Verity' stories gathered over the years of close observation amidst the intricacies of familial dynamics better left undescribed and unexplained. I will not regale you now with these delicious and revealing stories. But I do confess the wonder and pride of now seeing her stand before us this day, a woman of stature and great promise, seeking the church's ordination to a future of ministerial leadership for the church.

We are here, then, to ordain Verity Augusta Jones: a solemn act by the church and, like marriage, to be entered into 'reverently and in the fear of the Lord.' And to do this act of ordaining this day and in these times should occasion some serious questioning and pondering by us all.

Questions for us and questions for Verity:

1. Who are we who are engaged in this ordaining?
2. What sort of community is this gathered church that intends to ordain?
3. What is the real identity and character of the church?
4. Why do we ordain persons to special leadership?

I would suppose that many of the churches today in North America might have grave difficulties in trying to grasp and articulate just who they are and what their most distinctive character and identity is. And just *who are we* who are here to participate in this profound ordaining act?

These questions are crucially important and invite us to consider briefly this passage from Paul's second letter to the beleaguered church at Corinth. Paul, the Apostle of Jesus Christ with a primary mission to the Gentile or non-Jewish world, writes to his Corinthian fellow Christians by everywhere using the inviting and inclusive pronoun 'we'—even though we readers know that throughout the letter it is a rhetorical 'we' intending to appeal to and persuade his Corinthian readers of what is properly involved in a 'ministry of reconciliation' as 'ambassadors for Christ.' Perhaps it would be helpful if we who are gathered here today consider ourselves included in the 'we' of this provocative passage.

So Paul says: "*We regard no one from a human point of view.*" Literally translated it means we regard no one "*according to the flesh.*"

And this fleshy way of regarding folk is in contrast to the way 'we' regard folk when we regard them from the point of view of their being in Christ. Hence, this fleshy human point of view seems to have once been held by the Corinthian Christians—and even by us—but has now been abandoned as we have come to see persons in anew through Jesus Christ.

It should be instructive for us who have presumably abandoned this *fleshy point of view* to pause for a bit and ask just what is this human, all-too-human, point of view. It appears that the fleshy view is quite commodious and includes those many ways of seeing others with the eyes of the worlds in which persons live and move and have their being. These worlds of human conjuring are the ones in which all of us were raised and that beckon and shape us day by day. These are the *worlds of principalities and powers* that are quite expert at telling persons exactly who they are and what they are to become, what they are to consider the range of the real possibilities of their lives. These fleshy powers are ready and eager to stamp us all with an *identity and destiny* that serves their interests and their hopes. The human points of view are *legion*, and they are persistently powerful in their maneuvering and effectiveness. In fact, none of us has escaped their pervasive and formative power: from these worlds of social arrangements and provisions *we have a fleshy identity and place*. These powers never let up, they never sleep, their vigilance is stunning, they are intent on winning their ways among us, they are not easily disarmed or defeated. And we adopt their point of view about ourselves and about the others who make up the world. *We become this fleshy, human world.*

Hence, when we ask about our identity this day in the church, we want to be the 'we' who have adopted Christ's point of view and have thereby defeated and given up the fleshy naming and valuing of ourselves and all others. And isn't this just the dilemma of the church in our time: we are overwhelmed with the identities and values that the world has assigned to us and which we have made our own? 'We' struggle to grasp an identity in Christ, but the flesh is so strong and attractive and seductive.

There are at least *two fleshy worlds* that live in the midst of the churches in North America and constantly threaten the church's identity in Christ.

First, there is quite simply the identity the church is given by *the world of U.S.A. citizenship*. When push comes to shove in how we intend to live our lives and make decisions, this world of citizenship, with its markets, jobs, politics, pecking orders, and its distribution of goods is so definitive

PART FOUR—Sermons Ventured on Behalf of the Witness

and 'creator-like' that we are thoroughly shaped by it. I fear that the churches of the U.S.A. are given their most basic identity, values, and mission by this powerful and commanding world. And this world expects the church to be its emissary and promoter.

Second, there is the *world of global and pluralistic visions and aspirations* that seems intent on dismantling the world of U.S.A. sovereign citizenship. The church in this fleshy world of naming and sanctioning is no more than *one limited group among many other groups and religions* and therefore it should diminish its truth claims and identity. Whatever the talk of the divine might involve, it should be relatively hushed and humble and nonevangelistic. Indeed for the powers of this self-conscious pluralistic world, the church should be an emissary of limited claims.

It seems to me that both of these *human renderings and regardings* have found conflicting residences in the church of today. They do indeed war within the church, within us, within the '*we*' that Paul is addressing and trying to persuade to another point of view. Both of these worlds, precisely because they seem so persuasive to us, lay heavy claims on the church, and each beckons the church to become its emissary.

So, then what is this other point of view that Paul wants to differentiate from the all too attractive and powerful human points of view?

First, this *alternative view* is that of persons who have an overwhelming sense of the old passing away and having been graciously given a *new identity, a new creation*. How is that? All this gracious giving of the new is accomplished by the God who acted in Jesus, the Jew from Nazareth, to reconcile the whole world of creatures to Godself.

And again how did 'we' come to this? This God has acted in the cross and resurrection of Jesus Christ to show persons that they need no longer be subject to their fleshy worlds of judging themselves and others by their various standards of worldly deviance and sin. These worlds of human judgment are evacuated of their power to tell 'us' who we are and what we are worth and what we are to become. This is to us 'goods news', even as it is peculiar and odd news when compared to the daily news of the principalities and powers.

So, Christians, 'we' stand or fall according to the truth and power of this *Gospel of God's work in Jesus Christ*. We are given a new point of view that sweeps away the other points of reference and determination. And therefore, we are given a task: we are given a *ministry of reconciliation*.

On Being Identified as Ambassadors for Christ

We are called to be the community of persons who have the *defining and identifying aim* of declaring in word and deed, that is, in declaring with our very lives, that the Creator of all things has graciously loved and acted to save the world from its self-chosen but finally fruitless, hopeless, and violent ways of living.

Indeed, as the church, we are called to be a community of new creatures, to be ambassadors for Christ, to be emissaries of mercy and peace to this human world of misery and lostness. But as emissaries of Christ, we have nothing to boast of, nothing of our own superiority. We are merely the forgiven sinners who, in saying 'yes' to the Gospel, entrust our lives to this crucified Savior as the One who *resurrects hopes* and *buries the kingdoms of death*.

We are not emissaries of the world of U.S.A. citizenship and power, nor are we emissaries of the world of pluralistic dismantling. We are emissaries for Jesus Christ, the Savior of the world. As the Christ's ambassadors, we are carriers of a message of peace and justice, of a message of *God's life of reconciliation* among the people of the various worlds.

Can we bear this point of view, can we truly know ourselves as reconciled in Christ and thereby know ourselves as called to works of love on behalf of all the humans we now know as *neighbors in Christ*?

This is our ministry, the ministry of all those who have a new identity in Jesus Christ. This is not simply the ministry of the church's ordained ministers. As we ordain Verity to the leadership of the church of Jesus Christ, we know she is an ambassador, an emissary with us for the world.

So, we come to ask what it means for this all too human church of Jesus Christ, which struggles daily in the world to claim its identity and mission as witness to God's reconciling Gospel—what does it mean to *ordain* persons for leadership within the church?

The 'Free Church' traditions which are ordaining Verity today have been loath to make too high claims about the status and separateness of the ordained minister. It thus becomes important to be clear as to just what these traditions are ordaining Verity for and to. Let me state a few bold points.

We are calling and entrusting Verity to the special responsibility of keeping us the church clear and committed about our purpose and identity as ambassadors for Christ who is God's reconciliation of the world to Godself.

PART FOUR—Sermons Ventured on Behalf of the Witness

We are calling and entrusting Verity to *preach and teach* this Gospel of Jesus Christ in such wise that we may have our lives graced and forgiven and our daily paths illuminated by the light of this sovereign grace. Among other things she is entrusted to teach us the witness of Holy Scripture as a living and authorizing witness today.

We are calling and entrusting Verity to be a vibrant and articulate *visionary* for us, to point to God's surprising possibilities for us as agents of reconciliation. We need her vision as a dedicated and trained Christian *woman* to lift up the hope that calls us into action on behalf of the world's forgotten and neglected and calls us to be parables of God's ultimate redemption of all.

We are calling and entrusting Verity to be a muscular and truth-telling *prophet* in our midst, to remind us of our wandering and befuddling omissions, of our inclinations to be conformed cowardly to the world, of our propensity to tell and enjoy the lie about ourselves, the neighbor and about human well-being.

We are calling and entrusting Verity to be our caring *pastor*, who loves us with a steady openness to our weaknesses and sufferings, to be our friend and companion in discovering daily how to become God's new creation in the midst of a troubled and stressed world.

These callings and entrustings are, of course, impossible just in themselves. They become graciously empowered possibilites by the movement of the Holy Spirit in Verity and in the church.

As a not-so-neutral observer, I declare my conviction that Verity is equipped and ready to take on these challenging tasks of Servant Leadership. She has already been a rich blessing to many of us, and her promise is great to become a blessing and a gift to the future of the church of Jesus Christ.

In this ordaining, then, we pray for the Holy Spirit to continue to renew us, to empower us to give up the old lives we learned from the worlds in which we have lived, and to empower us to live as free ambassadors of reconciliation among the warring people of the various worlds of human conjuring. And we pray for Verity that she may live from the new creation she is in Christ and live toward the redemptive future God is bringing for the worlds.

All this dear friends, who are the *'we' of Paul's church*, I have dared to preach in the Name of the Father, the Son, and the Holy Spirit, One God, Mother of us all. Amen.

22

Jesus, the Family, and the Summons of the Kingdom

A sermon preached on June 26, 2005 at St. Paul United Methodist Church in Muskogee, Oklahoma. Published in Encounter, *vol. 67, no. 2 (Spring 2006), 199–206.*

Matthew 10:34–39

> Do not think that I have come to bring peace to the earth; I have not come to bring peace, but a sword. For I have come to set a man against his father, and a daughter against her mother, and a daughter-in-law against her mother-in-law; and one's foes will be members of one's own household. Whoever loves father or mother more than me is not worthy of me; and whoever loves son or daughter more than me is not worthy of me; and whoever does not take up the cross and follow me is not worthy of me. Those who find their life will lose it, and those who lose their life for my sake will find it.

This passage from the Gospel according to Matthew must surely strike us as strange and shocking. At the very least it must challenge some of the loose and careless assumptions that seem to be rife in the life of the church today.

One of those assumptions is that the Bible is easy to read and accessible in its meaning to any earnest individual. To be sure, much of our Holy

Jesus, the Family, and the Summons of the Kingdom

Scripture is quite transparent in its meaning, but so too there are many passages that remain obscure to any facile interpretation.

For those who think the whole Bible must be interpreted 'literally,' this passage is a stumbling block. Are we to believe that Jesus—who is represented elsewhere in Matthew and all the other Gospels as blessing peacemakers and bringing peace to his followers—has now changed his mind and is literally saying he "has not come to bring peace to the earth"; rather he has come to bring "a sword"? Are we to believe that Jesus is literally advocating the sword and the dismemberment of the family, as a condition for being his followers?

We will explore these questions in this sermon today. We will worry about the practice, often performed by Christian interpreters, of taking Bible passages out of context and as sentences that can stand alone with clear meanings.

Another of those easy assumptions in the life of the church is that the care and nurture of family is first and foremost for the disciple of Jesus. There is a whole movement today that seems to emphasize what it calls "family values" as being at the heart of Christian faith. But this passage in Matthew does seem to raise the question of just what is the relation between following Jesus and being a member of a family.

If this passage is supposed to be literally transparent in meaning, then where does it leave us in our understanding of discipleship to Jesus and our assumed responsibilities to our families? In our time many church folk do talk as though they believe that family obligations are front and center in Christian faith and practice.

In light of these consternations arising from this passage, I propose that we aim to work our way through them and thereby hopefully discern what divine Word there might be for us amidst the complexities of this scriptural passage.

First, let us say something about the Gospel of Matthew as a whole. It is generally agreed among scholars of the church that Matthew's Jesus is wrestling with God's summons to prepare for the coming of God's Kingdom in the midst of a Judaism that was itself under continual assault from its surrounding and dominating Gentile world. Jews were striving to be faithful to their God, who had covenanted with them and given the commandments by which they were to live.

In this Gospel, Jesus stands before us as a Jew in the prophetic tradition of Israel, who is bringing the life of Israel under prophetic critique. Something is profoundly amiss in Israel's life as God's elected people. Jesus is himself summoning the people of Israel to respond to what God is doing in bringing a new Kingdom to birth in Jesus' own time and in his own work and preaching in the midst of Israel. While the coming of God's Kingdom is a blessing for the people, it also demands new commitments to the Kingdom's radical character. The whole of this Gospel is about discipleship to Jesus as the One who is bringing God's Kingdom.

There are, therefore, repeated occasions in Matthew in which Jesus the Jew is in conflict with other Jews over what it means to be the people of God. It is clear that Jesus is not attacking the Jewish belief that God has elected Israel and has given special commandments to Israel. But sometimes Jesus is challenging the way those commandments have been interpreted in Israel, and sometimes he makes the commandments even more strict and severe than many other rabbis would make them.

With these general remarks in our minds, let us look closely at our passage for today. Matthew represents Jesus as saying:

> Do not think that I have come to bring peace to the earth;
> I have not come to bring peace, but a sword.
> for I have come to set a man against his father,
> and a daughter against her mother,
> and daughter-in-law against her mother-in-law,
> and one's foes will be members of one's own household.
> (Matt 10:34–35)

It might appear, then, that Jesus is setting himself over against the fifth commandment in the Ten Commandments, namely, "*Honor your father and mother*" (Exod 20:12). In the life of Israel, honoring father and mother was part of a *social system* in which fathers and mothers and children had kinfolk who made up an extended family, who then also made up a clan and then a tribe and then a nation bound together by family loyalties. These familial relationships were crucial to Israel's sense of solidarity and identity. When this familial system was undermined, the very life and identity of Israel was distorted and damaged.

Jesus, the Family, and the Summons of the Kingdom

We should also note that Israel's family system was decidedly patriarchal in character, in which the male was the dominant authority and decision-maker in and for the family.

So we must ask, "Is Jesus really demanding that this familial system be dismantled?" Most of us want to rush in and say, "Of course not; families are important to Jesus." And indeed in Matthew 15:4, Jesus explicitly affirms the commandment to honor father and mother.

But we must also look at another passage in Matthew 12:46–50 in which Jesus himself raises the question of who really is his "mother" and "brothers." Then Jesus points to his disciples and says, *"Here are my mother and my brothers! For whoever does the will of my Father in heaven is my brother and sister and mother."*

It should be evident to us that something *extraordinary* is being conveyed by Jesus about the *ordinary* ways in which Jews—and we might add, most cultural family systems—have talked about the priority of ethnic family and kinship. So, why is Jesus deliberately distancing himself from this priority of family obligations and systems?

Is it too much to suggest that Jesus, in all four Gospels, is consistently drawing attention to those given assumptions and practices in human societies that often are the sources of rivalry, enmity, violence, and armed conflict? Is it not true that Jesus knows that much violence is perpetrated in the name of protecting one's family and nation from an alien enemy that is outside the family? Does Jesus correctly discern that family pride and honor are repeatedly at the root of the revenge and retaliation that literally populate the whole of human history?

Perhaps Jesus is aware of a dark side to family relationships that might thwart and stand in the way of a family member becoming a disciple of Jesus?

As a good Jew, Jesus would have been acquainted with the fragility and volatility of family life as seen in the Hebrew Scriptures: in the primordial family of Adam and Eve, Cain slays brother Abel; Jacob deceives brother Esau out of his inheritance; in a jealous rage, Joseph's brothers sell him into slavery and lie to their father, Jacob; King David and Absalom his son become rivals with fatal consequences. In Jesus' own parable of the prodigal son, the elder brother is consumed with jealous rivalry about the father's extravagant welcome home to the prodigal brother.

PART FOUR—Sermons Ventured on Behalf of the Witness

Even in our own time it is empirically evident that an overwhelming percentage of murders in America occur in domestic situations fraught with rivalry, anger, and conflict. Family intimacies and estrangements can be a terrible breeding ground for violence and the disfigurement of human life.

Now with regard to Jesus' apparent bringing of a sword, we must proceed with caution and care. Consider this: we simply cannot read Matthew's account in chapters 5, 6, and 7 of what we call the "Sermon on the Mount" and still believe that Jesus is intent on finding ways to justify violence of the sword within the family, or against folk who offend family honor and pride or find ways to justify violence against those who would harm family and tribe! While we—the people of the church down through the centuries—have continually tried to find ways to justify violence against some people whom we think deserve to die, there is nothing in Matthew's Jesus or the rest of the New Testament to suggest that the Kingdom of God that Jesus is proclaiming and enacting is one that initiates, inspires, and justifies violence against folk who resist the Kingdom.

Surely it is too much to suggest, however, that Jesus is out to dismantle the natural family and bring it to an end. But surely it is also too much to suggest that Jesus gives absolute priority to familial loyalties, relationships, and traditions.

The issue for Jesus is that following him in response to the impinging of God's Kingdom is the first priority in the life of the disciple. No other loyalty should intervene, delay, or undermine one's loyalty to God's Kingdom. Hence, there is an incessant urgency in how we are to respond to Jesus and his proclamation of the Kingdom. All other urgencies and loyalties are to be ordered to the priority of God's Kingdom summons.

This urgency and priority is expressed by Jesus in Matthew 8:21–22, in which Jesus responds to the request by a would-be disciple to delay following Jesus in order to go bury his father. To that request, Jesus says, "*Follow me, and let the dead bury their own dead.*" This is a tough saying for those of us who could not think of a more pressing priority than burying a dead parent.

Let us pause here, as I can feel a chill wind settling over us as we grapple with Jesus' words about family relationships and the Kingdom of God. Maybe we are afraid that Jesus is calling us to a *policy* of forgetting about

Jesus, the Family, and the Summons of the Kingdom

family, of abandoning the family, of refusing to bury the dead, of refusing to honor mother and father.

Certainly we should not conclude that Jesus is advocating an anti-family policy, but we must understand—as folk who think of ourselves as being disciples of Jesus—that such discipleship is not simply a reinforcement of society's mores and relationships. Jesus is bringing in something new, something that will turn the world upside down, that will reorient who we call brother and sister and who we are called to love. This new Kingdom will bring great tension and suffering into the world's ordinary arrangements of powers and loyalties.

To follow Jesus is to travel soberly down a narrow path that is not gladly endorsed by the powers of the world. The Kingdom of God is like a new household, a new family, a family of reconciliation and peace that is not under the control of the given and ordinary familial authorities and rulers of the world.

So, has Jesus undermined the family? It depends on the family system about which you are talking. Jesus certainly does subordinate the family, with its systems of obligations, to the priorities of discipleship and the Kingdom of God. It is within the priorities of the Kingdom of God that the disciple is to discover and enact what it means to be a good father or a good mother or a good son or a good daughter.

Listen again to Jesus' further words in our passage for today:

> Whoever loves father or mother more than me is not worthy of me; and whoever loves son or daughter more than me is not worthy of me; and whoever does not take up the cross and follow me is not worthy of me. Those who find their life will lose it, and those who lose their life for my sake will find it. (Matt 10:37–39)

Remember, this taking-up-the-cross is not a symbol for bravely bearing the various and miscellaneous miseries and sufferings of ordinary and everyday human life. Rather, the cross is the brutal symbol of the Roman world's power and dominance. Jesus was strung upon a cross as a sign that Rome was in charge and that this Jesus was a political offense against the authority and sensibilities of the Roman world and of some Jewish leaders.

In this passage in Matthew, Jesus is warning the would-be disciple that following him might well bring one into conflict with the established political and religious orders that intend to control human life and dictate what is the good and acceptable order. The disciple must expect a collision with the world—and possibly with one's family—that will bring suffering for the disciple. That collision might well set a son against his father to the extent the father expects the son to order his life to the father's authority and control. To take up the cross of discipleship to Jesus is to be willing to bear the costs of the suffering that may well befall the disciple as he encounters the ruling powers in the world and in the family.

Even so, discipleship to Jesus and its consequent cross-bearing is not to be understood as a punishing burden. Rather, cross-bearing is a blessing to the disciple insofar as it is teaching the disciple how to truly live before God and with family, with neighbors, with strangers, and with enemies and therewith to receive and gain her life. The world—and often the world of the family—would have the family member believe that a true and meaningful life is only accessible through those social networks that reward familial status and inheritance and achievement and honor.

Listen carefully to Jesus: the logic of losing and gaining life is different for the disciple from the logic of the world.

Perhaps we can put the priority of discipleship and the Kingdom in this way:

Follow Jesus, and, in so following, love your parents and your children and your family.

Follow Jesus, and, in so following, bury the dead.

Follow Jesus, and, in so following, refuse the instruments of violence and do not return evil for evil.

Follow Jesus, and, in so following, love the enemy and be a peacemaker.

Follow Jesus, and, in so following, you will learn how to live boldly under the grace of God's impinging Kingdom.

Follow Jesus, and, in so following, you may well experience the suffering that will come upon you when the world—with its familial and political loyalties—realizes that your following Jesus undermines your loyalty to the world's priorities, politics, and loyalties.

The peace Jesus is bringing is not a peace that will preserve the disciple from harm or suffering or death; it is not a peace that will leave the disciple and her world undisturbed; it is not a peace that encourages passivity and complacency.

Jesus, the Family, and the Summons of the Kingdom

The sword Jesus is bringing is not a sword for violently slaying the evildoer; it is the metaphorical sword that reminds the disciple that her discipleship will displace and reorient the previous loyalties of her life.

> *Narrow is the way of the Kingdom*
> *but glorious is the blessing that it bestows.*
> *May those who have ears to hear and eyes to see*
> *be blessed by these words.*

All this I have dared to preach in the name of the Father, and of the Son, and of the Holy Spirit, One God, Mother of us all. Amen.

23

Behold, The Lamb of God

A sermon preached at Marquand Chapel in Yale Divinity School on October 25, 2005, at the time I was Visiting Professor of Theology at YDS, 2005–2006.

Revelation 4:1—5:14

This lectionary reading for today from the Book of Revelation is bristling with imaginative language that can just as easily be abused as used fruitfully in the life of the church. As I try to make some sense of this passage, I suggest we bear in mind the following preliminary points:

1. The Book is written in that sort of imaginative language scholars call 'apocalyptic,' in which the impending future is the time of God's great reckoning with the destiny of the world.

2. While the text itself does not claim to be written by John the disciple, the author does assert that he has received a "revelation of Jesus Christ" sent to him by an angel, and he considers himself among those in the early church who prophesy in the name of Jesus.

3. The text is addressed primarily to seven churches in what was called Asia Minor, which were under severe persecution by Roman authorities, and the text aims to give the churches hope for the final triumph of Jesus Christ in the coming future, even if during the present times many have been persecuted and many more will be persecuted for their commitment to Jesus Christ.

4. The text itself had a difficult time being accepted into the New Testament canon and was one of the later texts finally deemed apostolic in faith and character, if not in authorship.

5. In our time this text has become the normative blue print of the 'End Times' for the folk on the right wing of the church, in which Jesus will return in judgment in the near future, at which time those who have not affirmed Jesus as Lord and Savior will be consumed by fire, even cast into lakes of fire.

For those of us in the middle or in the left wing of the church, this book seems to have a distinctly sour taste and foul odor, and we might wish the early church had left it among the non-canonical books and thereby relieved us of the unhappy burden of trying to interpret or even to preach from the text.

Everyone agrees that the Book intends to give consolation and hope to the churches being persecuted by the Roman Empire. Lest we think that persecution is similar to that social prejudice today in which persons of faith are thought to be irrational and obscurantist by their secular neighbors, hear what was written by a Roman provincial governor named Pliny to the Roman Emperor named Trajan in the early decades of the second century. Referring to the Christians that were being brought before him, Pliny writes:

> I have handled those who have been denounced as Christians as follows: I asked them whether they were Christians. Those who responded affirmatively I have asked a second and third time, under threat of the death penalty. If they persisted in their confession, I had them executed. For whatever it is that they are actually advocating, it seems to me that obstinacy and stubbornness must be punished in any case.
>
> Those who denied being Christians now or in the past, I thought necessary to release, since they invoked our gods according to the formula I gave them and since they offered sacrifices of wine and incense before your image which I had brought in for that purpose along with the statues of our gods. I also had them curse Christ. It is said that real Christians cannot be forced to do any of these things.

Part Four—Sermons Ventured on Behalf of the Witness

> Others charged by this accusation at first admitted that they had once been Christians, but had already renounced it; they had in fact been Christians, but had given it up, some as long as twenty-five years ago.[1]

So, these Christians were considered criminals by the empire, unwilling to be obedient to those practices in which the empire and its gods and its Caesar were worshiped and honored as the real powers that gave order and meaning to the lives of its citizens. At least the Romans recognized that the Christians, in refusing to renounce Jesus Christ as Lord and pay honors to the empire, were committing a treasonable political act punishable by execution. Perhaps Christians are just too radical and subversive of empire to be allowed to roam freely among the people.

How then might one build up hope among the beleaguered Christians facing such definite and drastic persecution, that sort of persecution that takes away one's life, not merely one's dignity and pride? It is not uncommon in human history that persons who have been unjustly treated exhibit uncommon courage and hold out against their oppressors in the hope that justice will finally be done and their oppressors will receive the just reckoning they deserve: the oppressors will ultimately get it in the neck.

At stake here is who we think God is and upon whom we base our hope for deliverance. In the Book of Revelation there are some competing images and themes about God, Jesus, hope, the future, and who finally reigns and who is finally saved.

One set of images goes something like this: The Lord Jesus Christ, the Lion of Judah and the root of David, will come soon and rescue the true believers who have remained faithful in good works and uncorrupted by the Roman empire and its ways of life. But not only will *Jesus the Lion* rescue and redeem the faithful, he will also slay the evildoers, the unfaithful, the fornicators, the liars, the cowards, the sorcerers, the polluted, the murderers, and the idolaters, casting them into a deservedly loathsome lake of fire and sulphur (21:8). Justice will finally be meted out when Jesus comes, displaying that fearsome and violent power—that sheer coercive force—that will administer just deserts to the living and the dead.

Something close to this has been an attractive picture that has echoed down through the centuries in the church as the defining outline of that ultimate judgment and consummation that awaits all humans: *a dual*

---

1. Quoted in M. Eugene Boring and Fred B. Craddock, *The People's New Testament Commentary* (Louisville: Westminster John Knox, 2004), 761.

destiny in which the Christians will be saved and the non-Christians will be damned.

To be sure it seems good and fitting that those being persecuted for their faithful lives should take comfort and strength in remembering the power and strength of Jesus Christ. Remain faithful, we can say, because the power of Rome and all the empires, all the cities that human beings might construct, are not the powers that can confer blessing and hope ultimately. They shall all, in their administering of their empires, finally wither and fall into corruption from lies and idolatry. Empires might protect the strong and mighty and destroy their enemies, but they cannot bestow everlasting redemption. Do not trust them to do so and therefore do not give them the power to confer final meaning and truth on your lives.

But then, in what do we Christians trust, to whom do we take comfort even when our lives are at stake? Is it the Lion Jesus who will finally avenge the death-dealing the evildoers have visited upon the faithful?

But listen there is another strand in Revelation that gets lost in this popular picture. Can we hear it, can we see it, can we imagine it?

In those heavenly realms in which ultimate matters are decided and justice meted out, there is a throne and through an open door John can see the throne. There is One seated on the throne, surrounded by a rainbow and by wise elders and dancing spirits, and lightning and thunder echo throughout the chamber of the throne. Many are the creatures gathered around the throne, and day and night without ceasing they sing about the One sitting on the throne:

> Holy, Holy, Holy, the Lord God the Almighty, who was and is and is to come. (4:8)

> You are worthy, our Lord and God, to receive glory and honor and power, for you created all things, and by your will they existed and were created. (4:11)

The Creator of all things is the One on the throne! But there is a scroll in the right hand of the Creator, and an angel asks:

> "Who is worthy to open the scroll and break its seals?" And no one in heaven or on earth or under the earth has been able to open the scroll and read what the future holds. (5:2–3)

PART FOUR—Sermons Ventured on Behalf of the Witness

The scroll of the future has been sealed up and unreadable. And John the prophetic seer begins to weep bitterly. Are we not lost in the midst of the travail of tears of this life of persecution and death if we cannot see into the future and know that upon which we can hope? The future is so dark and death so near at hand. Who can assure us about the future?

Then a wise elder says to John:

> "Do not weep. See the Lion of the tribe of Judah, the Root of David, has conquered, so that he can open the scroll and its seven seals." (5:5)

Ah, the Lion of Judah, the strongest among the creatures, who devours all challengers? Surely we can trust in his knowledge and strength.

And just as we are ready to heed the Lion and clutch his mighty mane and praise his ferocious jaws and teeth, John sees a extraordinarily strange sight:

> "A Lamb standing as if it had been slaughtered." (5:6)

A slaughtered Lamb close to the throne of the Almighty? But all those who surrounded the throne, upon seeing the Lamb, burst into song saying to the Lamb:

> You are worthy to take the scroll and to open its seals, for you were slaughtered and by your blood you ransomed for God saints from every tribe and language and people and nation; you have made them to be a kingdom and priests to serve our God and they will reign on earth. (5:9–10)

The One on the throne and the slaughtered Lamb are worthy of glory and honor, power and wealth, wisdom and might, as they reign forever and forever! The slaughtered Lamb is the one who unlocks and reads and is the scroll that is the key to the future and the ground of our hope.

There is much here for us to ponder. But consider carefully the image of the slaughtered Lamb, which of course the persecuted Christians know is the crucified Jesus. It is in him, precisely as one proclaiming an impinging peaceable kingdom of non-retaliation who was killed by the empire. Jesus the sacrificial Lamb, slain by and for the sins of the world!

Are we finally to trust in Jesus as the One who will bring real retaliatory justice in the approaching future? *Is the slaughtered Lamb finally to become the avenging Lion?* Is that the vision of the future and the triumph of God over the empires? Or *is the avenging Lion to become the sacrificial Lamb?*

But, listen as we hasten on to a later passage in John's text and ask ourselves whether an avenging Lion could bestow this vision on John?

> Then I saw a new heaven and a new earth . . . And I saw the holy city, the new Jerusalem, coming down out of heaven from God . . . and I heard a loud voice from the throne saying:
>
> "See the home of God is among mortals.
> He will dwell with them;
> They will be his peoples,
> And God himself will be with them;
> He will wipe away every tear from their eyes.
> Death will be no more;
> Mourning and crying and pain will be no more,
> For the first things have passed away."
> . . . "See, I am making all things new." (21:1–5)

So, John the prophetic seer, receiving a revelation of Jesus Christ from an angel, envisions a future in which the persecuted and slain will be healed and the God known in the crucified Jesus will be the Alpha and the Omega of all things and will be God over all the creation. God will make all things new and overcome all the great enmities and injustices that have reigned in human history. A new Jerusalem!

Is this, then, the One in whom the persecuted are to have hope and precisely this sort of transformative hope?

Surely the tension in the texts is palpable. What is the true map of the future and who is the One in whom the persecuted are to hope and trust? It seems so intuitive, given what we are inclined to think about justice, that the persecuted and executed will hope in their own restoration and in the final punishment of their persecutors.

But is this what it means to hope and trust in the slaughtered Lamb, the crucified Jesus? The Lamb that refused to take up arms against his crucifying butchers—is he now the avenging Lion commanding the final bloodbath to begin and casting the evildoers into the just deserts of a lake of everlasting fire? Will the New Jerusalem have as its backside the stench of violent retribution?

Part Four—Sermons Ventured on Behalf of the Witness

No, no, no! *Do not convert the slaughtered Lamb into the avenging Lion!* Is it really so counter-intuitive for Christians—even Christians under duress and suffering—to say with another John as we do regularly in our celebration of Holy Communion:

> "Behold, the Lamb of God who takes away the sins of the world."
> (John 1:29)

All this, dear friends, I have dared to preach in the name of the Father and of the Son and of the Holy Spirit, One God, Mother of us all. Amen.

24

Remembering a Friend

Charles Edwin Jones

A homily for a memorial service for Charles Edwin Jones at St. Paul United Methodist Church, Muskogee, Oklahoma, March 3, 2007.

Dear Family and Friends of Charles:

As we have already been reminded, we have gathered to *celebrate* Charles' life among us and thereby express our genuine gratitude for the many ways in which he was a gift to us. His unexpected death, even at age seventy-two, startled each of us, and we have also gathered to *grieve* his death and to deal with *our loss*. Whatever depths of gratitude we might have for our relationships to Charles, we cannot dismiss from our minds and hearts—and therefore from this Christian gathering—that we *grieve* his passing.

Our lives will go on—for how long only God knows—but they will go on without those intimate and mundane transactions with Charles in which we met life and death and shared concerns and joys with him. Perhaps in the images of memory we may recall how Charles might have responded to us in this or that situation, but he will not be there to exchange glances and gestures and words with us.

It should be crystal clear to us—gathering here in Charles and Madge's church—that *we need this service*. Charles has died unto the merciful arms of God and does not now need this memorial service. But we need it.

PART FOUR—Sermons Ventured on Behalf of the Witness

When loved ones die—and most of us have experienced such losses before—we feel the irrepressible *shadow of our own prospective deaths and the emerging questions* about our own lives. Lurking there for us are these questions: What's life all about? How is my life holding together and where is it going? Does my life have any integrity, any truthfulness? What am I to do about my betrayals and deceptions and my repetitious cowardliness? We are in church now and we dare not be dishonest about these questions and the shadows of doubt and fear.

As we all should know, *Charles had his shadows and doubts.* Consider the truly remarkable promise of the intellectual vitality and achievement of his degrees from Southern Methodist University and from Duke Divinity School and then his admittance to pursue a doctorate in philosophy from that venerable citadel of intellectual prowess and achievement, Oxford University. Such *promise,* such *hope,* such *sheer joy* in joining the exciting and exacting dialogue and conflict of ideas and beliefs. *Then that sudden and terrifying accident that shattered his body and plunged him into the darkness of coma— almost taking his life and seeming to sever his promise and banish his joy.*

Perhaps his dear and remarkable mother, Madge, is the closest witness to his long struggle to heal, to gather his senses, to retrieve his direction, to search for his hope, to grope for his joy. That he lived almost five decades longer is itself a testimony to his courage and indomitable spirit. But let no callous soul among us dare say it was easy nor pretend that death and destruction did not often present themselves to him as real and perhaps desirable possibilities.

Nevertheless, he persisted and vigorously engaged life, and he engaged us—his family and friends—perhaps sometimes disturbing our complacencies. And yet with us he often conveyed a surprising energy with his throaty and exuberant bursts of laughter. With courage and determination he did continue his educational pursuits, eventually earning two more advanced degrees. Through it all, Charles seemed to spend little time and effort licking his wounds and nursing his grievances.

Charles admired the work of the philosopher/theologian Paul Tillich, one of the most influential theologians of the mid-twentieth century. Our regular

Remembering a Friend

and energetic discussions often pivoted around Tillich's theology, and it was not seldom that we disagreed about the adequacy of Tillich's thought.

A little book of Tillich's entitled *The Courage to Be* (1952) was especially meaningful to Charles. The *courage* Tillich describes—and, I think, Charles lived—is that *refusal to give up or give in to despair* in the midst of the whirlwinds and tumults, the disappointments and grievous harms, that human beings so often encounter. It is the strong and consistent *resolve*— and thereby the *courage*—to *trust* that at the depths of life and death there is a *sense-making Presence* that cannot be defeated. It is a courage that is rooted in an *unsolicited but awesomely ecstatic sense of the mysterious and almost unbearable beauty and transcendent meaning of life*—in spite of the undeniable and innumerable ways life can appear to us as gnarled and difficult and seemingly tragic and futile.

We have just read together those stunning and remarkable words of St. Paul from his Epistle to the Romans. For this Paul—and I think for Paul Tillich and surely for our Charles—there is that *unconquerable sense and trust* that at the bottom—or, if you will—at the heights of all realities, *there is the gracious and abundant love of God that comes to vivid expression in Christ Jesus.*

It is a love that both *judges and forgives* us. It is not a love we must work to *earn*. It is not a love that might *disappear or be withdrawn* in terrible times. It is not a love that enemies and principalities and powers can control or administer or *defeat*. It is a love that is *constant* and not fickle like our human loves. It is a love so *strong and abundant* that it cannot be thwarted by our shadowy secrets and doubts or even by death or by our fear of death.

It is precisely this triumphant love of God in Christ Jesus that is the *Gospel—the utterly true and disarming good news that has been revealed to us in the life, death, and resurrection of Jesus of Nazareth*. It is this Gospel that is the core reason we Christians gather for worship and gather for worship even on occasions of death and grief and loss.

And it is this good news that we are called to *bear in our souls*—to bear in *how we live*, in *how we love*, in *how we hope*, in how we *refuse* to waste our lives or neglect the arduous yet joyful ways of living that are sheer gifts from God.

This *good news*, however, does not suggest we will never grieve, never feel overwhelmed by fear, never be harmed by others, never be crushed and disabled by accidents of life, never be afflicted with sadness and regret, never be stalked by recurring dubieties. Rather, *in Christ Jesus we trust that whatever comes upon us—whether we live or whether we die—we are finally, ultimately the Lord's*. We and Charles have been called to trust in the ultimacy of God's love as the Alpha and Omega, the beginning and the end, of all things.

Dear friends, *hear* these words and *nestle* them in your hearts and *nurture* them in your living.

And dear Madge, in your grief, be comforted by the fact that your family and friends gathered here today rejoice in the sheer magnificence of the gracious ways in which you embraced and dearly held your son, Charles, in the midst of his sufferings and his courageous living. May God's gracious and merciful love guide, console, and strengthen you in the days ahead.

And dear family and friends, listen again as St. Paul has so passionately written for us:

> I consider that the sufferings of this present time are not worth comparing with the glory about to be revealed to us.
>
> But if we hope for we do not see, we wait for it with patience.
>
> Likewise the Spirit helps us in our weakness, for we do not know how to pray as we ought, but that very Spirit intercedes with sighs [or groans] too deep for words.
>
> [So] if God is for us, who is against us?
>
> Who will separate us from the love of Christ? Will hardship, or distress, or persecution, or famine, or nakedness, or peril, or sword?
>
> No, in all these things we are more than conquerors through him who loved us. For I am convinced that neither death, nor life, nor angels, nor rulers, nor things present, nor things to come, nor powers, nor height, nor depth, nor anything else in all creation, will be able to separate us from the love of God in Christ Jesus our Lord. (Rom 8:18–28, 31–32, 34–35, 37–39)

Family and friends, may it be so with us all.

All this I have dared to preach in the name of the Father, and of the Son, and of the Holy Spirit, One God, Mother of us all. Amen.

25

Purity of Heart and the Vicissitudes of Aging

A meditation for a vesper service in the chapel at Epworth Villa Retirement Center in Oklahoma City, on June 7, 2012.

Matthew 5:1–10

What a pleasure it is to be asked to speak to the weekly vesper service in this remarkable chapel at Epworth Villa. Sarah and I started our move into our Epworth cottage on April 27 and today we are under the impression that we are almost moved in, if not fully settled in.

Perhaps like most of you, we have come seeking more proximate medical care and less upkeep of house and lawn.

And perhaps like many others, our aging bodies and minds have experienced their own malfunctions and dismaying declines. In the previous decade, we both had led extremely active lives: Sarah as a psychotherapist and spiritual director and I as a retired professor of theology and an author of some books and an ongoing website. Yet now, we are not as robust of body as we used to be, but we still feel the challenge of being robust of spirit.

Coming to Epworth is a bit like coming home, inasmuch as we were both raised in Oklahoma City, were high school sweethearts, and married while we were attending the University of Oklahoma. We have raised three daughters while living in such interesting places as New Haven, Connecticut; Dallas; Enid, Oklahoma; and Indianapolis. In 2000 we thought we were retiring to a family cabin—we called it "Anchor Point"—on Fort Gibson Lake in eastern Oklahoma and that we would see the end of our days right there on the lake. Alas, we are now here at Epworth Villa, almost home-again but not yet to the end of our days.

It is this—not yet to the end of our days—that is the context for my meditation today at this vesper service.

None of us—gathered here today in this chapel in a retirement center—have to be told that we are aging. And such aging did not begin suddenly yesterday. It has been going on for a very long time, to which our presence here today astonishingly testifies. The church has from its very beginnings, arising out of its Hebraic roots, also testified that human beings are embodied creatures who live in a specific time-span amidst specific spaces. None of us lived at the beginning of the twentieth century and none of us will be alive at the end of this present century. We are finite creatures located in this particular span of time.

But each of us—whatever age we might be—is faced with the everyday question of *how* we will live. *How* will we sort through the days and nights of our lives? And as persons acutely exposed to the vicissitudes of aging, this *how* of living is inescapable and crucial. *How* will we put our lives together over the days left to us?

It is here that the scripture read today from the fifth chapter of the Gospel of Matthew, that we encounter those pithy aphorisms, sometimes called "the beatitudes" in Jesus' so-called "Sermon on the Mount."

Throughout the life of the church these brief words, in their wistful beauty, have resonated with Christian souls. And yet—even in their beauty—they seem so impossibly ideal that we are inclined to *admire the beauty* of the blessings and ignore their bearing on *how* we live our lives.

Note that the blessings are pronounced upon those who have certain characteristic *hows* of their living:

> Blessed are the poor in spirit
> Blessed are those who mourn
> Blessed are those who hunger and thirst for righteousness
> Blessed are those who are merciful
> Blessed are the pure in heart
> Blessed are the peacemakers

Purity of Heart and the Vicissitudes of Aging

Yes, a certain wistful beauty or poetry of the spirit, but who among us—especially we the aging who have lived long and sometimes wretchedly—*who among us* would grasp themselves among the poor in spirit, among those who mourn, who hunger and thirst for righteousness, who are merciful, who are pure in heart, who have any history of being peacemakers in ways other than the historic all-too-human way of seeking peace by incarcerating or slaughtering those regarded as evildoers and enemies of 'good' social order?

I certainly feel the sting of those blessings when I honestly grasp how I have lived and am now living.

Consider especially: *the blessings of having a pure heart*. If the word 'heart' is referring to something other than that organ that pumps blood through our vessels and veins, then what are we talking about? When we say such words as 'George has no heart,' aren't we saying something like 'in relation to the desperate situations of other human beings, George has no disposition to sympathetic affections and no will to action to be at their side or to seek their well-being'? It would seem as though George's spring for affections and actions is thwarted or so divided that he has become incapacitated to respond to others or to God with any passion undiluted by self-interest—by that inclination well-known to us all when we calculate *'what's in this for me?'*

Many are those of us gathered here today who have physical hearts that are weakened and function poorly, but we know that having such weakened hearts is not one of the conditions that Jesus says are blessed. Now, what did I just say? That having a poorly functioning heart is not one of the conditions that Jesus is saying are blessed—to be commended.

The sort of *heart* that Jesus is blessing is that *how* of living in which the individual is free of guile and bile, free of hatred and deadly anger, free of that sort of self-interest that calculates outcomes and advantages. A *pure* heart, then, must be that sort of *how* of living in which a person can, without reservation, will the good of another human being as a hearty spirit whom God loves.

Are there any folk here today who are *pure in heart*? That very question seems too harsh for us, especially those of us for whom the *beauty* of the beatitudes is what is most admirable about them.

So, what do we folk who are aging do when a pure heart seems just too much, too remote, too far-fetched, too much to expect when so much pain and stress wracks our bodies?

Might a pure heart emerge when we, in our aging bodies, move beyond excuse-making and the self-deception that we will be a robust forty again and perhaps move beyond the enervating supposition that in our extremities of aging we have no capacity to will the good of another?

Might we become those who have at least glimpsed that sort of purity of heart that can honestly and freely confess the struggle and pains of the past, that can be released from the guilt of what was unfaithfully done or what was selfishly left undone?

Might it be possible that any of us could possess a pure heart whenever we can *confess and live* as though we live before God's forgiving and unrelenting grace? But we will only grasp this grace for ourselves when we also grasp that it is not a grace that has been *earned* by years of our living with a pure heart. And therefore, as unearned, it is weirdly and almost incomprehensibly an unearned grace even for our enemies.

It is a pure heart that can give up keeping and settling old scores, give up even that self-condemnation that can creep into our awareness when we grasp just how much our hearts have been in disarray and broken thereby.

Consider then this: the beatitudes are not to be seen as the ways in which we are to *earn* God's grace; rather they are the gifts of living that are bestowed so abundantly upon us when we actually live that sort of *how* that accepts and trusts the grace and love of God for us all.

Let those of us who are acutely aware of our physical and mental declines learn the *how* of receiving God's grace with unfeigned gratitude and a heart that trusts, come what may, in the ultimacy of God's grace.

May all who hear these words be blessed by grace and be hopeful.

All of these words in the name of the Father, and of the Son, and of the Holy Spirit, one God, Mother of us all. Amen.

26

In Gratitude for Gary Byrkit

Pastor Theologian Par Excellence

After moving to Oklahoma City in late April 2012, Sarah and I began searching for a church home. Sometime in mid-May we visited Southern Hills Christian Church in the nearby town of Edmond. We had over the years heard favorable remarks about the church's pastor, Gary Byrkit (MDiv, DMin), but we had never met him. His preaching was outstanding and genuinely upbuilding for Sarah and me. We placed our membership in the church in early summer and came to regard Gary as not only a dear friend but a profound pastor theologian who taught the faith week after week. It had been some time since I had felt so deeply and complexly addressed and challenged by the preached word.

As I listened to Gary's preaching over many months, I was repeatedly stirred to ask how many laity are ever privileged in their lifetimes to hear such faithful, profound, and theologically sound preaching. That Gary was exceptional, was a fact about which I have perhaps been obnoxiously vocal over many years.

Gary had come to Southern Hills some twenty-eight years ago, and it was known that at the age of sixty-six he was thinking of retiring in the yet-to-be-determined future. But we were utterly unprepared to learn on Tuesday, August 13, that Gary had suffered a massive heart attack and died suddenly, sitting at his computer in his home. No history of heart trouble, no lingering previous illnesses. Just gone, with no goodbyes, no farewell embraces.

At Gary's funeral on August 17, I was asked to make some reflective comments about Gary's ministry—in no more than five minutes! Below are those comments, too brief, to be sure, to capture the rich and faithful ministry Gary enjoyed at Southern Hills.

Part Four—Sermons Ventured on Behalf of the Witness

Dear Friends:

I confess before you now that I have been asked to say something about Gary Byrkit, the pastor theologian who suddenly entered into Sarah's and my aging lives about a year ago. I hope no one here today is worried about my calling Gary a *pastor theologian*.

Over the years of church life and teaching in seminaries, I have heard some lay persons say they just want their pastor to love them and leave all that theological stuff aside. And from time to time different pastors have said to me that 'I am no theologian,' to which I have been want to reply that I am sorry to hear he—usually a male!—is leaving pastoral ministry. And to which he replies, with increasing sense of danger, that he is quite happy being a pastor. To which I reply that it is a self-contradiction to claim to be a pastor of a Christian congregation and to admit that one is either ignorant of or simply uninterested in the theological language of the church concerning the reality of God and the life, death, and resurrection of Jesus of Nazareth. How can you even preach a sermon about the Gospel of Jesus Christ if you disclaim being a theologian and abstain from theological reasoning and language?

And have I not found myself from time to time listening to an ordained minister mimicking the gestures of earnest preaching while doing no more than gassing and guessing about life and death and how to get ahead with a nobody god.

Is it really possible that anyone might come to faith in the utter absence of any of language of the faith? And is it really possible that one might learn *how to be faithful* without learning the language of faith?

Of course I have been blessed many times by pastor theologians who proclaimed the Word with power, insight, luminosity, and passion.

It has also happened that as Sarah and I were moving back into our hometown seeking medical care and wisdom, we came upon Gary Byrkit as he was preaching one Sunday morning in May of 2012. I had never met Gary before, or at least I do not remember it. But neither did he! But when some really wise persons from our past urged us to come to worship and listen, we came and listened as Gary enacted a startlingly truthful and honest witness to the Gospel, in that winsome style of so many previous saintly witnesses.

In Gratitude for Gary Byrkit

There he was, standing behind the pulpit reading the scripture for the day, without any of that pretense that he was the author of the text. He read it as though it was the text of an honored and authoritative witness that was worthy of our attention. Then he laid the Bible aside and walked away from the pulpit, laid his notes on the edge of the Communion table, and then turned to the congregation to rehearse and explore the wonders and puzzles that seem to surround the ways in which the church had previously understood the meaning of the text.

I should note here that during the succeeding fifteen months we were to listen to Gary's preaching, he always read a scriptural text and then invariably stayed with it, mulling its original setting and context, mentioning some of the authorities that have commented on the text. Or, to put it more sharply, I never heard him read the biblical text and then race on to some topic to which he was really interested, leaving the text slowly twisting in the wind. Gary might venture widely about the life of faith, but never without exploring what the scripture read might mean for us.

Then, from Gary, the stories began to emerge of life situations about which the text might apply or be illuminating. And then those long meandering and probing meditations about us—the gathered congregation—but now also we the folk who live where we live, who daily have to sort through lies and falsehoods and seductive temptations in the struggle to be faithful.

As Gary spoke it also became clearer that it is we—those of us gathered right there in the sanctuary—who live evasively and sometimes with cowardice and sometimes as liars and evildoers and yet are gripped by a longing for truth and purity and forgiveness. Perhaps it is a longing to get a new start, to get a new leg up on life and politics, on raising our children to be kind to the least of these in our world, and on learning to repent of the great harm we have done to others.

There we sat, our minds in movement and self-examination, as Gary deftly opened us to the text and how to think and live in the context of the church in this very contemporary world in which we also live. We were in the presence of a theologian of rare learning and skills. We were being taught about life situations and norms that previously we were fully convinced we had already learned to master. But in probing the vagaries of our lives, he did not explicitly accuse of being liars and self-deceivers. Yet we had a inescapable sense that we had been lovingly *unmasked and forgiven and challenged to live differently.*

PART FOUR—Sermons Ventured on Behalf of the Witness

And then there was that startlingly abrupt way in which Gary ended his sermons with sharp and pithy words and then turning his back on us and walking slowly back to his chair. It was abrupt but not angry or sarcastic. And it left us there to consider *what* had been said and *how* it had been said and *what it might mean for us.*

As we pulled ourselves together, received the Holy Communion of forgiveness and hope, we surely must have grasped that we were in the midst of theological language and practices. We were being taught how to use the word "God," how to construe Jesus hanging on a cross as one crucified by those—perhaps us—who think we are the arbiters of good and evil and social order. Perhaps we have been exposed to the fact that it is possible to use the word "God" in an idolatrous way.

As I have reckoned with Gary's style of preaching, I am reminded that he was well aware just how demanding and joyful it is to think and live in the theological language and practices of the church of Jesus Christ. The language of the church is not an add-on to something we already know and live. I am sure Gary would have resonated with the story—and would have wanted us to resonate too—of the elderly person who confessed that "it had taken him years to know how to say and mean *I know that my Redeemer liveth.*" Oh, the passion and depth and truthfulness embedded in that remark.

Might we remember that the God about whom Gary preached and taught is the One who is the Alpha and Omega of all things creaturely and the One who called Israel into existence and established it under covenant and who tabernacled among Jew and Gentile as Jesus of Nazareth, him crucified and dead at the hands of the powerful and yet raised from the dead, and who reigns with the Holy Spirit over all human life and history and will finally gather up all things into God's own eternal life.

Might I simply confess that for me—that cranky professor more critical of pastors than patient—Gary enacted a rare gift by addressing me among the gathered as struggling penitents hoping to hear from another the harsh but joyful assurance that God is finally gracious. None of us can really say that to ourselves. Only that trusted and authoritative other can venture to do it. But Gary has died and will no longer be there to preach judgment and grace.

Gary died so suddenly that we were deprived of saying our farewells and thanks for all he had done for and with us. We cannot quite admit that he is gone. But he will not be forgotten because from time to time each of us will recall the various ways in which he was a pastor theologian with rare spiritual skills that reminded us that there is a Gospel that he did not invent and to which he was only a witness, and that each of us is called to hear that Gospel and be empowered to be witnesses too.

Yes, we will miss him, miss his bold and earnest sermons and his lanky presence and shuffling gestures and wistful smile. Surely we will all thank God that Gary was a theologian and a gift to us all!

All this, dear friends, in the name of the Father, the Son, and the Holy Spirit, one God, Mother of us all. Amen

www.ingramcontent.com/pod-product-compliance
Lightning Source LLC
Chambersburg PA
CBHW031356230426
43670CB00006B/563